Charity Accounting and Reporting at a Time of Change

Charity Accounting and Reporting at a Time of Change

Ciaran Connolly, Noel Hyndman and Mariannunziata Liguori

CHARTERED
ACCOUNTANTS
IRELAND

Published in 2017 by
Chartered Accountants Ireland
Chartered Accountants House
47–49 Pearse Street
Dublin 2
www.charteredaccountants.ie

The publishers wish to acknowledge the support of the Chartered Accountants Ireland Educational Trust for the research included in this publication.

ISBN: 978-1-910374-80-1

Typeset by Datapage
Printed and bound by CPI Group (UK) Ltd, Croydon, CR0 4YY

Contents

Exhibits, Figures and Tables

Exhibits

Figures

Tables

About the Authors

Ciaran Connolly is Professor of Accounting at Queen's University Belfast and Subject Leader for the Accounting Group in Queen's Management School. A Fellow of Chartered Accountants Ireland, he holds a DPhil from the University of Ulster and an MBA from Queen's University Belfast. Ciaran's main area of research is in the field of public services, particularly the financial and performance measurement aspects of the charity and public sectors, and he has published in this area. He is currently on the board of a large Northern Ireland charity and was a member of the Department for Social Development (Northern Ireland)/Charity Commission for Northern Ireland Accounts and Reports Working Group during 2014 and 2015.

Noel Hyndman is Professor of Management Accounting (and Director of the Centre for Not-for-profit and Public-sector Research) at Queen's University Belfast. He has previously held professorships at the University of Ottawa in Canada, the University of Sydney in Australia and the University of Ulster. A Fellow of the Chartered Institute of Management Accountants, he was awarded a PhD for his research in financial reporting by charities. Noel was a member of the Annual Reporting Advisory Group established by the Charity Commissioners for England and Wales between 2003 and 2005 and has been a member of the Charity SORP Committee since 2006. He was a member of the Department for Social Development (Northern Ireland)/Charity Commission for Northern Ireland Accounts and Reports Working Group during 2014 and 2015. Currently, he is Chair of the British Accounting and Finance Association's Public Services and Charities Special Interest Group.

Mariannunziata Liguori is Senior Lecturer in Management Accounting and Director of the MSc Accounting and Finance at Queen's Management School, Belfast, where she moved after a visiting period at the University of Alberta in Canada. She was awarded a PhD, investigating processes and organisational dynamics of accounting change in the public sector, by Bocconi University in Milan, where she has also previously worked. Mariannunziata is a member of the editorial board of the public-sector and not-for-profit journal *Financial Accountability & Management*. She has been the secretary of the Public Services and Charities Special Interest Group of the British Accounting and Finance Association since 2015.

Preface

Charities exist to provide public benefit (such as the relief of poverty, the expansion of education, the advancement of religion or other purposes considered beneficial to the community), benefit that may perhaps not be provided, or not provided to the same extent, without charitable recognition. They are largely funded by individuals or organisations that receive no direct economic benefit from their funding. Charities exist in most countries and are encouraged and facilitated through various legal and regulatory frameworks. They often enjoy tax benefits over non-charitable organisations. Furthermore, charities make a distinctive and widely recognised contribution to the public good by building social capital in civil society. As such, it is a sector to be valued, nurtured, protected and encouraged by the whole of society, by those who receive the benefit of charitable activity, by those who work or volunteer in charitable organisations and by those who, in the spirit of altruism, seek to provide much-needed funds to generate public benefit.

In the United Kingdom (UK) and the Republic of Ireland (RoI), the charity sector comprises a vast and developing segment of economic activity. The influence of charities on everyday life is pervasive, through organisations like, for example, the National Society for the Prevention of Cruelty to Children, Macmillan Cancer Support, Oxfam and Focus Ireland. The growth in the size and influence of the sector has led to increased visibility and public scrutiny by diverse stakeholders, including government oversight agencies, private donors, clients, the media and the public at large. It is, therefore, a sector in which the fact and perception of the linked concepts of accountability, legitimacy, transparency and ethical behaviour are particularly important. In a similar way, it is a sector where trust and confidence among the general public are crucial as a basis for ensuring its health and growth. Calls for increased sector visibility and scrutiny have been persistent and widespread for many years with the need for charities to operate transparently, discharge accountability appropriately and act ethically being widely articulated. Given that a considerable amount of charitable work is supported by the general public (either as donors, volunteers or indirectly through taxation), it is critical that there are appropriate systems in place, not only to ensure that public money is not misappropriated and is fittingly and effectively spent for the communities for which the funds were intended, but also to sustain the health and longevity of both the sector and the groups and communities that charities seek to serve.

However, charities also operate in a society that is continually changing. Societal and business norms, legal and regulatory frameworks, and economic and social pressures are constantly in a state of flux. Pressure on funding and demands on services have intensified; the adoption of more 'business-like' practices has been encouraged (not always with positive outcomes) and governments, in a period of austerity, have sometimes viewed charities as useful vehicles through which services previously delivered by the public sector can be provided. Charities react and adjust to such changes, with a danger being that such reactions and adjustments have the potential to undermine their distinctive mission focus and result in unintended consequences. Appropriate responses to change can cement, solidify and provide further legitimation of the roles of charities; it can also help build trust and confidence in the sector. Conversely, inappropriate responses can jeopardise their lofty and valuable roles, and undermine focus, value and trust. Perhaps recent publicity surrounding a variety of scandals of various hues within charities in both the UK and RoI is evidence of this, notwithstanding the fact that such incidences are relatively rare.

At a time of such change, the importance of good management, good accountability and good governance processes within the charity sector cannot be overstated. Good accounting and reporting is central to this and is central to the building of trust and confidence. Poor accounting and reporting (and, as a consequence, the possibility of scandals) can severely undermine confidence in the charity sector and reduce both charitable giving and charitable activity. The widespread adoption of appropriate accounting and reporting practices, and the ongoing renewal of such, has the potential to provide a basis for greater faith in the control processes within charities and result in a more accountable and more legitimate sector. As a result, public confidence can be enhanced. Such may be a desirable, or indeed necessary, condition for the continuing health of the sector.

However, good accounting and reporting by charities should not be assumed; history provides clear lessons. In 1981, a study of charities' annual reports and accounts by Bird and Morgan-Jones (*Financial Reporting by Charities*) cast significant doubt on their usefulness as a means of providing accurate, reliable and comparable information to stakeholders. It revealed a sector where non-compliance with accounting standards was prevalent, and where the behaviour of accountants and auditors appeared cavalier. A range of creative and questionable accounting ploys was used that made it difficult for a user of accounts to understand the significance and meaning of the information. (Indeed, it was suggested that users were being deliberately misled.) Ultimately this research led to the publication of a Statement of Recommended Practice (SORP) for charities in 1988, and its subsequent revisions in 1995, 2000, 2005 and, most recently, in 2014 (*Accounting and Reporting by Charities: the FRS 102 SORP* – effective for accounting periods beginning on or after 1 January 2015). This SORP is mandatory for most large UK charities, and is best practice for RoI charities.

Spotlighting the UK and RoI charity sectors, this book seeks to examine the evolution of charity accounting and reporting and suggest how it might evolve in the future. It is a book that is useful to a range of readers, including:

- those within the charity sector charged with implementing the latest SORP requirements (as it contains the detail of such requirements and a profusion of examples of reporting from UK and RoI charities, and from regulatory guidance);
- academics with an interest in research of the sector as it contains a presentation of the main theories and themes that underpin research in this area, a summary of previous charity-reporting academic research, and the results of detailed field research conducted by the authors (focusing on the internal legitimation of charity-accounting changes and the performance accountability of charities); and
- policy makers and regulators who are engaged in debates and decisions impacting on the accountability of charities (often directed towards the goal of achieving a more accountable and more trusted charity sector).

Acknowledgements

The authors wish to express their gratitude to those individuals, whose comments and views are reported in Chapter Five, who kindly agreed to be interviewed. Furthermore, we would also like to thank the Chartered Accountants Ireland Educational Trust for the financial and research support of this project.

Abbreviations

ASB	Accounting Standards Board
ASC	Accounting Standards Committee
CAF	Charities Aid Foundation
FRS	Financial Reporting Standard
GAAP	Generally Accepted Accounting Principles
IAS	International Accounting Standard
IASB	International Accounting Standards Board
IFRS	International Financial Reporting Standard
NCVO	National Council for Voluntary Organisations
NFP	Not-For-Profit
NFPO	Not-For-Profit Organisation
NI	Northern Ireland
NPM	New Public Management
OSCR	Office of the Scottish Charity Regulator
RoI	Republic of Ireland
SOFA	Statement of Financial Activities
SORP	Statement of Recommended Practice
UK	United Kingdom

Chapter 1

The Charity Sector and Changing Accountabilities

The charity sectors in both the United Kingdom (UK) and the Republic of Ireland (RoI) are significant socially and economically. Their activities are pervasive, and often highly visible, and include such well-known names as Cancer Research UK and the Royal Society for the Protection of Birds (in the UK), and Trócaire and Focus Ireland (in RoI), as well as a plethora of smaller charities in each jurisdiction. The sector represents the sphere of social activity undertaken by organisations that are non-profit and non-governmental. It is quite different from the private or public sectors in terms of its orientation and motivation, the nature of its activities, its access to resources and the manner of its contribution to the public good.

Regardless of their size, charities play a significant and vital role in society, often serving and helping those who are most disadvantaged, marginalised or helpless. Increasingly, charities are used to deliver public services to tackle social exclusion. In both the UK and RoI, an organisation is considered to be a charity if its purposes are deemed to be 'charitable' and it fulfils a 'public benefit' (with the law in each jurisdiction specifying how such factors are determined).[1] More widely, charities exist in most societies and are facilitated through various legal and administrative frameworks by, for example, major tax benefits and differing, and possibly lighter-touch, law and regulation. Charities are different from general not-for-profit organisations (NFPOs) in that they focus on goals of a philanthropic nature that are deemed by individual societies to serve the public interest or common good. As a result, the definition of a charity can vary according to the jurisdiction in which an organisation operates.

The purpose of this chapter is to:

- provide a brief overview of the scope and size of the charity sectors in both the UK and RoI (**Section 1.1**);
- examine major changes that impact on a charity's (and the sector's) accountability (**Section 1.2**);

---

[1] The main pieces of legislation in the UK relevant to this determination are: the Charities Act (England and Wales) 2011, the Charities and Trustee Investment (Scotland) Act 2005, and the Charities Act (Northern Ireland) 2008. In RoI, it is the Charities Act 2009.

- introduce the concepts of performance accountability and internal legitimation (**Section 1.3**) that will be used later in the book to investigate field evidence relating to extant reporting by charities; and
- outline the key aims and structure of the book.

1.1   An Overview of the Sector in the United Kingdom and Republic of Ireland

The charity sectors in the UK and RoI are vast and growing segments of economic activity with substantial assets at their disposal. In the UK there are over 200,000 registered charities with an estimated total annual income approaching £80 billion (Charity Commission, 2016; Charity Commission for Northern Ireland (NI), 2017; Office of the Scottish Charity Regulator (OSCR), 2017). In addition, there are many exempt charities (mostly universities, educational institutions and national museums) and excepted charities (including religious charities), which are not required to register (therefore total numbers and economic significance is even higher).[2] In RoI, it is more difficult to get accurate estimates of the numbers and economic significance (partly because of a regulatory framework more in its infancy), although Breen and Carroll (2015) suggest that there may be over 8,000 charities, which themselves are a subset of a larger not-for-profit (NFP) sector of 12,000 organisations with an annual income of approximately €6 billion (about £5 billion).

The growth in the size and influence of the sector (Cabinet Office, 2002), combined with a number of highly publicised scandals, has led to increased sector visibility and public scrutiny in both the UK and RoI (Beattie *et al.*, 2002; Pratten, 2004; Katz, 2005; Burke-Kennedy, 2013; O'Brien, 2013; Hind 2017). Likewise, the need for the sector to operate transparently and discharge accountability has been widely articulated in the academic literature and practice (Charity Commission, 2000a and 2005; Brody, 2001; Ebrahim, 2003; Home Office, 2003; Pratten, 2004; Accounting Standards Board (ASB), 2007; Breen and Carroll, 2015).

Indeed, under the 2006 Charities Act, the Charity Commission in England and Wales has been charged with the responsibility to enhance charitable accountability, increase public trust and confidence, and also promote the effective use of charitable funds. In Scotland and NI, major changes in the regulatory environment have emphasised similar themes.

---

[2] In England and Wales exempt charities do not register with the Charity Commission but are subject to another regulator; excepted charities have been excepted from the requirement to register with the Charity Commission but are still subject to the Commission's oversight.

The Department of Justice and Equality is responsible for charity regulation in RoI, where, until recently, no charity-specific regulator for the sector had been established. Although a change in this position was anticipated in the RoI Charities Act 2009, elements of this are still awaiting legislative commencement.[3] The Charities Regulatory Authority (CRA) was eventually established in October 2014, although, at the time of writing (June 2017), the task of creating a register and implementing a robust system of regulation and oversight was still in its early stages. A key task of the new CRA is to improve the accountability and transparency of the sector. While the conceptual framework for charity and other NFP reporting has been guided by the accountability paradigm (ASB, 2007), the focus has principally been on financial reporting. Recent literature has, however, emphasised the significance of narrative and non-financial quantitative disclosures in the discharge of charity accountability.

A number of studies of charity activity by jurisdiction have identified both the UK and RoI as particularly generous nations and ones in which charitable activity is pervasive. For example, the World Giving Index (Charities Aid Foundation (CAF), 2016) identifies the UK as the most generous country in Europe, followed by RoI. The UK charity sector employs over 600,000 people — up 25% over the last decade — and the public is increasingly engaged in voluntary activities, with 45% of the public volunteering at least once a year and 29% at least once a month (National Council for Voluntary Organisations/CAF, 2012). While there is a growing reliance on earned income (50% of total income) within the sector, voluntary income continues to play a significant role (40%), with the remaining 10% largely consisting of dividend and interest income (Cabinet Office of the Third Sector, 2009). Individuals and government are important sources of income for the sector, contributing 37% and 34% respectively of the total income in the UK. In RoI, the NFP sector as a whole employs more than 100,000 people and has over 560,000 volunteers. Almost 80% of these organisations use volunteers, with the proportion of charities using volunteers (and relying on such inputs) increasing over time (INKEx, 2012).

In the UK, statutory sources and individuals' donations provide important flows of revenue, but in RoI the proportion from statutory sources is more pronounced (52.7% statutory sources versus 25% by individuals) (The Wheel, 2014). Consequently, since in both the UK and RoI a considerable amount of charitable work is supported by the general public – either directly through donations and/or through voluntary activities, or indirectly through taxes – it is critical that there are appropriate systems

---

[3] See the legislation section of the Charities Regulatory Authority website for the current status: http://www.charitiesregulatoryauthority.ie/en/CRA/Pages/Legislation.

in place, not only to ensure that public money is not misappropriated and is fittingly and effectively spent for the communities for which the funds were intended, but also to sustain the health and longevity of both the sector and the groups and communities that charities seek to serve.

1.2   Changing Times, Changing Accountability

Changing Times

Charities comprise a sector where the fact and perception of the linked concepts of accountability, legitimacy, transparency and ethical behaviour are particularly important. The trust and confidence of the general public are crucial for ensuring its health and growth. Calls for increased sector visibility and scrutiny have been persistent and widespread for many years, with the need for charities to operate transparently, discharge accountability appropriately and act ethically being widely articulated.

In addition, it is a sector that is changing, or perhaps, more correctly, it is a sector that is being changed by external pressures. For example, pressure on funding and demands on services have intensified. These, often triggered by the recent financial crisis and subsequent programmes of austerity with respect to public spending, have created a 'perfect storm' for charities, whereby they try to do more with less (Charity Finance Group (CFG), 2012; The Wheel, 2014). This has necessitated, among other things, major changes in strategies for seeking and using precious funds (CFG, 2013), although the ethical stance of certain charities in this regard is not always viewed as being of the highest standard (Hind, 2017). Furthermore, expansion of the charity sector has frequently been openly endorsed by government, sometimes based on policy objectives related to a perceived 'appropriate' balance of government and non-government activities. The financial constraints and crises of the last few years have encouraged governments to engage more with the charity sector (not always in the most considered and controlled manner) in relation to services previously provided by government. Indeed, the withdrawal of certain public-sector services has often put pressure on charities to respond to increasing beneficiary needs. Such factors increase the risk of inappropriate interference and steering by the government, with potential negative consequences to a range of stakeholders, including the public at large.

As outlined above, recent scandals, of various hues and in a variety of jurisdictions, have undoubtedly undermined trust and confidence in the sector in both the UK and RoI (and elsewhere). Some charity regulators have moved quickly to recognise the potential damage this can cause and have identified the need to respond by adjusting regulatory and control processes. Such changes reflect shifting expectations regarding regulation, accountability, trust and transparency (although each of these terms is capable of a variety of interpretations), and the trend towards strategic regulation. Whether such is required, or whether it reflects moves towards a 'Big Brother-type' audit society, remains uncertain and debated. However, it does suggest, at the very least, a degree of momentum towards greater engagement with a variety of stakeholders.

Changing Accountability and the Role of the Annual Report

Accountability can be viewed as the requirement to be answerable for one's conduct and responsibilities, a concept that comes more into focus when faced with a changing and dynamic external environment (influenced by, for example, funding pressures and high-profile scandals). While accountability is wider than accounting (no matter how widely we define accounting), good accounting and reporting is a key aspect of a good system of accountability. In this regard, since the early 1980s the UK has developed (in 1988) and periodically 'refreshed' (in 1995, 2000, 2005 and 2014) a Statement of Recommended Practice (SORP) relating to charity accounting and reporting. The SORP, over time, has become mandatory for most large UK charities and best practice for RoI charities. This has emphasised both the important 'financial account' and, arguably, the even more important 'performance account,' or 'telling the charity's story' (see Connolly *et al.*, 2013). While the original SORP (Accounting Standards Committee, 1988) largely sought to reduce diversity in charity financial statements (based almost entirely on applying business accounting principles), subsequent revisions required financial statements to be much more charity-specific (and very distinctive when compared with business financial statements) and focused attention on the content of narrative information (in recognition of its significance in discharging accountability).

A key feature of this evolutionary process in the charities-SORP development has been the way stakeholder engagement has been utilised (for example, involving, among others, such stakeholder groups as donors, funders and beneficiaries), both as a method of improving reporting and as a means of legitimating the SORP itself and the charities that use it (Connolly *et al.*, 2013). While it may be the case (particularly in businesses) that tensions exist between the differing stakeholder groups in terms of information needs (and the possibility exists for resource providers, particularly shareholders, to be in a privileged position), this is much less likely to be the situation in a charity context where there is often close alignment between, for example, donors' interests and beneficiary needs (Connolly and Hyndman, 2017).

Moreover, key stakeholders (such as government and large institutional funders) have been identified as instrumental in driving developments in non-financial (including impact) reporting, a feature capable of serving a wide range of stakeholders, particularly beneficiaries and individual donors (Hyndman and McMahon, 2011; Yang *et al.*, 2017). Indeed, the increased highlighting of non-financial performance measures (with 'impact' seen as the ultimate expression of performance) as a means of discharging appropriate accountability has been a continuing and developing theme of recent years (Charity Commission and OSCR, 2014a). While the difficulties of measuring performance in such terms is recognised as being fraught with challenges (indeed, the concept of performance in charities is frequently viewed as a contestable notion), the potential for it, not only to support the discharge of accountability but also to improve charity management focus, has been widely recognised.

A charity's trustees are responsible for the preparation of an annual report and financial statement (hereon referred to as an 'annual report'), which together are generally recognised as key documents in the discharge of accountability to external users. The purpose of preparing an annual report is to discharge the trustees' duty of public accountability and stewardship. As statutory documents, they have a validity that is missing from other flows of communication. Among other things, the annual report should enable a reader to appreciate a charity's structure, activities and achievements, as well as its financial transactions and financial position. This is not to say there are no other valuable and much-used channels of communication between a charity and its stakeholders, but the annual report holds a legitimacy and importance that is unsurpassed (Connolly and Hyndman, 2013).

A *leitmotif* in a range of academic and official publications has been that annual reports (and the accounting and reporting that they comprise) are an important aspect of how a charity engages with its stakeholders (Charity Commission, 2004a, 2004b; Charity Commission and OSCR, 2014a; Charity Commission for NI, 2016; Mack *et al.*, 2017). A key argument is that good accounting and reporting underpins good accountability, good accountability supports the building of trust between the charity and its stakeholders, and trust is essential to ensure the continuing health of the charity (including its ability to access funding). Conversely, poor accounting and reporting undermines accountability, undermined accountability damages trust, and damaged trust weakens a charity (and makes it more difficult to access funding).

1.3 Legitimating Accounting Changes and Performance Reporting

Legitimation of Accounting and Reporting Changes

In order to explain why the introduction of a new practice (such as a new or revised SORP), succeeds or fails to be adopted, embraced and embedded within a certain institutional field (such as the charity sector), it is essential to understand how actors (such as charity accountants and charity managers) legitimate (or justify) the change. Such internal legitimation could be viewed in terms of conformity to the law or to rules (formal or informal), or the ability to be defended with logic or justification.[4] Change can be imposed, but if it is not seen as legitimate (or having substantive justification) in the context in which it is applied, it is likely to be resisted.

How rhetoric and legitimation strategies shape the implementation and reproduction of generally accepted changes within organisations has received limited attention in the past, especially in a charity setting. The rhetorical arguments and strategies used during a process of change can strengthen or weaken the adoption of new practices and the way key charity actors make sense of the change. Indeed, the more persuasive the justification for the introduction of a new practice (such as a SORP), the more reasonable its adoption will be perceived, and ultimately accepted. Therefore, in the case of a revised SORP, the greater the legitimation of the changes proposed by those charged with implementing the changes, the greater the likelihood that substantial change will occur.

While a few accounting studies have investigated the rhetoric and legitimation strategies used to make sense of accounting practices (see **Chapter 5, Section 5.1**), these have not been focussed on the charity sector. It should be realised that the introduction of a SORP (or the revision of an existing SORP) is not merely a mechanistic application of a new practice into formal organisational structures, procedures and mechanisms. Such change requires the interaction of individuals and units inside and outside of the organisation. In the light of these considerations, it seems particularly important to study legitimation processes in relation to changes in charity

---

[4] This can be contrasted with external legitimacy, which is linked to ideas of legitimacy theory (Suchman, 1995), whereby an organisation tries to align its actions with social norms and stakeholder expectations – see **Chapter 2** for a fuller discussion.

accounting and reporting at their development stage (as in the case of the FRS 102 SORP (Charity Commission and OSCR, 2014a)), when they are discussed but have yet to be implemented. By doing so, it may also be possible to support their actual introduction and predict their impact on the charity (and the sector at large). This important issue, which has not previously been explored in a charity setting, is examined in detail in **Chapter 5,** where field evidence from the charity sector (on the basis of interviewing charity accountants in the UK and RoI) is presented and analysed.

Performance Reporting

Over time, recommendations on performance and governance reporting (arguably having greater importance to many charity stakeholders than traditional financial statements) have been progressively added to the SORP. Key aspects of this have related to: explaining a charity's objectives and the strategies mobilised to achieve these objectives; providing information about achievements and performance, and disclosing descriptions of the role and contribution of volunteers (a key input to the work that many charities do).

Performance accountability refers to managerial effectiveness and impact of the organisation on society (i.e. organisational success). With respect to it, there has been considerable debate as to how performance can be measured and how such accountability can be discharged. Frequently, performance reporting and the components of that reporting have been explained using a production model of performance utilising such terms as input, process, output, outcome and impact. The importance of outcome or impact measurement and reporting (impact, arguably, being the ultimate expression of the performance of a charity) has, despite major measurement difficulties, gained high profile. Although not specifically referred to in earlier iterations, the latest SORP (the 'FRS 102 SORP') (Charity Commission and OSCR, 2014a), while clearly acknowledging the challenges, explicitly encourages charities to develop and use impact reporting as a basis for discharging performance accountability. This could be viewed as one of the most radical aspects of the FRS 102 SORP (Charity Commission and OSCR, 2014a) and it is an emergent theme that is explained and developed in the book. This issue is examined in **Chapter 6**, where extant performance reporting is investigated (through an analysis of annual reports and annual reviews) and related to past evidence and current pronouncements.

1.4 Key Aims and Structure of the Book

Focusing on the UK and RoI, the overall aim of this book is to present and explore how charity accounting and reporting (and accountability) has evolved over time (and is likely to evolve going forward). Key aspects of this (which are investigated empirically) relate to the importance — and current state — of performance (including impact) reporting, and the view that during processes of accounting change (such as the introduction and evolution of the charities SORP), it is important to not only understand accounting technicalities but also the way they are interpreted and legitimated.

The book is structured as follows:

Chapter 2 explores the meanings and links between governance and accountability and their connections to accounting and ideas such as trust, legitimacy and transparency. Overall, it provides a brief summary of some of the main theories and ideas that underpin much of what is presented in **Chapter 3** (which traces the development of the SORP) and **Chapter 4** (which examines previous related research). In particular, it presents ideas that are expanded upon in the field research reported later in **Chapter 5** (which examines internal legitimation of accounting and reporting changes required by the most recent SORP) and **Chapter 6** (which explores the current state of performance reporting by UK and RoI charities).

Chapter 3 analyses the development of charity accounting and reporting since the 1970s. In particular, it traces and analyses the development and content of the SORP in its various iterations, focusing particularly on the requirements of the FRS 102 SORP (Charity Commission and OSCR, 2014a) in terms of both financial accounting and wider reporting.

Chapter 4 examines previous charity accounting and accountability research. As such it provides a reference point for the later empirical research on internal legitimation of accounting changes (**Chapter 5**) and performance reporting (**Chapter 6**). While a range of studies on charity accounting, accountability and governance exists, research in this chapter is organised into three broad categories relating to: the extent to which charity financial statements comply with SORP requirements; disclosure patterns of the information accompanying annual financial statements (mainly performance reporting); and the extent and impact of stakeholder engagement with respect to reporting frameworks for charities.

Chapter 5 contains field evidence exploring how key charity actors (i.e. accountants in charities, who are responsible for the SORP implementation and accounts/report compliance) involved in the introduction of the new FRS 102 SORP (Charity Commission and OSCR, 2014a) understand, interpret and legitimate (or delegitimate) the changes required. It is argued that the way and the extent to which this occurs will affect the ultimate influence of the SORP in changing accounting and reporting. The chapter reports and analyses the results of 21 semi-structured interviews conducted in the UK and RoI.

Chapter 6 reviews the concept of performance in the context of charities, indicating the importance — and difficulties — of reporting in such terms. It then presents an empirical analysis of a matched sample of performance disclosures by large UK and RoI charities (in their annual reports and annual reviews) and discusses the results in the context of performance accountability and changes over time.

Chapter 7 details the main themes from the book, summarises the key findings from the empirical analysis in **Chapters 5** and **6** and makes suggestions for policy, practice and further research.

Chapter 2

Governance and Accountability in Charities

The issues of governance and accountability increasingly come to the fore when discussing the growth and development of the charity sector, and when debating the ways in which charities should operate and report (Charity Commission, 2013). Notwithstanding this, the terms 'governance' and 'accountability' have a range of meanings and can be seen as overlapping and, at times, rather vague. Yet their importance is undisputed. In addition, how concepts like accountability and governance are applied (and operationalised) in a charity context may be distinctively different from how they are applied in other contexts (such as a business setting). This chapter explores the meanings and links between governance and accountability, and their connections to accounting and ideas such as trust, legitimacy and transparency (terms that frequently emerge in discussions regarding charity accounting and reporting). References to such notions are clearly seen in the rhetoric relating to the development and evolution of the charity accounting and reporting Statement of Recommended Practice (SORP) (detailed in **Chapter 3**) and in previous charity accounting and accountability research (presented in **Chapter 4**).

This chapter begins by contrasting the meaning of governance in business and charity (not-for-profit (NFP)) settings (**Section 2.1**). This is followed by an examination of the links between accounting and accountability, and how these ideas connect to both agency theory and notions of transparency and legitimation (external and internal) (**Section 2.2**). The subsequent sections examine in greater detail the concept of accountability as relating to questions concerning to whom, and for what, a charity might be accountable (**Section 2.3**), and the direction and form of that accountability (**Section 2.4**). Overall, the chapter provides a summary of some of the themes that underpin much of what is presented later in the book and, in particular, presents ideas that are expanded upon in the field research reported later regarding internal legitimation strategies used by accountants with respect to SORP changes (**Chapter 5**) and the current state of performance reporting by charities (**Chapter 6**).

2.1   Governance and Charities

Meaning of Governance

The word 'governance' comes from the Latin word 'gubernare', meaning 'to direct, rule or guide', which was in turn derived from the Greek term 'kybernan'. This means 'to steer or pilot a ship'. Using this definition, if one imagines an institution as a ship, then governance is the process of steering or guiding the ship towards its destination or goal. Choosing a destination and making sure the crew and passengers arrive safely is the responsibility of a ship's pilot, just as determining the objectives and regulating the relationship between all the various parties involved with an organisation may form part of the modern understanding of 'governance'. Viewing governance as the act of steering or directing constitutes a major part of this understanding. For example, Osborne and Gaebler (1992) provide a useful analogy when they distinguish between governing (steering) and implementing policy or operations (rowing).

Governance in Businesses and Charities

Although charities are clearly not part of the commercial sector, the concept of governance (usually referred to as 'corporate governance' in the for-profit sector) adopted in the literature relating to businesses may provide a useful indication of what governance might encompass for charities. In this respect, principal-agent theory or 'agency theory' (Jensen and Meckling, 1976) is often used. This focuses on the relationships between a principal and an agent, where the principal transfers resources to the agent, thereby generating the need to monitor and assess how this latter's actions are performed and reported. From an agency perspective, Shleifer and Vishny (1997, p. 737) provide a concise definition of corporate governance as dealing 'with the ways in which suppliers of finance to corporations assure themselves of getting a return on their investment'. Immediately, it is apparent that this definition is inappropriate for use in a charity, as charities do not return their funds to donors; instead donors provide them so that the charity may carry out some philanthropic service (focusing on a specific beneficiary group or society as a whole). Therefore, within the charity sector, donors' 'return' could be viewed as the money being used for the purpose for which it was donated.

With respect to charities and, more widely, to not-for-profit organisations (NFPOs), Cornforth (2003, p. 17) refers to governance as 'the systems by which organisations are directed, controlled and accountable'. In doing so, it is argued that the methods by which organisations are accountable may be a particularly important part of governance in the charity sector. However, rather like governance itself, accountability is a concept that may have more than one meaning (see **Sections 2.3** and **2.4** below). Stone and Ostrower (2007), in exploring the various facets of governance in NFPO and public-sector organisations, argue that many ideas come within its boundaries, including:

- accountability for performance;
- its multi-layered (or nested) nature;
- the network of formal and informal relationships that exist inside and outside of the organisation; and
- boards as primary actors influencing organisational effectiveness.

Reflecting on the above issues, Hyndman and McDonnell (2009) suggest that charity governance could be viewed as: relating to the distribution of rights and responsibilities among and within the various stakeholder groups involved, including the way in which they are accountable to one another; and also relating to the performance of the organisation, in terms of setting objectives or goals and the means of attaining them. This ties together the idea of governance as a set of relationships between stakeholders with the idea of governance as ensuring the organisation is effectively run in terms of attaining its objectives (defined, in this case, as meeting the needs for which the organisation was created, which in charities have a beneficiary or society-at-large focus). In addition, it recognises the importance of groups other than the board of trustees in delivering good governance in a charity.

2.2 Accounting, Accountability and Transparency

Accounting and Accountability

As argued above, accountability is an important aspect of governance. Conventional views of accounting see it as a purposive activity, directed towards a specified end, which is the meeting of users' (or stakeholders') information needs, with a stakeholder being defined as any 'group or individual who can affect or is affected by an organisation's achievements' (Freeman, 1984, p. 46) (for example, beneficiaries, donors, regulators or the public at large). It is viewed as being concerned with providing information to satisfy the needs of users/stakeholders (Accounting Standards Committee, 1975; Accounting Standards Board (ASB), 1999), and interpretations of this in the context of NFPOs (ASB, 2007) highlight a similar thrust. While accountability is more than accounting, focusing on the information needs of users/stakeholders seems clearly linked with ideas relating to accountability.

In considering what accountability means, Jackson (1982) emphasises the importance of explaining or justifying one party's conduct to another party through the giving of information (p. 220):

> "Basically, accountability involves explaining or justifying what has been done, what is currently being done, and what has been planned ... Thus, one party is accountable to another in the sense that one of the parties has the right to call upon the other to give account of his activities. Accountability involves, therefore, the giving of information."

In the context of charities, the Charity Commission (2004a) sees accountability in terms of a charity's response to the legitimate information needs of its stakeholders, an aspect of which is often made through annual reports and accounts, which should provide "adequate information to allow stakeholders to assess the overall performance of the charity" (p. 2). Emphasising a wider perspective, Roberts and Scapens (1985) describe accountability as a relationship where parties are required to explain and take responsibility for their actions through "the giving and demanding of reasons for conduct" (p. 447). In a similar light, Fry (1995) views accountability in terms of "public account-giving" that might include "justifications, rationalisations, stories, excuses" (p. 184). Again in the context of NFPOs, Edwards and Hulme (1995) see accountability as a means by which individuals and organisations report to a recognised authority, or authorities, and are held responsible for their actions.

Accountability, Agency Theory and Transparency

The accountability relationship (or stakeholder/user-needs model) can, to an extent, be summarised in terms of a principal–agent relationship (see **Figure 2.1**, which is an adaptation of Laughlin's (1990) skeletal model). The principal often transfers to an agent resources and expectations regarding the transfer. These expectations form the basis of the accountability relationship. As Laughlin highlights, these expectations are complex and may be written and explicit or unwritten and implicit. In a charity context, the principal could be viewed as a donor or major funder (often considered a key stakeholder in a charity setting) who transfers resources (without any direct economic benefit to themselves anticipated) to an agent (the charity).

With such a transfer comes expectations (frequently not specifically detailed in anything resembling contractual terms) on the part of the donor (principal) that the resources will be used to further the mission and objectives of the charity (often expressed in terms of supporting beneficiary need, or creating a wider public benefit); and expectations that information will be provided as to what a charity has done or plans to do (possibly in terms of activities, programmes, stories, spending, etc.). Accountability is discharged (or an account is given) as such information is communicated (through a variety of mechanisms and channels) to the donor (principal) regarding this. On this basis the principal (donor) holds the agent (the charity) to account by responding to such information through action (for example, continuing to provide funds or ceasing to provide funds) or communication (for example, by congratulating or censoring the charity).

Figure 2.1   **Accountability Relationship**

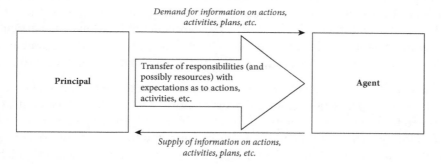

Demand for information on actions, activities, plans, etc.

Principal

Transfer of responsibilities (and possibly resources) with expectations as to actions, activities, etc.

Agent

Supply of information on actions, activities, plans, etc.

In addition, accountability has often been linked with ideas relating to transparency, which is frequently considered in terms of one party (possibly the public or a donor) gaining information about another party (possibly a charity), including: its processes and performance; its structures; and knowledge regarding who gains from, or pays for, its activities (Heald, 2006a; Etzioni, 2010). While transparency is often associated with (but not fully synonymous with) openness and disclosure, the importance of meaningful communication is critical. O'Neill (2006) argues that disclosure will achieve little "unless the material disseminated is made accessible to and assessable by relevant audiences, and actually reaches those audiences" (p. 84). Notwithstanding the generally positive thrust that charities (and organisations in general) should be transparent (Charity Commission, 2004a and 2004b), it has been argued that transparency may not always support accountability (and organisational performance) in all contexts; with Heald (2006b) analogising transparency as having the potential to act as sunlight (with positive illuminating and disinfectant properties) or, less positively, as searchlight or torch: "when sunlight becomes searchlight it can be uncomfortable and when it becomes torch it may be destructive" (p. 71).

External and Internal Legitimation

The above ideas on accountability and transparency can be related to concepts from legitimacy theory, with legitimacy viewed in terms of the extent to which an organisation's actions align with social norms and (stakeholder) expectations (Suchman, 1995). This could be considered as external legitimation. Engagement with stakeholders, including processes relating to the discharge of accountability, might, to an extent at least, be based on a need to convince external stakeholders of the legitimacy of the charity. Legitimacy theory suggests that an organisation can only survive in the long term if society perceives the organisation as legitimate, or operating in accordance with social norms (Suchman, 1995). Charities therefore need to demonstrate compliance with social norms and institutional rules, and this can be achieved through various mechanisms (including those relating to the discharge of accountability). Convincing stakeholders of legitimacy is particularly important in a charity sector which relies on public trust to sustain and develop its activities (Alexander *et al.*, 2010; Saxton *et al.*, 2012; Hind, 2017).

The idea of legitimation can also be considered from the perspective of those within an organisation (internal legitimation) and, in a charity context, related to the evolving changes in the charities SORP. The implementation of accounting change is not a mechanistic process, and the perceptions of actors within the organisation is likely to impact on how and the extent to which (and the manner in which) externally 'required' changes are likely to be implemented and embedded. The argument is that the effective implementation of accounting and reporting changes (such as the SORP requirements) requires key actors (such as charity managers and charity accountants) to see them as appropriate and useful. The degree to which such individuals view the changes as being justified (legitimated), or the extent to which such changes are questioned (or delegitimated), is likely to impact on the embedding of the changes themselves. Green (1994) and Green and Li (2011) identify a range of individual legitimation (and delegitimation) strategies: authorisation, rationalisation, normalisation, pathos, moralisation and narrativisation. Using these strategies as a framework for considering the perceptions of change, individual legitimation of the FRS 102 SORP (Charity Commission and OSCR, 2014a) is explored in detail later in this book as field research relating to charity accountants (**Chapter 5**).

2.3   To Whom and for What?

In considering accountability, two key questions emerge: to whom is a charity accountable; and for what is a charity accountable?

To Whom is a Charity Accountable?

In terms of the 'to whom' question, and specifically with respect to accountability and accounting, the meeting of stakeholders' (or users') information needs is a *leitmotif* in both *Transparency and Accountability* (Charity Commission, 2004a) and *Charity Reporting and Accounting: Taking Stock and Future Reform* (Charity Commission, 2009). It is this language that is much in evidence in communications from the Charity Commission (and other charity-sector bodies) in recent years in discussions of governance in charities, and these discussions have mirrored similar debates in respect of both public- and private-sector governance and accountability in the UK (see, for example, the Cadbury Report, 1992).

Several authors have identified (or speculated about) a range of stakeholders who, in the language of Freeman (1984), are 'affected' or 'affect' the operation of NFPOs (including charities) (Bouckaert and Vandenhove, 1998; Friedman and Mason, 2004; Hyndman and McDonnell, 2009). In these studies (which are often framed mobilising stakeholder theory, Freeman, 1984), key external stakeholders identified include: beneficiaries, government and regulators, donors/funders and the public at large. The central argument of stakeholder theory is that if organisations engage with stakeholders on a basis of mutual trust and cooperation, those organisations would build legitimacy and reputation that would give them competitive advantage. Given the breadth of parties who might be considered stakeholders, the issue of how organisations can identify 'who or what really counts' and prioritise competing stakeholder claims is considered by Mitchell *et al.* (1997, p. 853). They argue that the salience of stakeholders (or the degree to which they and their arguments are perceived to count) depends upon the stakeholder possessing three attributes: power, legitimacy and urgency. It is suggested that the most salient to the organisation are the stakeholders who are perceived to have the greatest amount of these attributes; and the claims of these 'definitive stakeholders' (p. 878) are likely to be prioritised.

While developed in the corporate sector, there is an obvious read-across of stakeholder theory and ideas of stakeholder salience to charities (although this should be done carefully, taking account of the differences between sectors — see Connolly and Hyndman, 2017). For the UK charity sector, in particular, the language of stakeholder theory resonates with the Charity Commission's advocacy of: developing good relationships with stakeholders as one of the *Hallmarks of an Effective Charity* (Charity Commission, 2004b); needing to report to meet the information needs of stakeholders (Charity Commission, 2004a); and involving key stakeholders in governance, such as including beneficiaries on boards of trustees (Charity Commission, 2000b).

For What is a Charity Accountable?

There are different bases of accountability. As Stewart (1984) argues in relation to the activities for which accounts have to be given (p. 16): "the purpose of the account and hence the basis of accountability can vary." He then goes on to develop a 'ladder of accountability' relating to public accountability which contains a number of 'rungs'. These are summarised in **Table 2.1.**

Table 2.1   **Stewart's Ladder of Accountability**

Base	Concerned with
Accountability for probity and legality	Concerned with the avoidance of malfeasance, ensuring that funds are used properly and in the manner authorised, and that the powers given by the law are not exceeded.
Process accountability	Concerned with ensuring that there has been no maladministration, and in particular no maladministration leading to injustice.
Performance accountability	Concerned with ensuring that there is no waste in the use of resources (efficiency) and, in a wider sense of performance, whether performance achieved meets required standards.
Programme accountability	Concerned with establishing whether a particular organisation has met its objectives and the goals set for it.
Policy accountability	Concerned with the policies that the organisation has pursued and those that it has failed to pursue.

From a reporting perspective, Stewart (1984) argues that an accountability information system should report on all levels of accountability. However, two main types of information that may be particularly important in this regard with respect to charities are: financial information as contained in traditional financial reports (to indicate, for example, that the money raised has been used for the appropriate purposes, that the charity has 'lived within its means', and the level of resources available to the charity for future service provision); and wider performance information, often of a non-financial nature (possibly relating to the goals, objectives, output, impact, efficiency and effectiveness of the charity; for a fuller explanation and discussion of this, see **Chapters 3** and **6**).

Regarding accountability, the information needs, and desired engagement (if any), of each stakeholder group (for example, beneficiaries/users of services, regulators and donors/funders) is likely to be different. For example, beneficiaries (and possibly donors) may emphasise the output, or effectiveness, of a charity, while the concern of regulators may be more on efficiency and probity.

It has been suggested by a number of writers that with charities specifically, and NFPOs generally, there may be temptation to focus accountability reporting on traditional financial accounts at the expense of wider performance reporting. This is possibly because of the existence of standard rules and templates, and the fact that accountants (who are often central to the information-provision process) may be particularly 'comfortable' and 'familiar' with such accounts. In addition, the determination of what is appropriate performance information (and the capturing of this information in an objective manner) is much more contestable and difficult than well-established financial interpretations. However, it has been argued that such a focus might undermine accountability by concentrating on the less important (Gray, 1983; Connolly and Hyndman, 2013). Gray (1983, 1984), in particular, highlights this danger, arguing that financial accounts only fully discharge accountability in 'special cases', the best example of which is the business enterprise/shareholder relationship. He suggests that, with charities, such reporting can only go a small way towards supporting the discharge of accountability.

2.4   Directions and Forms of Accountability

Upward and Downward Accountability

By being accountable to funders/donors and regulators (upward stakeholders), possibly by focusing on financial probity, efficiency and impact on beneficiaries and societies, charities can gain external legitimacy from such parties (Ebrahim, 2003; ASB, 2007). This has become increasingly important as charities are being placed under growing scrutiny and the need to maintain (or reinstate) public trust and confidence, either voluntarily or on demand, is particularly emphasised (Hind, 2017). To an extent, charity supporters and funders are somewhat akin to shareholders of commercial organisations (ASB, 2007). Yet while charity supporters and funders are arguably less likely to monitor charities as closely as shareholders may monitor commercial organisations, they are more likely to terminate their support if their trust and confidence wanes as their personal welfare is not necessarily dependent upon this support. Accountability and transparency are, therefore, critical attributes through which to gain and maintain public/funder support and trust.

Mechanisms for discharging accountability also enable charities to achieve external legitimacy from their downward stakeholders (for example, beneficiaries/users of services). In contrast to upward stakeholders, there is often a disparity in the relative power of charities (who may have, and may exercise, power) and downward stakeholders (who may possess little power). However, this power should not be exercised to avoid accounting to these stakeholder groups, but, rather, recognising the weak position of downward stakeholders, charities (as value-driven organisations) should choose to prioritise them in the discharge of accountability. Accounting to and for downward stakeholders enables charities to develop intangible sources of external legitimacy such as credibility, reputation, trust and integrity, which, in turn, are likely to engender the trust and support not only of beneficiaries but also of donors/funders (Slim, 2002; Connolly and Hyndman, 2017). In other words, consistent with the notion of a broad accountability paradigm, charities have an 'upward' accountability to their funders and financial supporters, government and oversight agencies and the public at large, and also a 'downward' accountability to the beneficiary groups and clients who use their services.

Contractual and Communal Accountability

It has been suggested (Laughlin, 1996) that an organisation's style of accountability will depend upon the relationship between the organisation's principals (for example, possibly donors/funders) and agents (possibly the charity and its managers/employees), categorising accountability as either contractual or communal. Laughlin argues that contractual accountability exists in formal relationships, where expectations of action, and information demand and supply are clearly defined and specified. At its most extreme, it involves entering into a legally binding agreement over standards of performance by laying them down in writing and in specific enforceable terms, often through the judicial process (Dubnick, 1998). In contrast, it is opined that communal accountability occurs in less formal relationships, where expectations over conduct and information demand and supply are less structured and defined. The communal accountability process involves meeting stakeholders' needs through consultation and seeking their involvement in the decision-making process.

These different forms of accountability are attributed by Laughlin (1996) to the potential for trust–value conflict between principals and agents in particular settings. It is contended that formal mechanisms of accountability are less important (and less pronounced) where high levels of trust exist between parties, and where it is expected (and assumed) that the agent (the charity) will fulfil the expectations of the principal (donors/funders). Alternatively, where there are low levels of trust, the principal (donors/funders) is likely to give much greater attention to establishing and utilising formal (and contractual) mechanisms to exert control over the behaviour of the agent (the charity). In a similar manner, and with respect to the values of principals and agents, where these align closely, communal accountability is more likely. However, if this is not the case, contractual forms of accountability will tend to dominate.

Chapter 3

Charity Accounting and Reporting: The Development and Content of the Statement of Recommended Practice

As was seen in **Chapters 1** and **2**, the charity sector is large, significant and one in which the fact and perception of accountability is particularly important. As was discussed, the importance of appropriate sector visibility and the ability for key stakeholders to scrutinise charity activity (in terms of, for example, finances, activity and performance) is vital in terms of legitimating the sector and individual charities within it, and in building trust (which is essential to the health and growth of the sector). It was argued that accountability can be viewed as being related to the requirement to be answerable for one's conduct and responsibilities. While it is recognised that this is more than merely accounting (no matter how widely we define accounting), good accounting and reporting is nevertheless a vital part of a good system of accountability.

Despite the importance of good accounting and reporting to the sector, until the 1980s the framework for such was extremely weak. In the UK and RoI, regulation was much less developed than it is today, with the lone regulator at that time (only England and Wales had such a functionary) not focusing to any significant extent on the reviewing and monitoring issues relating to accounting, reporting and accountability. Charity law was diverse and had little to say about charity accounting and the publication of financial statements.

While charities were often under an obligation to keep proper books of account and to prepare financial statements regularly, such statements frequently did not have to show a 'true and fair view,' and were not required to be audited. While this was not the case with charities incorporated as limited companies (these being subject to the reporting requirements of the Companies Acts), in practice the detailed application of accounting standards to the financial statements of such incorporation was commonly ignored (and auditors rarely commented on lack of adherence to such standards) because of misunderstanding and inertia (Pearson and Gray, 1978; Austin and Posnett, 1979). Overall, in the UK and RoI, there was limited pressure to improve charity reporting from legislation, accounting standards or an effective regulatory body, and wider reporting (such as that relating to governance and performance) was rarely on the agenda.

This changed considerably in the UK in the 1980s, with the development in 1988 – and subsequent periodic 'refreshing' – of a Statement of Recommended Practice (SORP)[1] relating to charity accounting and reporting. The charities SORP, which eventually gained considerable legal backing, also became a benchmark for good charity accounting practice in RoI. After outlining the early problems identified with charity reporting (**Section 3.1**), this chapter explains the subsequent development and evolution of the charities SORP (**Section 3.2**). Then, after summarising the background and principles underlying the FRS 102 SORP (Charity Commission and OSCR, 2014a) (**Section 3.3**), the detailed form and content of the trustees' annual report (TAR) and financial statements are discussed with the use of extensive examples in **Sections 3.4** and **3.5**, respectively.

3.1   Early Problems with Charity Accounting and Reporting

Goodman Committee (1976) and Austin and Posnett (1979)

During the 1970s, interest in financial reporting by charities began to grow. For example, in examining legislation relating to charitable organisations in the UK, the Goodman Committee (National Council of Social Service, 1976) argued that with respect to accounting and reporting, charities should be subject to disciplines consistent with the size of their assets and their responsibilities. It was contended that (p. 112):

> "At the highest levels, disciplines as strict as those applicable to a public company under the stringent provisions of the Companies Acts may well be appropriate."

Moreover, the report suggested a number of requirements in addition to those obligatory at the time for charities of 'any significant size' (p. 113). These included, among other things: separate reporting of expenditure on fundraising, administration and charitable objectives; more categorisation with respect to income; the requirement that larger charities be audited; and greater engagement of the Charity Commission in terms of examining charities' financial statements. Furthermore, the Committee encouraged charities to produce, as a supplement to financial statements, a report which explained in 'general language' (p. 114) activities and future plans.

[1] SORPs are recommendations on accounting practice for specialised industries or sectors, and they supplement other legal and regulatory requirements. Where a separate SORP exists for a particular class of charities (for example, for the Further and Higher Education sector or Registered Social Landlords), those charities should adhere to that SORP. Large UK charities (including those that form the basis of the research reported in **Chapters 5** and **6**) must comply with the extant charities SORP, with compliance in RoI being considered best practice. At the time of writing (June 2017), the extant charities SORP is the 'FRS 102 SORP' (Charity Commission and Office of the Scottish Charity Regulator (OSCR), 2014a), which is discussed further in **Sections 3.2–3.5**.

At a similar time, concern was expressed about the availability and usefulness of charity financial statements, with the information, when available, frequently being inaccurate, unreliable and/or lacking comparability (over time and between charities). For example, Austin and Posnett (1979), utilising 1975 data, found that many charities were simply failing to provide information at all. In their survey of almost 400 large charities in England and Wales, they found that the vast majority did not have up-to-date financial statements filed with the Charity Commission (despite the requirement in law for charities of the size surveyed to do so). Moreover, where financial statements were supplied, these often lacked quality, consistency and compliance with extant accounting standards. Austin and Posnett cited numerous examples of questionable reporting practices; for example, showing fundraising income net of costs and failing to value and depreciate fixed assets.

Bird and Morgan-Jones (1981)

A major piece of research that provided a catalyst for the greater attention that was to come was provided by Bird and Morgan-Jones (1981). Based on surveys of financial reporting by 85 charities of different sizes during the mid-1970s, they highlighted major failings in charities' transparency and accountability. The study revealed a sector where non-compliance with accounting standards was prevalent, archaic accounting treatments were used and there was a wide disparity in accounting practices between charities. Stark examples of these failings were given, which were often strongly contrary to the relevant accounting standards or normal practice, and which frequently had the effect of understating surpluses and assets or overstating losses and liabilities. Examples of such practices included:

- recording legacy income (in full or partially) to capital rather than income. The majority of charities that received legacies (that is, most charities in the survey) either credited them directly to capital, or split the credit between revenue and capital (often through the use of a 'legacy equalisation account');
- immediate expensing of fixed asset purchases (rather than capitalising and depreciating such assets over their useful life). Indeed, in a small number of cases, even freehold property was written off on acquisition; and
- creating provisions for future expenses which were charged to the income statement to reduce surplus/increase deficit of the period (contrary to the rules on provisioning).

This perceived bias towards treatments that made charities seem more in need of funds led Bird and Morgan-Jones (1981, p. 196) to suggest that:

"Management is fearful that, if they report truly and fairly, fundraising activities will be adversely affected, and therefore ways and means are found for tucking away revenue and charging expenses which would not be tolerated in business accounts."

Moreover, Bird and Morgan-Jones concluded that this situation was tolerated, and indeed perpetuated, because there was "no effective monitoring of the public accountability of charities by ensuring prompt filing of financial statements and by expert review of a significant proportion of these" (p. 225). In the conclusions to their report, they focused on the information needs of the users of charity reports (including funders, managers, boards/ trustees, auditors and regulators). While rejecting a prescriptive, rigid approach to preparing charity financial statements, they opined that: "users of charity accounts, as well as their producers and auditors, are ... strongly in favour of moves towards greater consistency and comparability in the accounts" (p. 146). Accordingly, in the appendix to their report they outlined possible detailed reporting guidelines which championed adherence to applicable accounting standards and offered specific guidance on problematic items identified in their work (such as with respect to legacies and fixed assets).

Response to Bird and Morgan-Jones

The research of Bird and Morgan-Jones (1981), which had been funded by the Institute of Chartered Accountants in England and Wales (ICAEW), stimulated much debate in the sector and among sector commentators. For example, Falk (1981), writing a comment piece in the ICAEW's members' journal *Accountancy*, highlighted the particular information needs of current or potential funders. He suggested that a funder needed not only financial information on income raised, sources of funds, costs of fundraising and administration, but also detail on how extensive the work and influence of the charity was; this, he acknowledged, would require an assessment "beyond financial matters" (p. 74). Falk suggested that if such information was clearly stated in charity reports, a range of stakeholders, including funders, would be able to compare charities and their relative efficiency. Gray (1984, p. 84), writing in the same publication, went further in arguing that wider reporting beyond financial reporting should be the focus of charity reporting: "there is a role for financial accounting but it is a role subsidiary to the main task of providing effectiveness information".

3.2   The Development and Evolution of the Charities Statement of Recommended Practice

Overall, the findings of the Bird and Morgan-Jones (1981) research were widely regarded as a 'wake-up call' for the UK charity sector. In April 1982, in a stated response, the Accounting Standards Committee (ASC) – the regulator and standard-setting body of the UK accounting profession at that time – began a lengthy consultation process on the issues raised. A charities' working party was set up by the ASC, with representatives from various stakeholder groups, including the accounting profession, charities, foundations and the Charity Commission. This was tasked with exploring ways of enhancing the usefulness and comparability of charities' annual reports and financial statements. Ultimately, this resulted in the release of the first SORP for charities in 1988 (ASC, 1988).

The First Charities Statement of Recommended Practice in 1988

The findings of the charities' working party were published as a discussion paper (in 1984) and an exposure draft (in 1985). Ultimately, *Accounting by Charities, Statement of Recommended Practice 2* (ASC, 1988) was issued (the practice of numbering SORPs later ceased). It focussed on addressing the financial reporting deficiencies that had been identified in the Bird and Morgan-Jones (1981) report, often closely following that report's recommendations and interpreting existing UK reporting standards. In the majority of cases it clarified best practice, for example: donated assets should be included as incoming resources at a reasonable estimate of their value to the charity; and fixed assets should be capitalised and depreciated. However, in a number of cases, SORP 1988 allowed discretion and emphasised that presentation should be made in a manner appropriate to the charity.

Despite having recognised that users "need to know about the resources entrusted to the charity and how efficiently and effectively the charities have used them in fulfilling their objectives" (ASC, 1988, p. 2), SORP 1988 provided few guidelines on how to report such efficiency and effectiveness. This lack of recommendations on broader narrative reporting attracted criticism in the sector (Randall, 1989). Hyndman (1990) argued that SORP 1988 would do little to meet the information needs of key stakeholders (particularly donors) because of the focus on the technicalities of audited financial statements (which were not the central interest of many stakeholders) at the expense of other types of reporting. However, the small step of recognising the need for additional reporting was nonetheless seen as significant; for example, Mumford (1990) argued that it represented the first time that the ASC had given any guidelines beyond the financial statements aspect of annual reports.

An enduring criticism of SORP 1988 was that, as recommendations, its impact on charity reporting was always likely to be (and actually was) marginal, and that a more rigid regulatory framework and strengthening of SORP 1988 were needed: "there must be the weight of legislation behind the charity accounting requirements" (Randall, 1989, p. 72). Moreover, in the consultation process leading up to the publication of SORP 1988, while many respondents recognised the need for guidance, there was some criticism that the SORP's commercial focus and its either/or approach could reduce the potential for positive impact. In retrospect, it was suggested that these weaknesses contributed to the rather limited impact that SORP 1988 had on the sector (Charity Commission, 2009).

The Evolution of the Charities Statement of Recommended Practice from 1988 to 2015

Since the publication of the first SORP (ASC, 1988), ongoing efforts have been made to refine it and align it more closely to not only prevailing (and changing) financial accounting standards, but also the context to which it applies (the charity sector) and the key concerns of stakeholders. This has resulted in a series of revisions. Since 1990 the successor to the ASC, the Accounting Standards Board (ASB), has no longer engaged in the preparation of SORPs; its role is now restricted to the approval of SORPs prepared by other bodies. Such approval is based on whether the SORP provided an appropriate interpretation of the ASB's reporting standards. At this time, preparation of the charities SORP passed to the SORP Committee of the Charity Commission, the regulatory body for charities in England and Wales (in 2006, the SORP Committee was widened to become a joint SORP-making body of the Charity Commission and the Office of the Scottish Charity Regulator (OSCR)). Subsequent iterations of the SORP were issued:

- *Accounting by Charities, Statement of Recommended Practice 2* – SORP 1995 (Charity Commission, 1995);
- *Accounting and Reporting by Charities, Statement of Recommended Practice* – SORP 2000 (Charity Commission, 2000a);
- *Accounting and Reporting by Charities, Statement of Recommended Practice* – SORP 2005 (Charity Commission, 2005); and
- *Charities SORP (FRS 102) Accounting and Reporting by Charities: Statement of Recommended Practice applicable to charities preparing their accounts in accordance with the Financial Reporting Standard applicable in the UK and Republic of Ireland (FRS 102) (effective 1 January 2015)* (Charity Commission and OSCR, 2014a).[2]

[2] The Charity Commission and OSCR, as the joint SORP-making body for charities, developed two SORPs in 2014 to deal with different size categories of charities: (i) the FRS 102 SORP (Charity Commission and OSCR, 2014a); and (ii) the Financial Reporting Standard for Smaller Entities (FRSSE) SORP (Charity Commission and OSCR, 2014b). However, for reporting periods starting on or after 1 January 2016, all charities must follow the FRS 102 SORP, as the FRSSE SORP, which was developed for smaller charities, has been subsequently withdrawn. This is discussed in more detail in **Section 3.3**.

During the process of evolution since 1988, the SORP has developed virtually beyond recognition. Of particular note was the name change – with the document becoming an 'Accounting and Reporting' SORP from 2000 onwards, rather than purely an 'Accounting' SORP. This reflected an emerging emphasis in the later incarnations of the TAR (which required a greater focus on the disclosure of non-financial information, including information relating to performance and governance). Other significant changes (as shown in **Figure 3.1** and subsequently discussed below) related to: the strengthening of legislative requirements; a much greater charity-specific focus; the emphasising of performance reporting; and a reduction in the degree of preparer discretion.

Figure 3.1   **Evolution of Charities Statement of Recommended Practice**

Accounting by Charities (SORP 1988)		Accounting and Reporting by Charities (FRS 102 SORP)
Recommended practice	⟶	Mandatory for large UK charities (best practice for RoI charities)
Commercial basis	⟶	Charity-specific basis (although aligned with FRS 102)
Financial reporting focus	⟶	Increased performance reporting focus (including encouragement for impact/outcome information)
High degree of preparer discretion	⟶	Reduced preparer discretion

Legislative Force

Initially, while charities were encouraged to apply the recommendations of SORP 1988 (ASC, 1988), they were not required to do so. However, since SORP 1995 (Charity Commission, 1995), changes to the legislative framework have made compliance mandatory for larger charities. In England and Wales, the Charities Act 1960 was replaced by new Charities Acts in 1992 and 1993; these contained expanded accounting regulations for charities, extended again in the Charity Accounting Regulations 1995.

Significantly, compliance with the SORP has become a legal requirement for non-company charities with incomes in excess of £250,000 (see Charities (Accounts and Reports) Regulations 2008). In 2006, compliance with the SORP was required for the first time in Scotland (for all charities preparing accruals accounts) after the implementation of the Charity Accounts (Scotland) Regulations 2006. Here again, the income threshold is £250,000. Similarly (and at identical income thresholds), since 1 January 2016 in Northern Ireland (NI), the SORP has become mandatory for non-company charities (*Charities (Accounts and Reports) Regulations (Northern Ireland) 2015*). At the time of writing (June 2017), the SORP remains best practice (though not required) in RoI. However, recent developments, most notably the Charities Act 2009 and the establishment of the Charities Regulatory Authority (which commenced work in October 2014), may require mandatory adoption in the future.

Therefore, in effect, compliance with the SORP is now mandatory in large charities in the UK; in RoI it is best practice. The 'Recommendations' have become 'Requirements' for large UK charities (which account for a significant proportion of the economic activity of the UK charity sector). Empirical evidence shows a high level of engagement with the SORP by these charities: among others, Connolly and Hyndman (2000, 2004) have provided evidence that compliance has increased over time, presumably caused, at least in part, by the more mandatory nature of the SORP.

Charity-specific Focus

Rather than creating a set of charity reporting standards aligned with the specific context and issues faced by charities, the initial charities SORP (ASC, 1988) focussed on interpreting the existing commercial reporting standards of the time and demonstrating how they could be applied to charities. Given the findings of the Bird and Morgan-Jones (1981) report that triggered the highlighting of the deficiencies of charity reporting, and the analytical approach adopted by the researchers, this was perhaps not particularly surprising. While the SORP remains, in part, an interpretation of extant financial reporting standards (although it also requires additional disclosures that go far beyond financial reporting standards), changes to the SORP over time have led to charity financial statements becoming substantially different from commercial financial statements. One of the most radical changes was the introduction of the statement of financial activities (SOFA) in place of the income and expenditure statement in SORP 1995 (Charity Commission, 1995).

The SOFA, which has evolved since its introduction, is unlike income and expenditure statements of companies; for example, it is columnar, separately showing income and expenses related to restricted and unrestricted funds (an important distinction under trust law), and it shows income of different types together with the expenditure associated with that income (rather than showing only one type of income and many types of expenditure in 'natural categories' – such as wage costs and interest costs). The adoption of the SOFA as the primary income statement was an extremely significant step in that a SORP had never before recommended such fundamental changes, in particular changes which were so sector-specific. Connolly and Hyndman (2000) saw these modifications as a direct result of criticisms levelled at SORP 1988, including the criticism that commercially based financial statements were not fully appropriate for charities.

In addition, through the evolution of the SORP, charity-specific terminology has been introduced, has evolved and has become a natural part of the language of the SORP and the language of charity accounting and reporting. For example, terms like restricted funds, designated funds and endowment funds have no meaning or comparator in the commercial sector. This has necessitated clarity as to definition and significant guidance on their use. The increased use of charity-specific terminology, the provision of definitions of that terminology and the augmentation of the SORP with clear examples has lengthened the document considerably: from a 30-page, A5-sized[3] stapled pamphlet in 1988 to a 193-page A4-sized bound book in 2015 (when viewed in its published, paper format).

Performance Reporting Emphasised

As discussed above, the original SORP (ASC, 1988) focussed on improving financial reporting by providing guidance on such matters as, among others, best practice relating to the treatment of fixed assets, legacies and restricted funds. Recommendations relating to any type of performance reporting were extremely limited. However, research at the time indicated that this focus on traditional financial accounting issues would inadequately meet the information needs of key stakeholders; for example, Hyndman (1990) had identified that the disclosures that resource providers (recognised as a key user of charity annual reports and accounts) found most useful was information that allowed them to assess the performance of the charity in terms of its goals and objectives. Important information relating to effectiveness

---

[3]   These refer to international standard paper sizes. A5 paper is 148.5 mm × 210 mm, A4 paper is 210 mm × 297 mm.

(relating to whether objectives had been achieved) and efficiency (relating to the relationship between the input, often costs, and output, often units of service provision) was rarely disclosed. It was argued that SORP 1988's focus on the technicalities of audited statements at the expense of other types of reporting represented a mismatch between the information which users perceive as most useful and the information which is provided to them. Moreover, it was argued that such not only weakened accountability, but also undermined the efforts of a charity's management in seeking to steer operations.

Progressively, recommendations on performance reporting (and wider governance issues) have been added to the SORP, usually argued for in terms of allowing the reader to judge the performance of the charity. For example, SORP 1995 (Charity Commission, 1995) promoted reporting on the general progress of the charity and what it had been able to achieve during the year (supported by statistical information, if available) and encouraged the provision of examples, such as the number of beneficiaries reached. Notwithstanding the above, concern continued to be expressed that many charities gave scant attention to the performance recommendations contained in both SORP 1995 and SORP 2000 (Charity Commission, 1995, 2000a) (Connolly and Hyndman, 2004).

Given this concern, which was widely expressed over a number of years, the UK Government took a much more proactive role through the publication of *Private Action, Public Benefit* (Cabinet Office, 2002) based on a review of charities and the wider not-for-profit sector. While its coverage was much broader than accounting and reporting, Chapter Six of the study focused on the need for better information as a basis for building trust and confidence in the sector, and on supporting the sector in improving performance. The report highlighted a lack of credible information on performance (including impact/outcome), and a lack of meaningful comparison between similar organisations; it was argued that such information would boost public confidence and assist decision making. In an attempt to address this issue, it advocated a new document, the Standard Information Return (SIR, later renamed the Summary Information Return) for charities with annual incomes greater than £1 million to provide "qualitative and quantitative information on how the charity sets its objectives and measures performance against them" (Cabinet Office, 2002, Para. 6.11). It also recommended that improvements should be made to the SORP to strengthen its focus on performance reporting.

As a result of this, the Charity Commission formed a sub-committee of its accountability implementation group, with a wider membership than the SORP Committee, to focus on governance and performance reporting.

This Annual Reporting Advisory Group was instrumental in helping to develop the detail for the SIR and recommendations for the TAR that were eventually included in SORP 2005 (Charity Commission, 2005). This resulted in significantly more comprehensive recommendations on performance reporting than had been seen before. It included detailed recommendations on:

- the need to explain the charity's main objectives for the year and to provide a description of the strategies for achieving those objectives;
- the provision of qualitative and quantitative information about the achievements and performance of the charity in the year, to include summaries of any measures used by the charity to assess its performance; and
- disclosure of sufficient information to allow readers to understand the role and contribution of volunteers.

More recently with respect to charity performance, debate has been dominated by calls for charities to focus on (and report) their impact (or outcome), i.e. the effect of their activities on beneficiaries and society. This disclosure has been particularly suggested as having potential to strengthen both upward accountability to donors and funders and downward accountability to beneficiaries (Benjamin, 2012; Connolly and Hyndman, 2013). In the FRS 102 SORP this call has been reinforced and made particularly explicit, albeit the challenges of reporting in such terms are clearly acknowledged (Charity Commission and OSCR, 2014a, para. 1.43):

> "In reviewing achievements and performance, charities may consider the difference they have made by reference to terms such as inputs, activities, outputs, outcomes and impacts, with impact viewed in terms of the long-term effect of a charity's activities on both individual beneficiaries and at a societal level. Charities are encouraged to develop and use impact reporting (impact, arguably, being the ultimate expression of the performance of a charity), although it is acknowledged that there may be major measurement problems associated with this in many situations."

Preparer Discretion Reduced Considerably

Considerable discretion was allowed in SORP 1988 (ASC, 1988) with respect to a range of issues (for example, the carrying cost of investments could be cost or market value). SORP 1995 (Charity Commission, 1995) was described as being significantly more prescriptive than its predecessor (Williams and Palmer, 1998), and this trend continued in subsequent SORPs. As an example, SORP 1995 eliminated the previous choice of valuation bases, and stated that investments should be shown on the balance sheet at market value. Over time, the SORPs have provided more clarification, more detailed technical guidance and more examples, reducing reliance on the judgement of the preparing accountant and lessening the scope for variability in charity practices. The fact that scope has been 'defined away' has been informed by the ASB's (1999) discussions on the *Statement of Principles for Financial Reporting* as they relate to public benefit entities.

3.3 The FRS 102 Charities Statement of Recommended Practice: An Introduction

This section provides a further backdrop to the publication and principles underlying the FRS 102 SORP, which applies to accounting periods beginning on or after 1 January 2015 (Charity Commission and OSCR, 2014a), with **Sections 3.4** and **3.5** then addressing the detailed form and content of the TAR and financial statements respectively.

By way of background to the publication of the FRS 102 SORP (Charity Commission and OSCR, 2014a), when EU-listed companies were required to prepare their consolidated financial statements in accordance with International Accounting Standards (IASs)/International Financial Reporting Standards (IFRSs), the expectation was that the UK and RoI would universally adopt IASs/IFRSs. However, although most UK and RoI accounting standards are now closely aligned with international standards, these are primarily written for listed companies; in contrast, the majority of UK and RoI companies are small or medium-sized, without the need for, among other things, the more detailed disclosures often required under IASs/IFRSs. Consequently, full convergence with IASs/IFRSs never materialised in the UK and RoI, resulting in an assortment of standards with their roots in UK and RoI standards and also IASs/IFRSs. Thus, the ASB (and subsequently the Financial Reporting Council (FRC)) began a project to consider the future of UK and RoI Generally Accepted Accounting Principles (GAAP). This culminated in the publication of a set of new UK and RoI standards, which are colloquially referred to as 'new Irish/UK GAAP', and include FRS 102 *The Financial Reporting Standard applicable in the UK and Republic of Ireland* (FRC, 2015a) and the Financial Reporting Standard for Smaller Entities (FRSSE) which applied to small companies or groups (FRC, 2013).

FRS 102 replaces the 'old' Statements of Standard Accounting Practice (SSAPs) and Financial Reporting Standards (FRSs). It is a single standard, with 35 sections covering the various different items previously addressed in separate standards, and it is designed to apply to the financial statements of entities (including those that are not constituted as companies and those that are not profit-oriented) that are not applying EU-adopted IASs/IFRSs.

However, the FRSSE (FRC, 2013) has been withdrawn with effect from 1 January 2016 and replaced by Section 1A of FRS 102 (FRC, 2015a) or FRS 105 *The Financial Reporting Standard applicable to the Micro-entities Regime* (FRC, 2015b), which applies to reporting periods starting on or after 1 January 2016. Consequently, from 1 January 2016, all entities reporting under UK and RoI GAAP have to decide, *inter alia*, whether to adopt IASs/IFRSs, FRS 102 or, if applicable, FRS 105.

Charity accounts may be prepared either on the receipts and payments basis or the accruals basis. Which of these is needed will depend on the income of the charity and whether or not it has been set up as a company. The receipts and payments basis is the simpler of the two methods and consists of an account summarising all money received and paid out by the charity in the financial year, and a statement giving details of its assets and liabilities at the end of the year. Charitable companies are prohibited by company law from adopting this method. Thus, non-company charities above a certain size,[4] and all charitable companies, must prepare their accounts on the accruals basis. If a charity prepares its accounts on an accruals basis, then it should do so in accordance with the extant charities SORP, which provides recommendations for accounting and reporting; in particular, how accounting standards should be applied in the context of charities and how to account for charity-specific transactions.

As the role of the charities SORP is to provide guidance on how charities apply GAAP, the changes referred to above with respect to UK and RoI GAAP necessitated the development of new reporting guidance for charities to reflect those changes. This led to the publication of: (i) the FRS 102 SORP (Charity Commission and OSCR, 2014a); and (ii) the FRSSE SORP (Charity Commission and OSCR, 2014b). However, the withdrawal of the FRSSE (FRC, 2013) had similar consequences for the FRSSE SORP. Consequently, for reporting periods starting on or after 1 January 2016, all charities in the UK (including those that applied the FRSSE SORP in 2015) that prepare accounts on the accruals basis to give a true and fair view of a charity's financial position and financial activities must follow the FRS 102 SORP (regardless of their size, constitution or complexity). In RoI, the FRS 102 SORP represents recommended best practice.

The FRS 102 SORP (Charity Commission and OSCR, 2014a) sets out how charities are expected to apply accounting standards to their particular activities and transactions, and explains how charities should present and disclose their activities and funds within their accounts. It also describes the content

---

[4] Different reporting requirements apply depending on: (i) the jurisdiction in which the charity is registered; (ii) whether the charity is a company, non-company or charitable incorporated organisation; and (iii) the size of the charity. See **Appendix 1**.

of the TAR which accompanies the financial statements. The FRS 102 SORP includes charity-specific requirements that are additional to those of national accounting standards devised for businesses; in particular, requirements relating to the TAR, fund accounting, the format of the SOFA and additional disclosures aimed at providing a high level of accountability and transparency to donors, funders, financial supporters and other stakeholders.

As charities are not owned by shareholders, they do not seek to provide a financial return to shareholders. In addition, there is no equivalent for profit after tax or earnings per share for charities. Therefore, in order to understand a charity's TAR and financial statements, it is important to appreciate the 'type' of charity being reviewed. Some common 'funding models' are explained below.

Donation Model

This model typically applies to charities that raise funds primarily through appealing for donations, deciding how to spend them once they have been received; a variant of this approach is appealing for donations for a specific purpose. In both scenarios, such charities are likely to build up cash reserves during the period in which they are accumulating funds and then in a particular year spend more than their annual income, possibly on a major capital asset. For example, a hospice that needs to build an extension may launch an appeal which takes two years to attract sufficient donations. During those two years, the hospice is receiving income but not spending it (i.e. the income is being added to reserves). In year three, the charity may then build the extension. Therefore, looking at one year's financial statements in isolation may give a misleading impression.

Endowment Model

This model typically applies to charities whose funds come primarily from legacies. Typically, endowed charities will invest the legacies and spend the income on the charitable purposes. If this is through grant-making, the charities' costs will be limited to those associated with administering the grant-making process, supporting the board's meetings and compliance activities such as audit.

Contract Model

A charity that focuses on delivering specific services may operate in a more 'business-like' manner than those that adopt one of the other models. In this scenario, operational costs are primarily funded through contract income. 'Margins' are likely to be low with contract income only just covering costs. Such charities bid for contracts and may compete with profit-orientated private-sector organisations.

Retail Model

Charity may raise funds through various retail activities, often in high street shops. This model often relies on volunteers and donated goods, and while the margins may be low compared to other forms of fundraising, the trading profit is important, especially when combined with income from one of the other models. Such charities are able to increase the return on their retail activities by claiming Gift Aid on the value of donations (which is also possible under the donation model).

In practice, a charity may adopt more than one of the above models. Focusing on the requirements of the FRS 102 SORP, the next two sections seek to provide an understanding of the format and content of the TAR (**Section 3.4**) and financial statements (**Section 3.5**).

3.4   Understanding the Trustees' Annual Report

The TAR is an opportunity for the trustees to take stock of how the year has gone compared to their plans and aspirations, to celebrate successes and achievements, and to reflect on difficulties and challenges. Its audience is not just trustees, donors and beneficiaries but also the wider public who may be interested in the activities and achievements of the charity. While the TAR need not be lengthy, it should bring the charity to life. The best TARs often combine case studies with output statistics when explaining the charity's activities and performance during the year under review. Some content of the TAR is mandatory for all charities. As a greater degree of public accountability and stewardship reporting is expected of a large charity, its report must also provide additional information.

The content of the TAR is summarised in **Table 3.1**, with information categories 1–5 (1. Objectives and activities; 2. Achievements and performance; 3. Financial review; 4. Plans for future periods; and 5. Structure, governance and management) subsequently being discussed in more detail and illustrated with examples. These examples are drawn from Arts

Theatre Trust, one of the sample charity reports (FRS 102 version) included on the Charity Commission website (Charity Commission, http://www. charitysorp.org/about-the-sorp/example-trustees-annual-reports/) (see **Appendix 2**). Arts Theatre Trust is a company limited by guarantee, operating a theatre and related activities, with one trading subsidiary (and is therefore required to prepare group accounts). The income of the group is £1.6 million, with the total net group assets being £1.5 million.

Table 3.1 **Content of the Trustees' Annual Report**

Information Category	All Charities	Larger Charities[5]
1. Objectives and activities	Charity Commission and OSCR (2014a, paras. 1.17–19) (see **Exhibit 3.1**) Information to help the user understand how the charity's aims fulfil its legal purposes, the activities it undertakes and what it has achieved.	Charity Commission and OSCR (2014a, paras. 1.35–39) (see **Exhibits 3.1** and **3.2**) Details of: • the issues the charity seeks to tackle and the differences it seeks to make; • how the achievement of its aims will further its purposes; • its strategies for achieving its aims; • the criteria or measures used to assess success; and • the significant activities undertaken and how they contribute to the achievement of its aims.

[5] 'Larger charities' is a term used in the FRS 102 SORP to identify those charities subject to audit under charity law in their jurisdiction of formation, registration or operation which the FRS 102 SORP requires to make additional reporting disclosures. In those jurisdictions where there is no charity law audit requirement, the reference to larger charities is construed as applying to those charities with a gross income exceeding £500,000 or €500,000 in the reporting period. Please see **Appendix 1** for details of the thresholds in England and Wales, Scotland, NI and RoI.

Information Category	All Charities	Larger Charities
2. Achievements and performance	Charity Commission and OSCR (2014a, para. 1.20) (see **Exhibit 3.3**) A summary of the main achievements of the charity, including the difference the charity's work has made to its beneficiaries and, if practicable, wider society.	Charity Commission and OSCR (2014a, paras. 1.40–45) (see **Exhibit 3.3**) A review of: • the significant charitable activities undertaken; and • achievements against objectives set, including for fundraising activities and investment performance.
3. Financial review	Charity Commission and OSCR (2014a, paras. 1.21–24) (see **Exhibit 3.4**) A review of the charity's financial position at the end of the reporting period, including its policy for holding reserves and the amounts held. Any uncertainties about the charity's ability to continue as a going concern should be explained.	Charity Commission and OSCR (2014a, paras. 1.46–48) (see **Exhibits 3.4–3.7**) Details of significant events affecting the financial performance and position of the charity, including: • their financial effect; • a description of the principal risks and uncertainties facing the charity, together with a summary of plans for managing those risks; and • any factors that are likely to affect the financial performance or position going forward. An explanation of the: • charity's principal funding sources and how these resources support the key objectives of the charity; • impact of a material pension asset or liability on the financial position of the charity; and • charity's investment and reserves policies.

Information Category	All Charities	Larger Charities
4. Plans for future periods	Larger charities only	Charity Commission and OSCR (2014a, paras. 1.49–50) (see **Exhibit 3.8**) A summary of the charity's plans for the future, including its aims and objectives and details of any activities planned to achieve them, together with how lessons learned from past or current activities have influenced future plans and decisions about resource allocation.
5. Structure, governance and management	Charity Commission and OSCR (2014a, paras. 1.25–26) (see **Exhibit 3.9**) Details of the governing document, how the charity is constituted and the methods used to recruit and appoint new charity trustees.	Charity Commission and OSCR (2014a, para. 1.51) (see **Exhibit 3.9**) Sufficient information to give the reader an understanding of how the charity is constituted, its governance and management structures, and how its trustees are trained.
6. Reference and administrative details	Charity Commission and OSCR (2014a, paras. 1.27–28) The charity's name, registration number(s) and principal office address, together with the names of those who were trustees on the date the report was approved or who served as a trustee in the reporting period.	Charity Commission and OSCR (2014a, paras. 1.52–53) Details of to whom the trustees' delegate day-to-day management of the charity and from whom trustees are taking advice.

Information Category	All Charities	Larger Charities
7. Exemptions from disclosure	Charity Commission and OSCR (2014a, paras. 1.29–31)	
		Where a report omits the name of a trustee, chief executive officer or senior staff member or the charity's principal address, it should give the reason for the omission.

Drawing on examples from Arts Theatre Trust (Charity Commission, http://www.charitysorp.org/about-the-sorp/example-trustees-annual-reports/) (see **Appendix 2**), information categories 1–5 per **Table 3.1** (1. Objectives and activities; 2. Achievements and performance; 3. Financial review; 4. Plans for future periods; and 5. Structure, governance and management) are now discussed and exemplified.

Information Category 1. Objectives and Activities

All charities are required to provide information to help users understand how the charity's objectives fulfil its legal purposes, the activities it undertakes and what it has achieved. Larger charities have also to provide details of:

- the issues the charity seeks to tackle and the differences it seeks to make;
- how the achievement of its aims will further its purposes;
- its strategies for achieving its aims;
- the criteria or measures used to assess success; and
- the significant activities undertaken and how they contribute to the achievement of its aims.

Exhibit 3.1 illustrates how the trustees might report the objectives and activities (Charity Commission and OSCR, 2014a, paras. 1.17 and 1.36) which are undertaken for the public benefit (para. 1.18).

Exhibit 3.1   **Objectives and Activities**

Our purposes and activities

The purposes of the charity are:

- to advance the education of the public in all aspects of dramatic art including the arts of drama, mime, opera, ballet, music, singing, dance and painting;
- the development of public appreciation of art by the provision of a theatre and the presentation of public performances; and
- to further the social and cultural welfare of the community of BF Borough.

The vision that shapes our annual activities remains the promotion and fostering of knowledge and appreciation of the arts by the provision of facilities for the education and recreation of the public in the fields of art, music and drama. The charity also has the general aim of contributing to the quality of life of the people of BF Borough by expanding their horizons through the provision of exciting, challenging and accessible professional and community drama and arts events.

In shaping our objectives for the year and planning our activities, the trustees have considered the Charity Commission's guidance on public benefit, including the guidance 'public benefit: running a charity (PB2)'. The theatre relies on grants and the income from fees and charges to cover its operating costs. Affordability and access to our programme is important to us and is reflected in our pricing policy set out in detail later in this report.

We endeavour to encourage all within our community to take part in our activities and to attend our theatre and/or to view our exhibitions. The drama and art we provide is to be enjoyed by all from those attending local schools or the higher education colleges through to our programmes with particular appeal to our older residents.

The strategies employed to achieve the charity's aims and objectives are to:

- present a broad range of theatre productions and art exhibitions for the enjoyment and education of our local community;

- offer opportunities for a broad range of people to get involved in arts activity exploring their own creative powers;
- provide facilities for amateur and professional artists to develop. Groups in the borough are given discounted rates for hire of space and access to professional advice;
- concentrate on involving young people in the arts to help encourage a culture in which different age ranges play a complementary part;
- celebrate the diversity of cultures in our society by programming presentations by, and with, artists of different cultural backgrounds.

Putting these strategies into action we have three major areas of activity which are: concerts and stage performances; educational programmes, including residences; and art exhibitions, including installations. Our programme of activities described below focuses very much on bringing the arts to the community of our Borough.

Source: Charity Commission, Model Trustees' Annual Report and Accounts: Arts Theatre Trust (FRS 102 version). Available at http://www.charitysorp.org/about-the-sorp/example-trustees-annual-reports/

While the value of volunteers as a resource to a charity is not included in the incoming resources, their contribution is often significant to a charity's ability to undertake a particular activity. However, while measurement issues, including attributing an economic value to their contribution, prevent the inclusion of their contribution in the statement of financial activities, larger charities should explain how the charity uses the services of volunteers (Charity Commission and OSCR, 2014a, para. 1.38) (see **Exhibit 3.2**). This information is important as the charity can only achieve its output with this additional input.

Exhibit 3.2   **Volunteers**

Our volunteers

The Trust is very involved in the community and relies on voluntary help. Besides those amateur performers and artists who display their talents at the Centre, over 40 volunteers assist with stewarding events and performances, enabling longer opening and lower staff costs than would otherwise be the case. Most volunteers are members of the company and it is at their suggestion that the 'Friends of the ATC Theatre' was formed in 2006 and we wish to thank our friends for their loyal support and service.

Source: Charity Commission, Model Trustees' Annual Report and Accounts: Arts Theatre Trust (FRS 102 version). Available at http://www.charitysorp.org/about-the-sorp/example-trustees-annual-reports/

Information Category 2. Achievements and Performance

All charities are required to summarise their main achievements and performance during the year, including the difference the charity's work has made to its beneficiaries and, if practicable, wider society. Larger charities should also review:

- the significant charitable activities undertaken;
- achievements against objectives set, including for fundraising activities and investment performance.

This information is illustrated in **Exhibit 3.3**.

Exhibit 3.3 **Achievements and Performance**

Achievements and performance

Attendances at the theatre fell marginally from 42,000 in the year ending 31 March 2015 to just over 40,000 in the current year. This was a major achievement given the economic backdrop and is a tribute to the quality of the artistic programme and the place the theatre has in the community and underpinned a challenging financial and creative year. Our staff deserve credit and praise for their skilful and enthusiastic efforts to provide a successful creative programme for our patrons.

The new Saturday matinees and weekday older people's programme proved very popular with average houses 70% full. Our revised concession arrangements for people on low incomes meant that the level of income per attendance has been reduced but overall this has offset the trend of declining audience seen by other theatres nationally. Maintaining a balance between patrons paying full price, accessibility for those of modest means, the encouraging of new young audiences, and maintaining a financial balance is an ongoing challenge. Our key financial aim remains a financially sustainable theatre and we remain very grateful to our sponsors for their support, without which the theatre would close.

Eighteen concerts and stage performances were held, including a very successful run of *Twelfth Night*. We maintained the mix established in 2015 of shows, plays, performances and concerts. *The Bristol Jazz Greats* were a sell-out and the highlight of the year was a return on his farewell tour of the famous Welsh tenor *Sir Roy Homes* whose *A Night for a Tender Heart* was a great Valentine's Night success. The repertoire combined a mixture of classical, jazz and popular rock and garage music with a combination of modern shows and a Shakespearian classic. Although ticket sales were below target for our contemporary play *Stuff Happens in LA* by David Hare, the performance was critically acclaimed following its opening in the West End of London.

The N Arts Trust sponsored residences programme included a residency for the famous artist Mr Keane Eye and our traditional residences from the *Shakespeare Travelling Company* and the *Roysdon Artists and Puppeteers* were all well received and financially successful. The number of schoolchildren and college students attending was 750 against a plan of 650. The Christmas installation *Visions of God, man and creation* included a number of sculptures, textile art and audio exhibits especially designed programme for children and adults with learning difficulties and these were very well received.

Volunteers from the *Friends* assist us in gaining the opinions of our patrons and customers through pre- and post-performance customer questionnaires and to identify the difference our events make to an individual's perception, enjoyment and involvement in the arts. Six surveys were carried out in 2016 and the overall result was an audience satisfaction rating with the performance of 85% compared to 75% in 2015. In summary, as the Table below shows, the audience reaction has generally been very positive and has returned to pre-refurbishment levels. The results for 2015 were affected by the refurbishment programme.

Audience experience:	2016	2015
Value for money	85%	65%
Booking process	65%	65%
Exceeded my pre-performance expectations	10%	–
Met my pre-performance expectations	85%	88%
Seats and auditorium comfortable	85%	65%
Sound quality satisfactory	80%	80%
Clear sight of the stage	99%	75%
Overall satisfaction	85%	75%

Source: Charity Commission, Model Trustees' Annual Report and Accounts: Arts Theatre Trust (FRS 102 version). Available at http://www.charitysorp.org/about-the-sorp/example-trustees-annual-reports/

Information Category 3. Financial Review

All charities are required to discuss their financial position at the end of the reporting period, including their policy for holding reserves and the amounts held. Any uncertainties about the charity's ability to continue as a going concern should also be outlined. Larger charities should explain significant events affecting their financial performance and position. **Exhibits 3.4** and **3.5**, which present a financial review and reserves policy respectively, illustrate this information.

Exhibit 3.4 **Financial Review**

Financial review

The completion of the building adaptations and staging alterations in 2015 with the assistance of N Arts enabled the Trust to provide the staging and auditorium facilities required by modern productions but did not add to our capacity for stage productions. Following the decision of BF Borough Council to withdraw its pledge of matched funding at a late stage, the Trust had to provide the matched funding and did so by taking out a secured bank loan. Unfortunately this increased financial pressure coincided with the continued freezing of our grant support in cash terms.

The Trust moved from a break-even position in 2015 to posting its first shortfall for six years of £161,000. The principal funding sources of income to the Trust itself were: admission fees and ticket sales of £392,000, income from art exhibitions and installations of £42,000, and grants of £671,000 including the separate grant award from N Arts Trust of £150,000 to finance the workshops and residences educational programme. The support of our partners continues to be essential to maintaining such a varied programme of creative arts. Not all the concerts and performances are not all self-supporting and the performing arts rely on a mixed economy of funding to ensure a vibrant and comprehensive programme.

The charity's wholly owned trading subsidiary, HTC Ltd, continued to trade well but experienced a sales fall in line with the theatre at ATC park itself generating a profit of £158,000 all of which was gift aided to the Trust. The trustees are pleased with the commercial success of the venture which operates the bar, coffee shop, conferencing and catering facilities and the profits generated assist the charity in meeting its objectives.

Despite to the increasing pressure on public expenditure the trustees understand that the support from our local authorities and N Arts will be kept at the current level of activity for at least the next three years. This means a fall in support in real terms, after allowing for inflation. To make good the shortfall the charity is expected to generate a larger proportion of funds from admission fees and commercial income generation or cost savings.

Since introducing our revised discount policy on 1 April 2014 we have noticed a growth in new audiences who have not visited us before and as anticipated we broke even with the revised pricing structure in the year to 31 March 2015. However, with major local employers still on reduced hours work we have found that demand for concessionary tickets rose as a proportion of sales increasing from 20% of sales in 2015 to 30% of ticket sales this year. A seat taken is a contribution to the running costs of the theatre and playing to full houses undoubtedly enhances the performance and audience experience, however this is an unforeseen change which we hope will prove temporary once the economy recovers.

Source: Charity Commission, Model Trustees' Annual Report and Accounts: Arts Theatre Trust (FRS 102 version). Available at http://www.charitysorp.org/about-the-sorp/example-trustees-annual-reports/

The unspent unrestricted funds of a charity are its reserves. While some charities may be able to operate on limited reserves (for example, endowed charities that distribute grants from the income earned), others may have significant committed expenditure. Many charities express their reserves policy as the number of days which could be funded by the amount held in reserves. For example, a charity with annual running costs of £365,000 might state that it holds £90,000 in reserve to provide three months' cover. However, it is not possible to judge whether this is appropriate unless the charity also explains the nature of the risks it faces and whether three months is sufficient cover. For larger charities, the reserves statement should also disclose the amount the charity holds at the end of the reporting period, identify any amounts that are restricted or designated and explain, where relevant, what steps are being taken to bring the amount of reserves held into line with the level identified as appropriate. **Exhibit 3.5** illustrates the reserves policy disclosure, explaining the target level of resources, the reserves held and the charity's plans to restore its reserves (Charity Commission and OSCR, 2014a, paras. 1.22 and 1.48).

Exhibit 3.5 **Reserves Policy**

Reserves policy and going concern

Reserves are needed to bridge the gap between the spending and receiving of income and to cover unplanned emergency repairs and other expenditure. The trustees consider that the ideal level of reserves as at 31 March 2016 would be £225,000.

The Trust had no reserves with a negative (£323,000) on unrestricted funds after allowing for those resources designated for property and props and setting aside funds to cover professional fees, the details of which are given in note 25 of the accounts. This situation is largely attributable an operating deficit and the need to finance the interest on the bank loan required to match the N Arts capital grant. The decision of B F Borough Council to withdraw their support to the refurbishment project in 2014 and the fall in income has resulted in an extremely difficult year financially. Whilst we understand the Council has had to prioritise its funds to urgent local needs, this has left the theatre in a difficult financial position.

Without the support of Cruffs Bank Plc it is doubtful that the Trust could continue operating. The trustees are endeavouring to ensure the success with a combination of measures by offering a creative programme that caters for broader audiences, rescheduling the secured loan and working with our local authority partners and N Arts to ensure their continued support. Our consolidated balance sheet remains strong with net current assets of £116,000 and the ownership of a long leasehold interest in our theatre. The trustees have reviewed the circumstances of the Arts Theatre Trust and group and consider that adequate resources continue to be available to fund the activities of the Trust and group for the foreseeable future. The trustees are of the view that Trust and group are a going concern.

The cash-flow outflows from operating activities of £126,000 from the charity in 2016 reflected the difficult trading circumstances faced by the theatre due to a shortfall in box-office income. The trustees are aware that the lack of free reserves, together with the economic backdrop, will provide a challenging environment in the year to come. The trustees have plans in hand to address this situation and restore the reserves to nil balance before accumulating reserves from 2017.

Source: Charity Commission, Model Trustees' Annual Report and Accounts: Arts Theatre Trust (FRS 102 version). Available at http://www.charitysorp.org/about-the-sorp/example-trustees-annual-reports/

In addition, larger charities should also describe the:

- principal risks and uncertainties facing the charity, together with a summary of plans for managing those risks (Charity Commission and OSCR, 2014a, para. 1.46) (see **Exhibit 3.6**);
- charity's principal funding sources and how these resources support the key objectives of the charity;
- impact of a material pension asset or liability on the financial position of the charity; and
- charity's investment policy (Charity Commission and OSCR, 2014a, para. 1.47) (see **Exhibit 3.7**).

Exhibit 3.6   **Risk Management**

Risk management

The trustees have a risk management strategy which comprises:

- an annual review of the principal risks and uncertainties that the charity and its subsidiary HTC Ltd face;
- the establishment of policies, systems and procedures to mitigate those risks identified in the annual review; and
- the implementation of procedures designed to minimise or manage any potential impact on the charity should those risks materialise.

This work has identified that financial sustainability is the major financial risk for both the charity and its subsidiary. A key element in the management of financial risk is a regular review of available liquid funds to settle debts as they fall due, regular liaison with the bank, and active management of trade debtors and creditors balances to ensure sufficient working capital by the Trust and its subsidiary company.

Attention has also been focussed on non-financial risks arising from fire, health and safety of artists and audiences, management of performing rights and food hygiene. These risks are managed by ensuring accreditation is up to date, having robust policies and procedures in place, and regular awareness training for staff working in these operational areas.

Source: Charity Commission, Model Trustees' Annual Report and Accounts: Arts Theatre Trust (FRS 102 version). Available at http://www.charitysorp.org/about-the-sorp/example-trustees-annual-reports/

Exhibit 3.7 **Investment Policy**

Investment powers and policy

The trustees, having regard to the liquidity requirements of operating the theatre, have kept available funds in an interest-bearing deposit account and seek to achieve a rate on deposit which matches or exceeds inflation as measured by the retail prices index. Due to wider economic circumstances deposit rates have been depressed and so this aim was not achieved in the year.

The invested funds held on deposit achieved an average rate of 0.5% against the retail price index of 2.8% for the year.

Source: Charity Commission, Model Trustees' Annual Report and Accounts: Arts Theatre Trust (FRS 102 version). Available at http://www.charitysorp.org/about-the-sorp/example-trustees-annual-reports/

Information Category 4. Plans for Future Periods

Larger charities are required to discuss their plans for the future, including their aims and objectives and details of any activities planned to achieve them, together with how lessons learned from past or current activities have influenced future plans and decisions about resource allocation. In **Exhibit 3.8**, the charity has identified that its financial sustainability is challenged, and has outlined the measures it is taking (Charity Commission and OSCR, 2014a, para. 1.49).

Exhibit 3.8 **Plans for Future Periods**

Plans for future periods

The strategic plan envisaged a second stage refurbishment of the foyer and booking hall at a cost of £800,000 to be carried out in 2016/17 but in the absence of grant support, the trustees have deferred a decision as to whether to proceed until early January 2017 when the extent of the economic recovery and the impact on the theatre's income is known. Until financial circumstances have improved the planned capital investment programme has been deferred.

A major financial concern for the trust will be ongoing financial sustainability given the lower level of support from our donors with the reduction in council funding over the past two years. The trustees have retained

Goodshires & Co as advisers to assist in a restructuring of the theatre business and anticipate introducing a voluntary severance programme to reduce the staff complement by five posts to save £100,000 annually. Goodshires will also assist in a procurement and non-pay savings review. In total target savings of £170,000 are to be achieved. In addition, a review of the theatre programme with a return of popular favourites and an extended Pantomime season to boost revenue is in hand.

The trustees have also successfully concluded discussions with our bankers, Cruffs Bank plc, to reschedule the loan repayment period by extending the repayment terms from five to eight years.

We continue to strengthen our links with the community, our patrons and customers through the *Friends of ATC Theatre*. The *Friends* are the members of the Company and have their own quarterly magazine and benefit from advanced ticket facilities with special discounts and *Friends* events. The Friends will also be key to the success of our plans for a public appeal in the summer of 2017 in support of the next phase of redevelopment of ATC Park which aims to ensure we remain a prestige arts venue.

Source: Charity Commission, Model Trustees' Annual Report and Accounts: Arts Theatre Trust (FRS 102 version). Available at http://www.charitysorp.org/about-the-sorp/example-trustees-annual-reports/

Information Category 5. Structure, Governance and Management

All charities are required to provide details of their governing document, how the charity is constituted and the methods used to recruit and appoint new charity trustees. Larger charities are expected to develop this information, including an explanation of governance and management structures, and how trustees are trained (Charity Commission and OSCR, 2014a, para. 1.51). This is illustrated in **Exhibit 3.9**.

Exhibit 3.9   **Structure, Governance and Management**

Structure, Governance and Management

Governing Document

Arts Theatre Trust is a company limited by guarantee governed by its Memorandum and Articles of Association dated 28 September 1950. It is registered as a charity with the Charity Commission. Anyone over the age of 18 can become a member of the Company and there are currently 137 members (145 in 2015), each of whom agrees to contribute £5 in the event of the charity winding up.

Appointment of trustees

As set out in the Articles of Association the chair of the trustees is nominated by N Arts Trust. BF Borough Council nominates five trustees and B Town Council nominates three trustees. Four trustees are elected annually by the members of the charitable company attending the Annual General Meeting and serve for a period of two years. The trustees have the power to co-opt up to two further members to fill specialist roles.

All members are circulated with invitations to nominate trustees prior to the AGM advising them of the retiring trustees and requesting nominations for the AGM. When considering co-opting trustees, the Board has regard to the requirement for any specialist skills needed, for example Mr D East is a qualified surveyor and joined the board to assist with the planned refurbishment programme and the recent bid to the Arts Council of England and BF Borough Council. Nominees appointed by B F Borough Council and B Town Council are subject to the appointment processes of those bodies and the guidelines on appointment to public office as they apply to Local Government nominees.

Trustee induction and training

New trustees undergo an orientation day to brief them on: their legal obligations under charity and company law, the Charity Commission guidance on public benefit, and inform them of the content of the Memorandum and Articles of Association, the committee and decision-making processes, the business plan and recent financial performance of the charity. During the induction day they meet key employees and other trustees. Trustees are encouraged to attend appropriate external training events where these will facilitate the undertaking of their role.

Organisation

The board of trustees, which can have up to 15 members, administers the charity. The board normally meets quarterly and there are sub-committees covering development, membership, finance and audit which normally meet monthly. A Chief Executive is appointed by the trustees to manage the day-to-day operations of the charity. To facilitate effective operations, the Chief Executive has delegated authority, within terms of delegation approved by the trustees, for operational matters including finance, employment and artistic performance related activity.

Source: Charity Commission, Model Trustees' Annual Report and Accounts: Arts Theatre Trust (FRS 102 version). Available at http://www.charitysorp.org/about-the-sorp/example-trustees-annual-reports/

Having examined the information that should be included in the TAR, the next section focuses on the financial statements.

3.5   Understanding Charity Financial Statements

One of the fundamental principles of charity financial statements is fund accounting, which requires all incoming and outgoing resources (see **Exhibit 3.11**) and assets and liabilities (see **Exhibit 3.12**) to belong to a fund, with the SOFA and balance sheet presenting income, expenditure, assets and liabilities in accordance with the relevant fund. The different types of funds are illustrated in **Exhibit 3.10**.

Exhibit 3.10   **Classes of Charitable Funds**

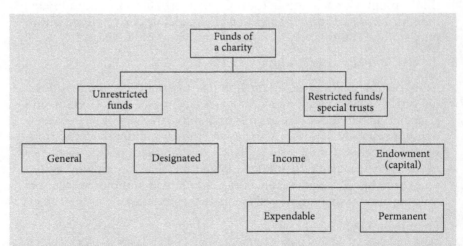

Source: Charity Commission and Office of the Scottish Charity Regulator (OSCR) (2014a), *Charities SORP (FRS 102) Accounting and Reporting by Charities: Statement of Recommended Practice applicable to charities preparing their accounts in accordance with the Financial Reporting Standard applicable in the UK and Republic of Ireland (FRS 102) (effective 1 January 2015)*, London. Available at http://www.charitysorp.org/media/619101/frs102_complete.pdf

Unrestricted funds are available to be spent as the trustees see fit in further-ance of the charity's objectives. General funds are unrestricted funds which have not been earmarked for a particular purpose by the trustees. In con-trast, designated funds are unrestricted funds that have been earmarked for a particular purpose. The notes to the financial statements should explain the purpose of designated funds.

Restricted funds may only be used for the purposes specified by the donor (including funds arising from a public appeal for a specific purpose). They may also include donated land, buildings or other assets. Unless specified, interest or other income earned on a restricted fund should be added to the fund. Expendable endowment funds are donations to be held as capital, but with powers being given to the trustees to use the funds as income (usually subject to certain conditions). Permanent endowment funds are donations to be held as capital with no power to convert the funds to income. Significant restricted funds should be separately disclosed in the notes to the financial statements.

The remainder of this section focuses on the main aspects of charity finan-cial statements, with **Exhibits 3.11–3.16** being drawn from Arts Theatre Trust, one of the sample charity reports (FRS 102 version) included on the Charity Commission website (Charity Commission, www.charitysorp.org/about-the-sorp/example-trustees-annual-reports/) (see **Appendix 2**). Charity financial statements comprise:

1. a SOFA (see **Exhibit 3.11**);
2. a balance sheet showing the charity's financial position at the end of the year (see **Exhibit 3.12**);
3. a statement of cash flows (a requirement for larger charities) (see **Exhibit 3.13**); and
4. explanatory notes (see **Exhibits 3.14–3.16**). Each of these components is now discussed in turn.

1. Statement of Financial Activities

As charity law requires charities to use all their funds in furtherance of their objectives, the profit concept, together with the distribution of profits to shareholders through dividends, is inappropriate for charities. Consequently, the traditional profit and loss account is replaced by a SOFA (see **Exhibit 3.11**), which presents the incoming resources available to the charity and shows how these have been used to fulfil the charity's objectives. Income therefore includes endowments and donated assets received by the charity during the period. However, as noted above, volunteer services, which can be significant for some charities, are excluded; although charities should explain in the TAR how the charity benefits from volunteer support.

Exhibit 3.11   **Consolidated Statement of Financial Activities (including consolidated income and expenditure account) for the year ended 31 March 2016**

	Note	Unrestricted Funds £'000	Restricted Funds £'000	Total Funds 2016 £'000	Total Funds 2015 £'000
Income:					
Donations and legacies	4	35	25	60	44
Income from charitable activities:					
Operation of theatre and arts centre	5	1,105	–	1,105	1,163
Income from other trading activities:					
Commercial trading operations	6	479	–	479	595
Investment income	7	18	–	18	16
Total income		**1,637**	**25**	**1,662**	**1,818**
Expenditure					
Costs of raising funds:					
Commercial trading operations		323	–	323	390
Expenditure on charitable activities:					
Operation of theatre and arts centre	8	1,475	9	1,484	1,422
Total expenditure		**1,798**	**9**	**1,807**	**1,812**
Net income/(expenditure) and net movement in funds for the year		(161)	16	(145)	6

Reconciliation of funds

Total funds brought forward	1,649	12	1,661	1,655
Total funds carried forward	**1,488**	**28**	**1,516**	**1,661**

The statement of financial activities includes all gains and losses recognised in the year.

All income and expenditure derive from continuing activities.

Source: Charity Commission, Model Trustees' Annual Report and Accounts: Arts Theatre Trust (FRS 102 version). Available at http://www.charitysorp.org/about-the-sorp/example-trustees-annual-reports/

The SOFA (**Exhibit 3.11**), which includes the results of the subsidiary consolidated on a line-by-line basis (Charity Commission and OSCR, 2014a, para. 24.25), reports the main charitable activities undertaken. Comparatives are provided for all columns in the SOFA either by way of adding additional columns or by providing this information in the notes (para. 4.2). A single-column SOFA for all funds is permitted where only one class of funds is material, otherwise unrestricted and restricted funds and endowment must be shown separately. In **Exhibit 3.11**, the charity is taking advantage of the concession (available under company law) to provide only a consolidated SOFA.

Exhibit 3.11 reports the charitable activities as single line (paragraph 4.7), with the expanded analysis in Note 8 to the accounts (para. 4.53) (not shown). To illustrate the net funding requirement or contribution by each activity, the costs and income of each activity have been compared in Note 9 (para. 4.29) (not shown). The analysis of the material components of income (para. 4.42) is given in Notes 4 to 7 to the financial statements (not shown, with the exception of Note 7 which is included in **Exhibit 3.15**). The results of the subsidiary alone are required by the SORP and are disclosed in Note 6 (para. 24.36) (not shown).

If the column for unrestricted or restricted funds shows net incoming resources, this represents a surplus; as noted previously, this may only be spent in furtherance of the charity's general objectives with respect to unrestricted funds and the specific purpose for which the funds were given in relation to restricted funds. If a charity is no longer able to use restricted funds for the purpose for which they were given, then it must offer the funds back to the donor.

With respect to the SOFA, the FRS 102 SORP makes a number of changes to SORP 2005 (Charity Commission, 2005). These are summarised in **Table 3.2**. For example, the treatment of gains and losses on investment assets has changed. SORP 2005 presented both realised and unrealised investment gains and losses as an item within 'other gains and losses' after striking a total for 'net incoming/outgoing resources'. FRS 102 requires that changes in the value of financial instruments (which includes investments) measured at fair value are taken through profit and loss. In order to comply with this requirement, gains and losses on investments are now shown in the SOFA before striking a total for 'net income/expenditure'.

Charities undertake a wide range of activities to raise funds for their cause. Some forms of fundraising require significant investment, some have high costs, and some are higher risk than others. Consequently, there is no single performance indicator. Many readers of charity accounts will look at the formula of fundraising cost over total income to measure the fundraising return. This would be misleading because some forms of income will probably not have required any fundraising input. Therefore, the charity could omit this income and just compare the cost of fundraising to the funds raised. While this is a more appropriate cost/income ratio, the following needs to be borne in mind.

- The fundraising costs reported in the financial statements are likely to be generating income in the following financial year or years (i.e. income is not necessarily matched to the relevant costs). This may not matter too much for a mature charity, but it will make a difference for a young charity or one that is embarking on new fundraising and so is in the investment phase.
- Income from legacies will fluctuate from year to year, but this is likely to have nothing to do with fundraising performance.
- Different forms of fundraising have different margins. For example, charity shops may have relatively small margins, but income is steady and unrestricted. Major donations might represent a much greater return, but they are unpredictable and often restricted. In order to assess the fundraising performance of a charity, it is important to understand more about the fundraising mix.

Often administration costs are seen as 'bad' costs. However, if a charity is to use its resources efficiently, understand its performance and pay its staff, it is going to have to spend money on administration. Just because a charity spends very little on administration does not necessarily mean that it is well run. Without good administration, it is likely that resources are wasted on activities that do not generate appropriate results. 'Administration costs' are not presented in a set of charity accounts. They are divided between support costs and governance costs. The support costs are the indirect costs of an activity or project; they are a necessary part of operations (for example, rent and wages). Governance costs are the statutory costs of running the charity and include the costs of trustee meetings (if any), audit and legal advice.

Table 3.2   **SOFA: SORP 2005 v FRS 102 SORP**

2005 SORP (SOFA extract) ●———————►	FRS 102 SORP (SOFA extract)
Voluntary income ●———————►	Donations and legacies
Activities for generating funds ●———————►	Other trading activities
Investment income ●———————►	*Income from* Investments
Incoming resources from charitable activities ●———————►	*Income from* Charitable activities
Other incoming resources ●———————►	Other *income*
Total incoming resources ●———————►	Total income and endowments
Costs of generating voluntary income ●———————►	***Expenditure on* Raising funds**
Fundraising trading: cost of goods sold and other costs ●	
Investment management costs ●	
Resources expended on Charitable activities ●———————►	***Expenditure on* Charitable activities**
Governance costs ●	
Other resources expended ●———————►	Other *expenditure*
	Net gains/(losses) on investments
Net incoming/outgoing resources before transfers ●———►	Net income/(expenditure)
Gross transfers between funds ●———————►	Transfers between funds
Gains on revaluation of fixed assets for charity's own use ●	Gains/(losses) on revaluation of fixed assets
Gains/losses on investment assets ●	
Actuarial gains/losses on defined benefit pension schemes ●———————►	Actuarial gains/(losses) on defined benefit pension schemes
	Other gains/(losses)
Net movement in funds ●———————►	Net movement in funds

Source: Charity Commission and OSCR (2014c).

Other changes on the face of the SOFA are:

Income
- The main heading 'Total incoming resources' is renamed 'Total income and endowments'.
- 'Voluntary income' is renamed income from 'Donations and legacies'.
- 'Incoming resources from charitable activities' is renamed 'Income from charitable activities'.
- 'Activities for generating funds' is renamed income from 'Other trading activities'.

Expenditure
- The main heading 'Resources expended' is renamed 'Expenditure on'.
- 'Costs of generating voluntary income', 'Fundraising trading: cost of goods sold and other costs' and 'investment management costs' are all combined in a new heading, 'Expenditure on raising funds'.
- 'Resources expended on charitable activities' is retained as 'Expenditure on Charitable activities'.
- The heading of 'governance costs' is dropped altogether, with these costs being included in 'Expenditure on Charitable activities'. For those charities reporting on an activity basis, governance costs are a separate component of support costs.
- 'Other resources expended' is renamed 'Other expenditure'.

2.   Balance Sheet

The basic structure of the balance sheet, with its columnar presentation distinguishing the classes of fund held (unrestricted income, restricted income and endowment), is retained from SORP 2005 (Charity Commission, 2005) (see **Exhibit 3.12**). The FRS 102 SORP (Charity Commission and OSCR, 2014a) requires that:
- investment properties are measured initially at cost and subsequently at fair value at the reporting date. SORP 2005 permitted 'any reasonable approach to market valuations', but the FRS 102 SORP requires valuations to be made by an independent expert, or disclosure that this has not been done;
- the class of mixed-use investment property is introduced with the property apportioned between its investment use and operational use unless this is impractical, in which case it is treated as a tangible fixed asset. SORP 2005 required such mixed-use properties to be classified based on main use of the property;
- property which is let or occupied by another group undertaking must now be treated as investment property;

- social investments are shown as a separate class of investment; and
- debtors recoverable more than 12 months after the year-end must be discounted to present value, if the effect is material.

Exhibit 3.12 **Consolidated Balance Sheet as at 31 March 2016**

	Note	Group 2016 £'000	Group 2015 £'000	Charity 2016 £'000	Charity 2015 £'000
Fixed assets					
Tangible assets	17	1,700	1,760	1,700	1,760
Investments	18	–	–	30	30
Total Fixed Assets		**1,700**	**1,760**	**1,730**	**1,790**
Current assets					
Stock	19	87	83	73	82
Debtors	20	207	206	252	206
Cash at bank and in hand		202	345	84	316
Total Current Assets		**496**	**634**	**409**	**604**
Liabilities					
Creditors falling due within one year	21	(380)	(333)	(323)	(333)
Net Current assets		**116**	**301**	**86**	**271**
Total assets less current liabilities		**1,816**	**2,061**	**1,816**	**2,061**
Creditors: falling due after more than 1 year	24	(300)	(400)	(300)	(400)
Net assets		**1,516**	**1,661**	**1,516**	**1,661**
The funds of the charity:	25				
Unrestricted income funds		1,488	1,649	1,488	1,649
Restricted income funds		28	12	28	12
Total charity funds		**1,516**	**1,661**	**1,516**	**1,661**

Source: Charity Commission, Model Trustees' Annual Report and Accounts: Arts Theatre Trust (FRS 102 version). Available at http://www.charitysorp.org/about-the-sorp/example-trustees-annual-reports/

3.   *Statement of Cash Flows*

The statement of cash flows required by the FRS 102 SORP (Charity Commission and OSCR, 2014a) is based upon the statement (IAS 7) developed by the International Accounting Standards Board (IASB). The FRS 102 SORP describes each of three mandatory headings (operating activities, investing activities and financing activities) (see **Exhibit 3.13**) and also gives examples of cash flows that fall within each heading, together with providing advice on the treatment of cash flows arising from endowments. The FRS 102 SORP continues to allow the choice of either the 'direct' or 'indirect' method.

Exhibit 3.13   **Statement of Cash Flows**

	Note	Group 2016 £'000	Group 2015 £'000	Charity 2016 £'000	Charity 2015 £'000
Cash used in operating activities	29	(39)	(41)	(126)	(41)
Cash flows from investing activities					
Interest income		18	16	16	16
Purchase of tangible fixed assets		(22)	–	(22)	–
Cash provided by (used in) investing activities		(4)	16	(6)	16
Cash flows from financing activities					
Repayment of borrowing		(100)	(100)	(100)	(100)
Cash used in financing activities		**(100)**	**(100)**	**(100)**	**(100)**
Increase (decrease) in cash and cash equivalents in the year		**(143)**	**(125)**	**(232)**	**(125)**
Cash and cash equivalents at the beginning of the year		345	470	316	441
Total cash and cash equivalents at the end of the year		**202**	**345**	**84**	**316**

Source: Charity Commission, Model Trustees' Annual Report and Accounts: Arts Theatre Trust (FRS 102 version). Available at http://www.charitysorp.org/about-the-sorp/example-trustees-annual-reports/

While the statement of cash flows in **Exhibit 3.13** includes the information for the charity and the group, the charity could have opted to disclose the information only for the group provided the required related party disclosures were made (Charity Commission and OSCR, 2014a, para. 24).

4.   Notes to the Financial Statements

The notes to the financial statements typically provide further detail for the amounts shown in the three financial statements discussed above (see **Exhibits 3.11–3.13**). While many of the notes are fairly standard, there are a number of changes as a consequence of the FRS 102 SORP (Charity Commission and OSCR, 2014a).

When first reporting under the FRS 102 SORP, a charity is required to explain how the transition from its previous financial reporting framework affected its reported financial position and financial performance (Charity Commission and OSCR, 2014a, para. 35.12). To comply with this, it is necessary to describe the nature of each change in accounting policy and reconcile the charity's retained funds determined in accordance with the previous financial reporting framework to the retained funds determined in accordance with the FRS 102 SORP. For example, in applying the FRS 102 SORP, the accounting policies now require the recognition of a liability for paid holiday pay, which involves restating opening balances at the date of transition and consideration of any change in that liability in subsequent accounting periods. This reconciliation is illustrated in **Exhibit 3.14**.

Exhibit 3.14   **Transition to FRS 102 Reconciliation**

b) Reconciliation with previous Generally Accepted Accounting Practice

In preparing the accounts, the trustees have considered whether, in applying the accounting policies required by FRS 102 and the Charities SORP FRS 102, the restatement of comparative items was required.

At the date of transition in applying the requirement to recognise liabilities arising from employee benefits, a liability was recognised for short-term compensated absence arising from employee entitlement of the parent charity to paid annual leave. The initial liability recognised at the date of transition was for the holiday entitlement carried forward and for the entitlement arising in the year which was due but not taken. The initial liability was for £37,685. No other restatements were required. In accordance with the requirements of FRS 102 a reconciliation of opening balances is provided.

Reconciliation of group funds and balances	1 April 2014 £'000	31 March 2015 £'000
Fund balances as previously stated	1693	1699
Short-term compensated absences	(38)	(38)
Fund balances as restated	1655	1661

Source: Charity Commission, Model Trustees' Annual Report and Accounts: Arts Theatre Trust (FRS 102 version). Available at http://www.charitysorp.org/about-the-sorp/example-trustees-annual-reports/

The FRS 102 SORP (Charity Commission and OSCR, 2014a, module 11) requires extensive disclosures for financial instruments (financial assets and financial liabilities). Rather than setting out these disclosures in a separate note, the disclosures are made in the Arts Theatre Trust example[6] in the context of the particular items in the accounts. For example, the:

- disclosure requirements (para. 11.35) are met in Note 1(k) – operating leases, Note 1(q) – financial instruments including loans, Note 7 – investment income, Note 11 – total interest expense and Note 27 – financial instruments at amortised cost (see **Exhibit 3.15**);
- significance of financial instruments (para. 11.35) is discussed in Note 27 (see **Exhibit 3.15**) and in the financial review section of the TAR, which is referenced from Note 27 (see **Exhibit 3.6**); and
- discussion of credit risk (para. 11.38) is included in Note 27 (see **Exhibit 3.15**).

---

[6] Source: Charity Commission, Model Trustees' Annual Report and Accounts: Arts Theatre Trust (FRS 102 version). Available at http://www.charitysorp.org/about-the-sorp/example-trustees-annual-reports/

Exhibit 3.15   **Financial Instrument Disclosures**

1 Accounting Policies

k) Operating leases

The charity classifies the lease of printing, specialist lighting and audio equipment as operating leases; the title to the equipment remains with the lessor and the equipment is replaced every 5 years whilst the economic life of such equipment is normally 10 years. Rental charges are charged on a straight line basis over the term of the lease.

q) Financial instruments

The trust only has financial assets and financial liabilities of a kind that qualify as basic financial instruments. Basic financial instruments are initially recognised at transaction value and subsequently measured at their settlement value with the exception of bank loans which are subsequently measured at amortised cost using the effective interest method.

7 Investment income

All of the group's investment income of £18,000 (2015: £16,000) arises from money held in interest bearing deposit accounts.

11 Net income/(expenditure) for the year

This is stated after charging	2016 £'000	2015 £'000
Operating leases-equipment	13	13
Depreciation	82	66
Bank interest payable	60	62
Auditor's remuneration:		
Audit fees	10	10
Accountancy services	5	5

27 Financial instruments

Financial instruments measured at amortised cost comprise the loan financing provided by Cruffs Bank Plc to the Trust.

	2016 £'000	2015 £'000
Loan payable falling due within 1 year	100	100
Loan payable falling due in more than 1 year but less than 5 years	250	300
Loan payable falling due after 5 years)	50	–
Total	**400**	**500**

The loan financing is in the form of a secured loan with a variable interest rate. The market risk facing the Trust is that it is widely expected that interest rates will rise as the economic recovery gains momentum. Refer to the risk management section of the directors' report for information as to how this risk is managed and to note 28 for information as to how the liquidity risk is being managed by rescheduling the loan.

28 Post-balance sheet events

The charity's bankers Cruffs Bank Plc agreed on 28 May 2016 to the rescheduling of the secured bank loan. The loan has been rescheduled so that the repayment of capital due in 2017 remains £100,000 but thereafter it is reduced to £50,000 with the overall loan term extended from 5 years to 7 years. The variable interest rate of base rate plus 7% is to be increased to base rate plus 8% from 1 June 2016. The trustees anticipate that the extra interest cost incurred will be £5,000 of the remaining life of the loan. Cruffs Bank plc has also agreed an overdraft facility of £300,000 on their normal commercial terms, reviewable six monthly.

On 7 June 2016 the trustees agreed with staff representatives a voluntary severance programme and optional reduction in hours programme, for booking office, administrative, hospitality and premises related staff, with a view to reducing the establishment by five whole-time equivalent staff, as part of the business recovery programme. The savings from the staffing are anticipated to amount to at least £100,000 annually and will make a major contribution to the business efficiency review being conducted for the charity by Goodshires & Co.

Source: Charity Commission, Model Trustees' Annual Report and Accounts: Arts Theatre Trust (FRS 102 version). Available at http://www.charitysorp.org/about-the-sorp/example-trustees-annual-reports/

Charities have to provide a narrative explanation in the TAR for the remuneration policy for senior staff (see **Exhibit 3.16**). In addition, charities have to disclose information about the numbers of staff paid at a rate greater than £60,000 in the reporting period (excluding employer pension contributions but including any other benefits), together with details of the aggregate pay of their 'key management personnel' or senior management team (see **Exhibit 3.16**).

Exhibit 3.16   **Remuneration Policy and Staff Costs**

Pay policy for senior staff

The directors consider the board of directors, who are the Trust's trustees, and the senior management team comprise the key management personnel of the charity in charge of directing and controlling, running and operating the Trust on a day to day basis. All directors give of their time freely and no director received remuneration in the year. Details of directors' expenses and related party transactions are disclosed in note 12 to the accounts.

The pay of the senior staff is reviewed annually and normally increased in accordance with average earnings. In view of the nature of the charity, the directors benchmark against pay levels in other provincial theatres of a similar size run on a voluntary basis. The remuneration bench-mark is the mid-point of the range paid for similar roles adjusted for a weighting of up to 30% for any additional responsibilities. If recruitment has proven difficult in the recent past a market addition is also paid with the pay maximum no greater than the highest benchmarked salary for a comparable role.

Analysis of staff costs, trustee remuneration and expenses, and the cost of key management personnel

	2016 £'000	2015 £'000
Salaries and wages	699	672
Social security costs	53	51
Pension costs	86	82
	838	805

No employees had employee benefits in excess of £60,000 (2015: nil). Pension costs are allocated to activities in proportion to the related staffing costs incurred and are wholly charged to unrestricted funds.

The charity trustees were not paid or received any other benefits from employment with the Trust or its subsidiary in the year (2015: £nil) neither were they reimbursed expenses during the year (2015: £nil). No charity trustee received payment for professional or other services supplied to the charity (2015: £nil).

The key management personnel of the parent charity, the Trust, comprise the trustees, the Chief Executive Officer, Finance Director and Artistic Director of Arts Theatre Trust. The total employee benefits of the key management personnel of the Trust were £165,301 (2015: £162,060).

The key management personnel of the group comprise those of the Trust and the key management personnel of its wholly owned subsidiary HTC Ltd. The key management personnel of HTC Ltd are the Chief Operating Officer and the Commercial Manager whose employee benefits total £73,001 (2015: £70,002). The employee benefits of key management personnel for the group was therefore £238,302 (2015: £232,062).

Source: Charity Commission, Model Trustees' Annual Report and Accounts: Arts Theatre Trust (FRS 102 version). Available at http://www.charitysorp.org/about-the-sorp/example-trustees-annual-reports/

This section has focused on the main aspects of charity financial statements (SOFA, balance sheet, statement of cash flows and explanatory notes). The chapter began by outlining the early problems identified with charity reporting, and discussing the limited pressure to improve charity reporting from legislation, accounting standards, or an effective regulatory body (**Section 3.1**). However, the situation changed considerably with the subsequent development and evolution of the charities SORP to the extent that it gained legal backing in the UK and became a benchmark for good charity accounting practice in RoI (**Section 3.2**). After explaining the background and principles underlying the FRS 102 SORP (Charity Commission and OSCR, 2014a) in **Section 3.3**, the detailed form and content of the TAR and financial statements were illustrated in **Sections 3.4** and **3.5** respectively with the use of extensive examples. Thus, having provided a suitable platform to more forward, the next chapter discusses key themes arising from previous charity accounting and accountability research in order to provide a reference point for the empirical research on the legitimation of accounting changes (**Chapter 5**) and performance reporting (**Chapter 6**) presented later.

Chapter 4

Previous Charity Accounting and Accountability Research

While a range of studies on charity accounting, accountability and governance exists, some key thrusts of past research (beyond the ground-breaking work of Bird and Morgan-Jones in 1981, described in **Chapter 3**) are considered here. This, together with the material in **Chapters 2** and **3**, as well as providing an analysis of key themes in accounting-related research in the charity sector, presents some reference points for the later empirical research on internal legitimation of accounting changes (**Chapter 5**) and performance reporting (**Chapter 6**). For convenience, in this chapter research is broadly categorised into studies that have investigated the:

- extent to which charity financial statements comply with the financial accounting recommendations of the extant SORP (**Section 4.1**);
- disclosure patterns of information accompanying annual financial statements (often in the Trustees' Annual Report – TAR) (**Section 4.2**); and
- extent and impact of stakeholder engagement with respect to reporting frameworks for charities (**Section 4.3**).

These categorisations are a convenient way to present the material, although many of the studies themselves relate to the three categories and more widely.

4.1 Charity Financial Statements and the Statement of Recommended Practice

Ashford (1989), Gambling, Jones, Kunz and Pendlebury (1990) and Hines and Jones (1992)

Three very different studies completed shortly after the publication of SORP 1988 (Accounting Standards Committee (ASC), 1988) (see **Chapter 3** for details of this and its subsequent evolution) concluded that the SORP had had very limited impact on the financial statements of charities.

Ashford (1989) investigated the compliance of the financial statements of large charities with the recommendations of SORP 1988, and highlighted that, notwithstanding some examples of good practice, many charities

were continuing to use accounting practices contrary to the recommendations (and, it was suggested, the spirit) of SORP 1988. They did this, he
argued, to present their position in a way that made those charities seem to
be more in need of funds; examples included failing to recognise income
from legacies in the income statement, and recording the value of investments at the (usually lower) cost value rather than market value. These
practices and motives were identical to those identified by Bird and
Morgan-Jones (1981) almost 10 years earlier.

In a study of six small charities, Gambling et al. (1990) identified, through
a series of semi-structured interviews, that not only were these smaller
charities not applying the recommendations of SORP 1988 (ASC, 1988)
but that awareness of the existence of the SORP was low. In addition, the
SORP 1988 recommendations were seen as adding additional compliance
costs with little or no perceived benefit to the charity. The authors suggested that this lack of awareness and perceived irrelevance of the SORP,
combined with the lack of resources then available to the Charity Commission to monitor or to enforce compliance, made it unlikely that the SORP
would impact significantly on the sector.

In a longitudinal study of the financial statements of large charities, Hines
and Jones (1992) found that while the vast majority of the charities prepared the statements recommended by SORP 1988 (ASC, 1988), dubious
accounting practices in the preparation of those statements remained
pervasive. Hines and Jones cited such basic examples as failure to capital-
ise and depreciate assets. They argued that non-compliance with the mere
recommendations of the SORP was unsurprising and opined that, for this
position to change, legislation mandating the SORP would be required.

Williams and Palmer (1998), Connolly and Hyndman (2000, 2001) and Palmer, Isaacs and D'Silva (2001)

The poor response of the sector to SORP 1988 (ASC, 1988) necessitated the
development of a more rigid regulatory framework and strengthening of the
SORP to ensure proper accountability in the sector. As detailed in **Chapter 3**,
after further review and consultation, a revised SORP was published in 1995
(Charity Commission, 1995) and this recommended more standardised
practice for financial reporting, rather than relying on the judgement of the
preparing accountant, with the most radical change being the introduction
of the Statement of Financial Activities (SOFA) in place of the income and
expenditure statement. Following this, Williams and Palmer (1998), in a
study reviewing the financial statements of a sample of small, medium and

large charities, identified a degree of increased compliance with SORP 1995. In particular, they observed significant improvement among larger charities since the early 1980s, but fairly extensive failure to comply with the SORP's recommendations among small and medium-sized charities.

Connolly and Hyndman (2000) analysed the financial statements of the top 100 fundraising charities in the UK before and after SORP 1995's (Charity Commission, 1995) revision. Referencing earlier studies, they contended that SORP 1988 (ASC, 1988) had had a significant, but lagged, impact on charity accounting practices. They argued that this delayed impact was as a result of a 'fairly gradual learning curve' (p. 96) in the accounting profession on the recommendations of the SORP. However, in respect of the new requirements contained in SORP 1995, only partial compliance was identified. Moreover, non-compliance was particularly observed in respect of some of the most significant changes, such as reporting on costs. Connolly and Hyndman (2000) commented that given the 'radical' nature of some of the SORP 1995 changes and the lagged impact of earlier recommendations, change would perhaps be seen, but it was likely to take time. Overall, they concluded that "charity accounts have improved significantly since the early 1980s, where improvement is seen in terms of increasing compliance with recommended practice" (p. 95).

In subsequent work comparing UK and RoI charities' compliance with SORP 1995 (Charity Commission, 1995), Connolly and Hyndman (2001) found that RoI charities' compliance with SORP 1995 was even more lagged and less complete than that of their UK counterparts. Suggesting reasons for these differences, they remarked that compared to UK charities, RoI charities (while also encouraged to apply the SORP) operated in a less regulated environment, with no legislative requirement on any charities to comply with the SORP and less scrutiny of their reporting.

Palmer et al. (2001) examined the first year of adoption of SORP 1995 (Charity Commission, 1995) by 125 'major' UK charities (all of which were registered with the Charity Commission in England and Wales, statutorily required to comply with the SORP and subject to full professional audit). The research found a number of major departures from SORP 1995's financial accounting requirements, few of which were identified and disclosed as such by the charity or its auditors. The authors concluded that charities and their auditors were largely aware of the SORP and that divergence seemed to occur because it suited the charity. Consistent with prior research, areas of non-compliance included the treatment of legacies, income being taken directly to capital, investment income being recorded on a receipts rather than an accruals basis and subsidiaries not being consolidated. Palmer *et al.* questioned whether auditors understood the requirements of the SORP or, if they did, why auditors did not report non-compliance. As a consequence, doubts were raised about the apparent reliance of the Charity Commission on the adequacy of auditors' reports. The authors (similar to Connolly and Hyndman, 2000) argued that while charity accounting had improved over time, there was still considerable diversity in practices, which needed to be reduced.

4.2   Disclosure Patterns of Information Other than Financial Statements

Over time, the focus of much empirical work on UK and RoI charities has shifted away from financial accountability (usually framed in terms of compliance with the extant financial requirements of the SORP — as discussed in **Section 4.1**) to accountability for performance and the provision of additional background information valuable to the users of charity reports. The potential importance of such information had been identified by Bird and Morgan-Jones (1981), but was not the focus of SORP 1988 (ASC, 1988). However, progressively, the performance and governance aspects of charities came more to the fore. Mirroring what was developing in the public sector at the time, a number of parties, including government, called for greater focus on performance measurement and performance reporting. For example, through the publication of *Private Action, Public Benefit* (Strategy Unit, 2002), government highlighted the need for better performance information as a basis for building trust and confidence in the sector, and to support the sector in improving performance. As seen in **Chapter 3**, as the SORP evolved, the performance and governance aspects were strengthened considerably (these were often required to be disclosed in a charity's TAR).

Hyndman (1990, 1991)

Based upon an analysis of the annual reports of 163 large UK charities and a survey of 133 donors to such charities, Hyndman (1990) sought to identify the information that was routinely made available to donors through the annual report, and the most important information sought by donors to charities. In the study, donors were asked to rank 14 types of financial and non-financial information, including frequently disclosed information, in terms of importance to them. This was compared with the information routinely made available to them in the annual report. He found that while audited financial statements dominated reporting by charities, donors viewed other information, particularly that relating to performance, as most important.

In a related study, Hyndman (1991) investigated whether the identified 'relevance gap', the difference between the information disclosed by charities in their annual reports (mainly audited financial statement information) and the information required by donors (mainly performance-related information) was due to a lack of awareness on the part of the providers of the information. The objectives of the paper were to identify the views of providers of information regarding the importance of donors as users of charity reports, and to ascertain the perceptions of such providers concerning the importance to donors of the 14 information types used as the basis for previous study (Hyndman, 1990). Two key groups involved in the provision of information to donors (charity officials and auditors) were surveyed. As well as confirming the importance of donors as the perceived focus for annual reports (with both groups of providers overwhelmingly identifying donors as the user group to whom such reports were primarily directed), the major part of each questionnaire asked charity officials and auditors to rate the 14 information types in terms of perception of importance to donors.

These perceptions were then compared with the actual importance to donors identified in the previous study. It was found that while providers of information were aware of the most important information required by donors (performance-related information), and donors were identified as the most important users of the annual report, the majority of charities did not disclose such information. Overall, the research discounted the possibility that the 'relevance gap' was caused by providers of information being unaware of the information needs of donors. Rather, it was argued that accountability to donors was not discharged in the most effective manner, with limited reporting of performance information as evidence of this. Moreover, it was speculated that there may be a general complacency among the providers of information with respect to the adequacy of existing reporting procedures, given that they knew what was important, but did not disclose it. Limited incentive and motivation of charities to improve accountability to donors was seen as a cause of such a scenario.

Connolly and Hyndman (2003, 2004)

In a study of the TARs of large UK charities over two accounting periods (pre- and post-SORP 2000 – Charity Commission, 2000), Connolly and Hyndman (2003), aware of the changes in the SORP and the pressure from various sources for charities to improve performance reporting, sought to identify the extent to which performance accountability was discharged. TARs were analysed using a checklist developed from the recommendations of the SORPs, the information types identified by Hyndman (1990) as being important to donors, and other sector guidance of the time (such as that provided by the Charities Aid Foundation, 2001). Categorising disclosures on this basis and comparing them to Hyndman's (1990) study, they identified that many charities were providing extensive background information (for example, on how the charity was constituted, its mission and the need area addressed) and that there had been some limited improvement over time in performance reporting (such as reporting on goals, objectives and output). However, their primary conclusion was that, despite the recognised importance of performance information to the users of charity annual reports, such information was still not widely disclosed.

A number of examples of charities' failings in this regard were given, including the fact that a significant proportion of charities failed to disclose a single measure of efficiency or of effectiveness (argued to be two of the key criteria for judging performance). Reporting of efficiency and effectiveness measures actually decreased in the two periods studied, against an increase in the reporting of more 'marketing-focused' (Connolly and Hyndman, 2003, p. 117) information. The authors contrasted this situation with significant improvements in reporting in the UK public sector in the same time period, and speculated that this deterioration may have been due to a number of factors, including a lack of willingness and pressure to report in the charity sector, combined with a paucity of guidance on performance reporting in charities. They also suggested that a concentration in the sector on discussing technical financial accounting matters "may have detracted from a meaningful debate relating to the relevance of the information content of charity annual reports" (Connolly and Hyndman, 2003, p. 117).

Applying a similar methodology, and distinguishing between size categories of charities, Connolly and Hyndman (2004) compared the reporting of performance information in UK and RoI charities. Analogous to their findings in respect of financial reporting (Connolly and Hyndman, 2001), the authors identified that for almost all types of performance reporting, and across both large and small charities, RoI charities reported significantly less than their UK counterparts. For example, measures of output were reported by 96% of large UK charities, 77% of small UK charities, 47% of large RoI charities and 29% of small RoI charities.

Connolly and Dhanani (2006)

Connolly and Dhanani (2006) investigated narrative reporting practices in the top 100 fundraising charities in the UK, including the disclosure of organisational information, financial management policies, financial infor-

mation, operational information and non-financial performance information. They found that while charities readily disclosed organisational
information and financial management policies, the quantity and quality of
disclosure tended to decrease in the reporting of financial information,
decreasing again in respect of operational information (including measures
of fundraising efficiency) and was lowest of all with respect to performance
information. Performance reporting tended to be dominated by information
on charitable activities (with 91% of the sample reporting at least one measure), reporting on input (73%), volunteer contribution (67%) and output
(66%). Significantly lower levels of disclosure were seen in respect of reporting on results (impact/outcome) (17%) or on effectiveness (3%). Moreover,
the authors commented that the charities tended to report using quantitative
or monetary measures (depending on what was being reported), but that
ratio analysis presentations were uncommon. Where the information was
disclosed, a key concern in respect of this reporting was that they "seldom
provided disclosures of comparative information, explanations of results
[impact/outcome] and plans for the future" (p. 59). It was argued that there
was considerable scope to improve reporting practices in this area.

Dhanani (2009)

Dhanani (2009) reviewed the reporting practices of 73 of the largest charities
reporting on the GuideStar UK website, and applied content analysis to
those charities' records to identify the existence and quantity of reporting
across four key disclosure types: charitable intent (or aims and objectives),
charitable activities (or programmes), charitable performance (subdivided
into output, impact, efficiency and effectiveness), and future intentions (or
plans/strategy). The study found that while all but one charity provided
information on aims and objectives, and 89% provided information on their
activities, reporting on performance and future plans was much less common. Dhanani highlighted that while 75% of charities provided some performance measures, these tended to be the 'lower order' measures, such as
simple quantifications of the services provided, rather than measures of efficiency or effectiveness. Additionally, only one-third of the sample provided
any information on future plans, indicating "a willingness to provide descrip-
tive information but hold back information that organisations may be held
to or questioned about" (p. 189).

Dhanani argued that this lack of reporting was particularly concerning
given the high levels of media attention and public scrutiny being focussed
on higher-order measures of performance, particularly on efficiency and
effectiveness. While these results demonstrated some improvement in

comparison with earlier studies (albeit acknowledging difficulties in making comparisons), they also suggested wide variations in practice between the charities investigated. For example, fundraising charities (as opposed to grant-making charities) were more likely to provide information on charitable activities, performance information and future plans (concurring with the findings of Connolly and Hyndman, 2003).

Connolly and Dhanani (2009)

Connolly and Dhanani (2009) carried out a content analysis of the annual reports and annual reviews of the largest UK charities, an examination of their websites and a series of interviews with representatives of those charities. Their results identified continuing problems with the discharge of accountability in the sector: at the most basic level, 36% of charities asked to supply a copy of their annual report failed to do so, and thereby contravened a statutory requirement. Comparing their analysis with earlier research, they commented that the demonstration of accountability in the annual reports of charities had weakened over time. They contrasted the increasing length and perceived importance of these reports to lower disclosure levels of information relating to fiduciary accountability, financial managerial accountability and operational managerial accountability. Considering operational management disclosures in more detail, they found that reporting was dominated by information on the charity's activities, rather than on their performance (including impact on society).

Connolly and Dhanani (2009) contended that "charities appear to seek legitimacy for their actions on the basis of the nature of their work (i.e. charitable activities and projects) rather than from evidence of the resulting societal change" (p. 7). From the interviews, conducted in tandem with their survey, they concluded that this was an identified problem among interviewees, who highlighted an information gap that existed both internally within charities in terms of how they assess their performance, and externally in respect of their reporting of that performance. They acknowledged some attempts to better report on the impact of charity activities and recommended that such efforts be supported to put in place holistic and formal systems of performance measurement within charities.

Jetty and Beattie (2009)

Jetty and Beattie (2009) conducted an in-depth analysis of the narrative element of the TARs and annual reviews of 10 UK charities. In addition, interviews with the preparers of these documents were undertaken in order to explore the motivations, drivers and constraints relating to public charity disclosure. Consistent with the findings of previous studies reported here (for example, Hyndman, 1990, 1991; Connolly and Hyndman, 2000, 2003; Connolly and Dhanani, 2006), Jetty and Beattie (2009) reported variations in charity reporting practices and a continuing lack of forward-looking information, especially in the TAR. However, there was some evidence that charities were beginning to provide more non-financial, non-quantitative and narrative information. In contrast to Connolly and Hyndman (2003), Jetty and Beattie's (2009) findings suggested that charities were disclosing more performance-related information than background data, with the former often being presented in a narrative story form (perhaps due to difficulties in measuring impact).

As called for by Bird and Morgan-Jones (1981) and Hyndman (1990, 1991), the authors presented a framework towards understanding the drivers and motivations for charity disclosure. They posited that there appeared to be various motivations for disclosure other than the accountability and user-needs arguments; for example, motivations relating to stakeholder influence (salience) and socio-political drivers, such as a desire to create a sense of empathy for the charity. Jetty and Beattie (2009) suggested that the main hindrance to improved charity annual reports was not only the lack of agreement about their content, but also the extent of the enthusiasm and engagement of preparers. They also advised that the annual review, the document favoured by users, should be subject to regulatory oversight, albeit one that was 'light-touch', to alleviate the risk of it becoming a clone of the annual report.

Hyndman and McConville (2016, 2017)

Using the lens of stakeholder theory, and focusing on the concept of transparency, the objective of Hyndman and McConville (2016) was to investigate the extent and manner of reporting on efficiency by large UK charities. To do this, a tentative framework for analysis was developed which took, as its starting point, O'Neill's (2006) suggestion that, for effective transparency, disclosures should address the information needs of the audience and be accessible to and assessable by that audience. The detail of the framework combined guidance from the charity and wider not-for-profit (NFP) sectors with recommendations from previous charity studies on efficiency measurement and reporting of efficiency. The developed framework (argued to be akin to a model for reporting on efficiency for charities) was not viewed by the authors as prescriptive for all charities; indeed, it was acknowledged that aspects of the framework were likely to be more suitable for some charities than others.

The empirical aspects of the study concentrated on the reporting of efficiency by the 100 largest UK fundraising charities via TARs, annual reviews and websites. Utilising the developed framework as a benchmark, key findings included:

- there was limited reporting of key efficiency measures and conversion ratios;
- few charities provided comparatives, explanations or diagrams relating to efficiency information (which, it was argued, would have supported transparent reporting);
- the vast majority of charities did not link the reporting of efficiency to their objectives; and
- there was little information indicating the reliability of the information (with these latter two aspects being construed as significant weaknesses in facilitating users in assessing reported indicators of efficiency).

Overall, the research provided evidence that reporting on efficiency in UK charities lacked transparency, in terms of both the extent and manner of disclosure. Moreover, it was argued that efficiency reporting was often more concerned with legitimating the organisations in the eyes of external stakeholders, rather than providing ethically-driven accounts of their efficiency.

In a parallel study (using the same sample charities), this time focusing on the reporting of effectiveness, Hyndman and McConville (2017) used a similar approach: the building of a model, and the analysis of effectiveness-information disclosures in the TARs, annual reviews and on websites of large UK charities. Again, transparency was explored in the context of stakeholder engagement, and it was argued that good effectiveness reporting can assist the charity sector in discharging accountability, gaining external legitimacy, and sharpening mission-centred managerial decision making. A major finding of the research was that although there had been increased reporting of effectiveness measures over time, there were still significant shortcomings in terms of making such reporting transparent. For example, few charities provided comparatives, explanations or links to objectives, and there was limited evidence relating to the reliability of the information and the engagement of stakeholders in the determination of what was measured and disclosed. It was argued that such inadequacies made assessing effectiveness information difficult for most users.

Overall, Hyndman and McConville (2017) argued that transparency on effectiveness by UK charities was partial and varied, although, to the extent that comparisons can be made with earlier studies, a journey of improvement (albeit from a very low starting point) was apparent. It was argued that, to a degree, these improvements (which largely related to the amount of disclosure rather than the manner of disclosure) may have been influenced by increased 'messaging' on the importance of transparency and effectiveness-related information (especially relating to impact/outcome) in sector debates, and more widely in society. In addition, it was suggested that the increased reporting of these effectiveness-related measures in publicly available communications may represent attempts by charity managers to respond to stakeholder needs and (in various ways) secure their continuing support.

This argument was supported in the paper by evidence that different information (in varying quantities and formats) was provided in different communications, potentially indicating that these communications were being used to engage with particular stakeholders and to respond to their specific needs. However, in many cases, even when more measures were provided, it was opined that often this was mere disclosure rather than meaningful transparency (Heald, 2006b; O'Neill, 2006), and stakeholder needs, the central focus in the development of the framework created by the authors, may not have been met.

4.3   Engagement with Stakeholders

Hyndman and McDonnell (2009)

Hyndman and McDonnell (2009) provided a critical analysis of 'governance' in the context of charities, and examined both the theoretical underpinnings and empirical investigations relating to it. Their focus was very much a stakeholder focus, and the importance of stakeholder theory was highlighted in the paper. By exploring the major themes that form the basis of much of the discussion of governance in charities, primarily looking from the perspective of the key stakeholders in the sector, the paper presented a broad definition of governance with respect to charities and discussed governance issues in relation to important external stakeholders (donors, regulators and beneficiaries). In addition, key aspects of governance pertaining to internal charity stakeholders were considered in terms of two key themes: board composition and board roles; and the relationships between the board and staff/volunteers. The authors argued that charity governance is a broad concept that includes, among other things, considerations of how stakeholder groups are accountable to one another, how performance is measured and reported, and how goals and objectives are set, and strategies devised, towards realising such goals and objectives. On the basis of this, a research agenda for those interested in adding to knowledge in this area was outlined (albeit acknowledged as partial).

Hyndman and McMahon (2010, 2011)

The objective of Hyndman and McMahon (2010) was to analyse the evolution of the UK charities SORP with insights from stakeholder theory. Stakeholder theory originated in the 1980s (this is discussed in more detail in **Chapter 2**), with a central argument advanced that organisations engage with stakeholders to build legitimacy and reputation. It was argued that for an accounting pronouncement such as a SORP, stakeholders might include groups or individuals who impact, or are impacted upon by a sector's reporting regime. They opined that these considerations have been central in discussions on accounting principles both in the commercial and charitable sectors over many years. Drawing on work relating to stakeholder salience, they explored competing stakeholder claims as they impacted on the evolution of the SORP since the mid-1980s.

Analysing a period of almost 20 years (see the evolution of the SORP detailed in **Chapter 3**), Hyndman and McMahon (2010) argued that the language of stakeholder theory, with its emphasis on identification of key stakeholders, their salience and their information needs, was used by the Charity Commission and others as a foundation for discussions on appropriate accounting and accountability frameworks within the charity sector. From their analysis, it was suggested that the two most salient and continuing stakeholder groups in this process have been government and the accounting profession. Furthermore, in each case, it was argued that these stakeholder groups began as rather passive and inactive with respect to charity accounting and reporting issues, but through time, as discussion built and awareness of the importance of these issues became clearer, they each engaged vigorously in shaping the SORP. Moreover, it was suggested that the perspectives of these two stakeholder groups had different focuses, with government being more concerned with performance and governance reporting, while the accounting profession's primary interest was more related to technical financial accounting issues.

This theme was later extended. Using insights from stakeholder theory and data from interviews with members of the various SORP Committees, Hyndman and McMahon (2011) focused on the influence of one highly salient stakeholder – government – in developing a regime of quality accounting and reporting in the charity sector. It was argued that, over time, government as a stakeholder became much more forceful and demonstrated considerable power and legitimacy as it sought to push through agendas it perceived as urgent. In addition, the authors contended that government's influence had been partly coercive (in creating the regulatory framework, through legislation requiring SORP compliance, and as an increasingly important resource provider exercising a direct disciplining effect on those charities to whom it provided funds) and partly persuasive (in giving greater prominence to measuring and reporting performance, and in facilitating the basis for the drafting of best-practice financial reporting).

The field data from the research suggested that government's increasing engagement with the charitable sector over time, often on the basis of a customer/provider relationship, had certainly influenced government demands relating to the 'giving of accounts' to themselves (and more widely to other stakeholders) and was evidence of the powerful hand of government shaping accounting and reporting. Moreover, it was argued that much of this had to do with government's view with respect to the correct conduit through which certain services should be delivered to the public, and the increased prominence afforded to the charity sector was evidence of it being viewed in a progressively more favourable light.

Connolly, Hyndman and McConville (2013)

Utilising data from a major consultation on a revised future charities SORP (which was eventually published as FRS 102 SORP – Charity Commission and OSCR, 2014a), Connolly *et al.* (2013) explored stakeholder engagement with respect to this (at the time) future publication. This consultation lasted for more than a year and involved approximately 1,000 stakeholders, including funders (such as charitable trusts, government agencies and individual donors), accounting professionals involved in preparing and auditing charity accounts, and academics. Data was generated from 28 roundtable events conducted throughout the UK, and evidence was presented of how this had influenced the SORP Committee's deliberations. The researchers concluded that this ambitious consultation exercise facilitated much wider stakeholder engagement than had previously been observed (particularly with funders), and that the extensive and much broader stakeholder engagement that was achieved had the potential to further legitimate the process and make the UK's unique sector-specific reporting framework (the SORP) an even more powerful tool with respect to charity reporting and accounting.

Connolly and Hyndman (2017)

Mobilising ideas from stakeholder theory, Connolly and Hyndman (2017) explored the motivations of charities in discharging accountability and the interplay of donor and beneficiary accountability needs. Drawing on 26 semi-structured interviews with four key stakeholder groups (charity auditors, beneficiaries, donors and charity managers), the researchers explored the extent to which concentration on one group may disadvantage another, something suggested by theory. On the basis of their findings, it was argued that, while in a corporate context, focusing on discharging accountability to finance providers may be detrimental to other stakeholders, this is much less likely in the charity sector because donors' (providers of finance) interests may (or perhaps should) be closely aligned with those of beneficiaries.

In addition, they suggested that if charity managers pursue an instrumental approach to the discharge of accountability by focusing on donors' interests (key providers of finance), this may, *de facto*, result in a multi-fiduciary orientation by default (as donors' interests are likely to be aligned with those of beneficiaries). Moreover, if charities embrace a multi-fiduciary approach (and pay particular heed to the needs of beneficiaries), this should not alienate donors (and consequently threaten long-term organisational survival) because of the motives of donors. They argued that 'managing paradox' in a charity context means embracing and exploring tensions and differences rather than choosing between them. Furthermore, they opined that much of what makes responsible decision-making difficult in the charity sector is understanding how there can be an ethical relationship between trustees/management and stakeholders that avoids being too weak (prioritising donors) or too strong (prioritising beneficiaries).

Using Mitchell *et al.*'s (1997) theory of stakeholder identification and salience, Connolly and Hyndman contended that charities have a fiduciary responsibility to account for the funds received to support their beneficiaries who, while having legitimacy and urgent needs, appear to lack power. In the language of Mitchell *et al.*, beneficiaries might be considered merely 'discretionary' or 'dependent' stakeholders; that is to say that it would be at charity managers' discretion to respond to their accountability needs, or they would rely on the power of other stakeholders to provide leverage. However, the research found that stakeholders commonly perceived as more salient, such as large donors (who have power, legitimacy and urgency given their ability to provide or withdraw resources), cede power and impute saliency to beneficiaries. In addition, charity managers, highlighting a 'felt' responsibility, often reflected on the desire to involve, and get feedback from, beneficiaries as a way of giving such individuals voice and sharpening service delivery. Indeed, it was suggested that the frequent close alignment between donors' and beneficiaries' interests may result in donors acting as proxies for beneficiaries (especially where beneficiary involvement and feedback is difficult to obtain).

Chapter 5

Legitimation and the FRS 102 Statement of Recommended Practice: An Investigation

As discussed in **Chapter 3**, the charities SORP has developed considerably over time, from an initial document that largely applied existing commercially based accounting standards to charities, to a much broader, charity-specific set of recommendations and requirements. Over its various iterations (Accounting Standards Committee, 1988; Charity Commission, 1995, 2000, 2005; Charity Commission and the Office of the Scottish Charity Regulator (OSCR), 2014a), it has evolved virtually beyond recognition. As explained previously, formal consultation has always been an integral part of the SORP-development (and reviewing/revision) process as a basis for, among other things, identifying user needs, encouraging best practice and eliciting buy-in and legitimation from key stakeholders. Indeed, as a basis for reviewing SORP 2005 (Charity Commission, 2005), there was extensive consultation across all key stakeholder groups (Charity Commission, 2009; Connolly *et al.*, 2013). The consultation, discussion and engagement emanating from this heavily influenced the shape and content of the FRS 102 SORP (Charity Commission and OSCR, 2014a).

It was clearly recognised by the SORP Committee (and more widely) that if key stakeholders were to be influenced by the accounting and reporting requirements contained in the charities SORP, then they would have to view the document (and its contents) as being appropriate and useful to them and to the charity sector (i.e. it would need to be seen as 'legitimate' or justifiable). This theme is explored in this chapter. Initially, relevant literature and theoretical insights are presented; with these being used subsequently to explore, analyse and understand the results of the empirical analysis shown in the chapter.

The main aim of the research presented in this chapter is to explore the process of internal legitimation by examining the way key organisational actors (i.e. accountants in charities, who are responsible for the SORP implementation and accounts/report compliance) involved in the introduction of the FRS 102 SORP (Charity Commission and OSCR, 2014a) in their respective charities understand, interpret and legitimate (justify) or delegitimate (question) the changes required. It is argued that how, and the extent to which, this occurs will affect the ultimate influence of the SORP in changing accounting and reporting. Indeed, the more legitimate the changes are perceived to be, the more likely they will be accepted and embedded, thus affecting charity management. To date, there have been no specific studies investigating the accountants' legitimation of accounting change in charities. The empirical research reported in this chapter focuses therefore on an area which has been less investigated: the way different actors translate and talk about accounting changes in the particular context of charitable organisations.

What is novel is that this research investigates legitimation strategies employed by accountants (key actors) working in charities when significant changes had been announced but, at the time of the interviews that form the basis of the empirical investigation, were not yet mandated (and, largely, not implemented). This study focuses on large charities in both the UK and the RoI. The chapter is organised as follows: **Section 5.1** discusses previous studies on accounting change and internal legitimation; **Section 5.2** presents the methodology on which the empirical research is based; **Section 5.3** presents the results and main highlights derived from the interviewees with charity accountants, and this is further discussed and interpreted in **Section 5.4**. Finally, **Section 5.5** discusses some of the study's implications for the charity sector.

5.1   Organisational Translation and Legitimation of Accounting Changes: An Overview

In order for any change to be implemented within a specific organisation, it is important that it is first understood and translated by the organisational actors who are responsible for its implementation. 'Translation' in this context is the transportation of meanings across different cultural contexts which may result in a change in that which is translated (Sahlin and Wedlin, 2008; Meyer and Höllerer, 2010; Czarniawska, 2011). With respect to accounting, not only is it important to understand the technicalities of what is being translated and the way it is being implemented, but also the way in which accounting practices are mobilised, the aspirations and ambitions attached to them and the roles that they play (Kurunmäki *et al.*, 2010). As accounting instruments are implemented, travel and spread, they come into contact with ideas which define different and variable relationships across space, people and aspirations. Individual translations may change a certain practice almost beyond recognition, and the institutional features or particular organisational contexts may be much more resistant to change than it is often wished for (Czarniawska, 2011). In addition, change can follow a more or less linear trajectory, where existing practices are replaced by new ideas and structures in response to contextual circumstances and competing institutional prescriptions (Broadbent and Guthrie, 1992; Romanelli and Tushman, 1994), or it can occur through sedimentation, reflecting a pattern of new emerging structures and ideas super-imposed (or layered) on pre-existing ones (Hyndman et al., 2014).

Legitimation of Change and Charities

In order to implement a new accounting practice or technique, this has to be first understood and legitimated at the organisational level. It has been suggested that in public-sector and not-for-profit (NFP) contexts, accounting changes do not always yield the expected results (Eldenburg and Vines, 2004; Liguori and Steccolini, 2012; Ellwood and Greenwood, 2016) and they tend to produce a layering, rather than a replacement, of practices over time (Hyndman et al., 2014). Only relatively recently has increased attention been devoted to understanding the impact and process of accounting change at the organisational and individual levels in different fields (Erkama and Vaara, 2010; Liguori and Steccolini, 2012; Järvinen, 2016). Most of the previous studies investigate private or public sector organisations, while how change is perceived, translated and legitimated within charities has received very limited attention.

Studies of legitimation in charities have mainly focused on the achievement of external legitimation following accounting disclosures (Connolly and Hyndman, 2001; Mack et al., 2017; Yang et al., 2017) or relating to fundraising activities (Guéguen et al., 2015; Hind, 2017). Liu et al. (2016) investigated the creation and legitimation process of the first Chinese independent charity foundation. They show that the coexisting and competing relationships among state, civil society, social mission and market logic provided impetus for organisational change and innovation. In the early stages, the main change leverages to gain external legitimation were financial resources, international experience and knowledge, charismatic leadership, and social influence. In the later stages, with change facilitating increased visibility and credibility, the organisational focus shifted towards cultural resources and constructing and mobilising societal discursive resources. Silver (2001) highlighted that funders tend to validate the impression of themselves (externally) as good citizens by supporting charitable organisations and their work. He found that regardless of whether strategic changes, aimed at improving external legitimation, actually increase the level of corporate donations or not, this instrumental role of charitable donations is often central for funders who want to achieve a socially responsible identity.

As discussed previously in **Chapter 2**, the process of external legitimation through which an organisation seeks approval (or avoidance of sanction) from society is the main focus of legitimacy theory (Suchman, 1995). In accounting, research adopting this perspective has mainly explored the impact of voluntary external disclosures. However, this approach only examines the external stakeholder perspective. This chapter proposes that focusing on internal legitimation (internal justifications) and, in particular, on the use of individual legitimation strategies, helps to highlight the importance of individuals and their construction of reality during a process of change.

From an organisational point of view, a preliminary (and extremely important) condition for the successful implementation of change (however that might be defined) is that it has to be considered as 'legitimate' within the very context in which it is to be applied (i.e. it has to have internal legitimation). At the individual level, legitimacy can be seen in terms of how 'reasonable', 'logical' and 'right' a change is perceived to be. The empirical research reported in this chapter explores the deployment and use of legitimation (and delegitimation) strategies by accountants in UK and RoI large fundraising charities with respect to the changes required by the FRS 102 SORP (Charity Commission and OSCR, 2014a). In doing so, it allows an assessment of the extent to which such changes are likely to be embedded.

Legitimation and Delegitimation of Change

In order to explain why the introduction of a new accounting practice succeeds or fails in a certain field, it is essential to understand how actors legitimate or delegitimate the change and the arguments they mobilise for it. Previous studies have often referred to this as the role of institutional entrepreneurship (Maguire *et al.*, 2004). As Scott (1995, p. 45) pointed out, "legitimacy is not a commodity to be possessed or exchanged but a condition reflecting cultural alignment, normative support or consonance with relevant rules or laws." The specific context conditions (historical, administrative or cultural) define "which ideas are considered 'sensible', which constructions of reality are seen as 'realistic', and which claims are held as 'legitimate' within a certain policy at a specific time" (Koopmans and Statham, 1999, p. 228). The extent to which new accounting practices are perceived as legitimate may be crucial in order to predict the likelihood of them embedding in the manner anticipated (Oliver, 1991).

In legitimating change, language can play an important role for its diffusion and implementation (Strang and Meyer, 1994; Green, 2004). The rhetorical arguments and strategies set in place during a process of change can strengthen or weaken the adoption of new practices and the way people make sense and justify the usefulness of the change itself (Hirsch, 1986; Green, 2004). The ambiguity regarding the process and the outcome of change induces individuals within organisations to use rhetorical arguments to construct reality and gain legitimacy on certain organisational structures and beliefs (DiMaggio, 1988; Clemens and Cook, 1999; Creed *et al.*, 2002; Suddaby and Greenwood, 2005). The more persuasive the supporting reasons for the introduction of a new practice, the more justifiable its adoption will be perceived, and ultimately accepted. However, how rhetoric and language shape the introduction and reproduction of change within organisations has been little investigated in the past and, in particular, how legitimation (or delegitimation) strategies are used to achieve change is still unclear (Vaara *et al.*, 2006; Green *et al.*, 2008).

Previous studies have looked at legitimation and organisational change by mainly focusing on particular fields, such as industrial restructuring and mergers and acquisitions (Vaara, 2002; Comtois *et al.*, 2004; Vaara *et al.*, 2006). Legitimation strategies have been found relevant in: processes of institutional change (Green, 2004; Suddaby and Greenwood, 2005); actors' struggles over controversial decisions, such as organisational shutdowns (Erkama and Vaara, 2010); contested issues, such as climate change (Lefsrud and Meyer, 2012) and shareholder value (Meyer and Höllerer, 2010); and corporate restructuring (Vaara *et al.*, 2006) and international corporate investments (Joutsenvirta and Vaara, 2015). Studies focusing on accounting have only seldom investigated the way these changes are framed (Chang *et al.*, 2008; Roberts and Jones, 2009; Bay, 2011; Andon and Free, 2012), more often limiting the analysis to accounting narratives and documents (Bettman and Weitz, 1983; Staw *et al.*, 1983; Salancik and Meindl, 1984; Clapham and Schwenk, 1991; Wagner and Gooding, 1997; Aerts, 2001; Tsang, 2002; Clatworthy and Jones, 2003).

In charities, change has been most often viewed as led by other sectors (for example, the private or public sectors) and potentially affected by conflicting pressures and risks of mission drift in terms of the fundamental objectives and goals of the organisation (Järvinen, 2016; Glennon *et al.*, 2017). Dynamics of legitimation and delegitimation may thus be particularly relevant in this context, where competing ideas and perceptions of what a charity should be doing exist. As suggested in previous chapters, charitable organisations have felt pressure to operate in a more 'business-like' manner (whether it is appropriate or not). Individual interpretations and translations of such ideas are important to understand and predict the development of this process of change and of the SORP itself.

Legitimation Strategies

The implementation of accounting change (such as a change introduced by a new or revised SORP) is not a mechanistic introduction of a new practice into formal organisational structures, procedures or mechanisms. Rather, it represents a translation of general ideas adapted to local circumstances and a local edition of more general ideas (Brunsson, 1989). In organisations which implement new tools and practices on the basis of pre-standardised templates, including new (or refashioned) accounting tools, change requires the interaction of individuals and units inside and outside of the organisation.

But how are legitimation and rhetorical techniques used to introduce new practices which potentially replace, or undermine, existing structures which are still embedded within an organisation? According to Green and Li (2011), this can be explained through the use of different legitimation strategies. In this sense, the active role of those individuals who are directly involved with the change is mirrored in the rhetorical arguments that are used and accompany the introduction of the new practice, affecting the way it is interpreted. Following Vaara *et al.* (2006), new techniques and ideas can be put forth relying on one of five discursive strategies (or a combination of these):

- authorisation, which refers to legitimation through authority of tradition, custom, law and persons upon whom institutional authority of some kind has been bestowed;
- rationalisation, related to legitimation by institutionalised social action and knowledge that society has constructed, giving the proposed change(s) cognitive validity. Such a strategy mainly focuses on the benefits, purposes or outcomes that a certain course of action can bring;
- normalisation, which legitimates by exemplarity that can involve 'retrospective' (similar cases, events or practices in the past) or 'prospective' (new cases, events or practices to be expected) references, which make the case at hand something 'normal' and professional;
- moralisation, which refers to legitimation by reference to specific moral values (such as the need to be accountable or transparent); and
- narrativisation, which is about legitimation conveyed through narratives. Indeed, telling a story can provide evidence of acceptable, appropriate or preferential behaviour.

Green (2004) also identified a route of legitimation via pathos, i.e. legitimation by appealing to emotions (Green and Li, 2011), which does not necessarily coincide with the above strategies. This may reflect legitimation because of a personal commitment to something (in this case, an accounting change), for whatever reason. In this chapter, we propose that the variation in the acceptance of a particular change depends upon the variation in the deployment of specific arguments and strategies in a particular situation.

Legitimation strategies, however, are not always intentional or conscious, and their use usually decreases with time, when justifications are less needed as a change becomes accepted or a new practice is taken for granted (Green, 2004). Legitimation strategies play a role in creating the organisational conditions that can help to restore or justify social status quos, or can even destroy them through delegitimation. Van Leeuwen and Wodak (1999) identified four macro-families, which summarise the way strategies can be used:

- constructive strategies to build or establish particular views;
- strategies of perpetuation and justification to maintain and reproduce existing ideas and identities;
- strategies of transformation to support change; and
- destructive strategies to delegitimate the new (in order to undermine or stop a change, different people might use antagonistic framings or destructive strategies, criticising the validity or ridiculing a specific source of information – van Leeuwen and Wodak, 1999; Lefsrud and Meyer, 2012).

Previous literature shows that legitimation strategies are often intertwined. For instance, normalisation seems to be strongly supported by other strategies, especially by narrativisation. Vaara *et al.* (2006) also found authorisation to be frequently linked with rationalisation and moralisation because authorities themselves symbolically represent specific institutions and viewpoints. Rationalisation seems to be often based on moral and ideological foundations, even when these are not stated explicitly; moralisation is often an attempt to put authorisation and rationalisation into a particular legitimating or delegitimating perspective, while narrativisation seems associated with multiple 'legitimations' (Vaara *et al.*, 2006). Green *et al.* (2008) opined that different individuals at different levels tend to use the same rhetorical sequences during successive periods of change inside an organisation. Moreover, movements from the status quo, or stable institutional arrangements, are often initially brought about by emotional appeals to redirect limited social attention. Hence, pathos arguments may have a part to play, particularly at the beginning of the change process, when a stronger push is needed to overcome the initial social and organisation inertia. Once a course of action is chosen, rational arguments more regularly justify the new arrangements as responsible and appropriate (Green, 2004).

5.2   Research Methods

This section introduces some of the concepts and measurements that underpin the subsequent empirical analyses used in the chapter. Unlike previous studies (see, in particular, Hyndman and Liguori, 2016b), this chapter investigates key actors' (charity accountants) understanding and legitimation of the new charity FRS 102 SORP (Charity Commission and OSCR, 2014a) before (rather than after) it is actually implemented. There is thus no *ex-post* rationalisation involved in this study, as individuals talked about the SORP changes as they were being considered for implementation within their own organisations.

With respect to the FRS 102 SORP (Charity Commission and OSCR, 2014a) implementation, two cases, the UK and RoI, have been chosen following an intensity sampling criterion (Patton, 2002). In particular, the research compares the case of the UK, where the SORP is a mandatory requirement, and RoI, where the SORP is often followed but only represents best practice, at least at present (June 2017). A different intensity of adoption, and different needs and translations are thus expected within the charities of the two jurisdictions. This allows variability in the dimensions under study in terms of both translation/legitimation and implementation of the same practice. In addition to the legitimation (or delegitimation) strategies of the actors (charity accountants), this research also considers how the national context may impact on the way in which the SORP is understood and implemented.

As seen previously (particularly in **Chapter 3**), FRS 102 SORP (Charity Commission and OSCR, 2014a) not only represents a set of requirements and recommendations to be followed, but also aims at aligning and strengthening comparability across charities. In particular, with respect to financial statements, this is facilitated by making reporting consistent with FRS 102 (Financial Reporting Council (FRC), 2013). The FRS 102 SORP applies to all reporting periods starting on or after 1 January 2015 (so for most charities, this will apply to the annual period ending December 2015, or their 2015/2016 reporting period). The transposition of rhetoric and legitimation strategies is, thus, analysed at the very start of the FRS 102 SORP implementation process and through the eyes of the main actors involved (financial directors and accountants who have the task of translating and implementing the new rules within their organisations).

Exploring legitimation strategies required asking charity accountants about their experiences and perceptions. This involved conducting semi-structured interviews to elicit the understanding and perceptions of these key actors as to the main SORP changes, in terms of the Trustees' Annual Report (TAR), financial statements and 'annual report' (i.e. the SORP as a whole) and the related (implicit) rhetorical strategies of legitimation or delegitimation. The main areas of investigation and the respective questions (and prompts) were identified on the basis of the SORP *Help Sheets* published by the Charity Commission and OSCR (Charity Commission and OSCR, 2014d), a comparison of the FRS 102 SORP (Charity Commission and OSCR, 2014a) with SORP 2005 (Charity Commission, 2005), and insights from the SORP Committee (responsible for drafting the new SORP[1]). The *Help Sheets* – aimed at supporting charities in the preparation of the new accounts – highlighted, discussed and exemplified the main changes that would come in place with the FRS 102 SORP (Charity Commission and OSCR, 2014a), such as, for instance:

- the changes in the value of financial instruments measured at fair value being taken to the SOFA, with gains and losses on investments now shown before striking a total for 'net income/expenditure';
- income to be recognised in the SOFA when its receipt is 'probable' rather than 'virtually certain';
- encouragement to report on impacts in the TAR; and
- an explanation in the TAR of any policy a charity has for holding reserves and a statement of the amounts of those reserves and why they are held.[2]

The questions asked related to overall perceptions of the SORP (past and present), origins of the SORP, and views on the main specific changes included in FRS 102 SORP (see **Appendix 3** for the complete interview guide). These included questions exploring the actors' (charity accountants') input in the process of change (if any), their understanding of specific changes, and their expectations in relation to the likely effects of such changes on their everyday activities and the sector more broadly.

Interviews were conducted in 11 charities in the UK (with a total of 14 interviewees) and 10 charities in RoI (with a total of 10 interviewees) between September 2015 and March 2016. The charities were identified through criterion sampling to ensure their comparability (Patton, 2002). Only large fundraising charities with incomes of over £5 million (or, in RoI, €6 million) were included in the sample. This ensured that all UK charities interviewed were subject to the FRS 102 SORP (Charity Commission and OSCR, 2014a) through legislation; in RoI, the SORP was best practice at this time (and many large charities had adopted it).

---

[1] Noel Hyndman, one of the authors of this book, has been a member of the SORP Committee since 2006.
[2] For a detailed discussion of the content of these changes, refer to **Chapter 3**.

Table 5.1 shows the distribution of charities for the UK and RoI samples classified by area of activity. This categorisation draws on the classification of the 'advanced search features' available on the Charity Commission website.[3]

The interviewees are identified in any quotations included in this chapter by the jurisdiction within which they operate (UK or RoI) and an interviewee number (for instance, 'UK1' indicates the first interviewee in the UK, 'RoI4' the fourth interviewee in RoI, etc.). The interviewees, accountants and financial directors, were identified through snowball sampling (i.e. on the basis of informants' suggestions, in order to get information-rich cases from those directly involved in the process of change) (Patton, 2002). Each interview lasted for about one hour and was recorded and transcribed in full for coding. A preliminary coding scheme was developed based on the relevant literature on change and legitimation strategies. Following an iterative process, the coding scheme was further refined and applied to ensure data consistency. The coding scheme was applied to each of the interviews independently by two researchers, with all cases of disagreement being reviewed and resolved as a team. Data coding was supported by software for qualitative data analysis.

Table 5.1   **Distribution of Charities by Area of Activity**

	Medical/Health/ Medical Research	Overseas Aid/ Famine Relief	Development/ Animal Welfare	Wider Social Objects
UK	2	2	1	6
RoI	2	2	1	5
Total	4	4	2	11

As far as the interview analysis is concerned, a specific argument was coded when a legitimation strategy was used with regard to at least one of the possible areas of change (i.e. TAR, financial statements or annual report). In distinguishing the legitimation strategies, the typologies proposed by a number of writers were combined, and resulted in six legitimation/delegitimation strategies being operationalised in this research (Green, 2004; Vaara *et al.*, 2006; van Leeuwen and Wodak, 1999). For each of the strategies indicated in the previous section, specific sub-strategies (i.e. possible types of arguments made by the interviewees)

---

[3] See apps.charitycommission.gov.uk/ShowCharity/RegisterOfCharities/AdvancedSearch. aspx.

were initially identified (and subsequently refined) to support the analysis. These were:

- authorisation (reported in the tables as AUT), based on the use of sub-strategies that reference external or internal authority, such as political pressures, mimetic pressures – when other countries or experiences in the same sector were taken as an authoritative example and reason for change – or benchmarking, financial crisis, external stakeholders, market pressures, the role of the EU, Government, law and regulation, internal management pressures, etc.;
- rationalisation (reported in the tables as RAT), based on the use of sub-strategies referencing rational managerial aspects, such as the importance of culture, effective planning and decision making, skills and education, resources, support of IT services, etc.;
- normalisation (reported in the tables as NOR), based on arguments and sub-strategies such as the importance of professional standards, the opportunity of comparisons with other non-charity sectors (for example, private or public sectors) deemed to be 'more advanced' in a specific matter, etc.;
- moralisation (reported in the tables as MOR), based on the use of sub-strategies that stress the importance of accountability, transparency, gender equality, social and environmental sustainability, good administration, etc.;
- narrativisation (reported in the tables as NAR), based on the use of organisational 'stories' or historic events, accounting scandals or exemplars of behaviour; and
- pathos (reported in the tables as PAT), based on sub-strategies that reference the role of elements such as organisational and personal commitment, career dedication and patriotism in strengthening or weakening the implementation of the changes.

Legitimation strategies were coded as '1', whereas delegitimation strategies were coded as '2'. For example, AUT1 would represent a positive legitimating strategy (justification) based on authorisation; whereas AUT2 would represent a negative delegitimation (questioning) strategy based on authorisation. In the UK, overall 1,314 interview arguments were coded and associated with at least one strategy; 1,093 of these were positive legitimation, while only 221 were relative to delegitimation arguments. In RoI, the total arguments coded were 1,119, where 910 used legitimation strategies and 209 delegitimation ones (see **Table 5.2**).

5.3   Understanding and Legitimating the FRS 102 Statement of Recommended Practice

This section presents the results of the empirical investigation relating to the interviews conducted with accountants in UK and RoI charities. The first two subsections introduce the overall results as far as legitimation and delegitimation of changes introduced in the FRS 102 SORP are concerned, while the third (and final) subsection presents more of the detail of the way the different areas of FRS 102 SORP (Charity Commission and OSCR, 2014a) – namely the TAR, financial statements and annual report – were talked about by the interviewees. **Table 5.2** distinguishes between the UK and RoI and shows the counts for each strategy used by the interviewees. The relative frequencies are computed on the overall total of the strategies used. As discussed earlier, the areas of change highlighted by the interviewees were the TAR, the financial statements and the annual report (i.e. the overall SORP being referred to). These are specifically reported in **Table 5.3**, which shows, for each jurisdiction, the absolute counts and relative percentages of the frequency with which each SORP area was mentioned by the interviewees (a total of 548 hits in the UK and 492 hits in RoI). The area most talked about was the TAR in both the UK and RoI (respectively, 47.6% and 48% of the times an argument was made), followed by the financial statements and the overall annual report (the overall SORP).

It has to be noted that in **Table 5.2** the number of occurrences for each strategy was computed so that a repetition of the same argument (or substrategy) within the same answer was only counted once. However, a number of strategies could co-exist and be used at the same time in relation to a specific area of change that was being mentioned. Moreover, more than one area of change (TAR, financial statements and annual report) could be referred to in the same answer. As a consequence, the total counts reported in **Table 5.2** and **5.3** may present different totals, with the former showing a higher number of total hits because of this.

Legitimating the FRS 102 Statement of Recommended Practice in the United Kingdom and Republic of Ireland

As can be seen from a comparison of the two jurisdictions in **Table 5.2**, the first interesting finding is that the results are similar, regardless of the SORP being compulsory in the UK and only best practice in RoI. All interviewees in both jurisdictions talked about the SORP changes in mainly positive terms, with criticism and delegitimation strategies much rarer (these represented only 16.8% of the total strategies used in the UK and 18.7% in RoI;

see **Table 5.2**). In both jurisdictions, the main legitimation strategy used was authorisation (33.9% in the UK, 37.3% in RoI; **Table 5.2**), followed by rationalisation (21.8% in the UK, 18.8% in RoI) and narrativisation (15.7% in the UK, 15.5% in RoI). Moralisation and normalisation arguments were present, although were perhaps different from what would be expected when dealing with accounting techniques. It is also interesting to note that despite the fact that the charity sector is the focus of study (where moral and commitment issues are often to the fore), the interviewees showed very little personal commitment and pathos (both in positive and negative terms) towards the changes. Indeed, pathos was the least used strategy among all (**Table 5.2**). This was perhaps due to the changes being made in what might be described as a technical area (accounting), for which the specific sector (the charity sector) does not, in this instance, appear to have a particular influence on the actors' perceptions.

Most interviewees believed the provisions of the FRS 102 SORP (Charity Commission and OSCR, 2014a) to be, although useful, largely incremental adjustments to an evolving system of accounting and reporting. This view was prevalent in both jurisdictions, but particularly in the UK where large charities have had to comply with previous SORPs and were all accustomed to, and aware of, most of the major adjustments necessary to comply with the FRS 102 SORP (Charity Commission and OSCR, 2014a). For instance:

> "They are all incremental adjustments, all of it [the FRS 102 SORP] as far as I am concerned. I can't think of a single forced change..." (UK4)

Although, in the UK, rationalisation strategies were employed slightly more often than in RoI, the specific arguments used by the interviewees in each jurisdiction to legitimate change were similar. In terms of authorisation (the most recurrent strategy in both jurisdictions), the implementation of the FRS 102 SORP (Charity Commission and OSCR, 2014a) was first of all explained through reference to the importance of mimetic behaviours, such as aligning themselves with what other charities were doing in the jurisdiction or in other jurisdictions (this was especially the case for RoI charities). This sub-strategy (as an aspect of an overall authorisation strategy), was perceived as facilitating increased comparability across charities (something pushed by external authorities). It was frequently mentioned as a reason for the development and adoption of the SORP. For example, one charity highlighted the usefulness of benchmarking against similar charities, something facilitated by the SORP:

> "So you have an interesting compare and contrast when you're talking to [charity's name – a charity working in the same area], because, in a lot of

ways, we are a very similar charity. From starting within a couple of years of each other in the 1860s; and in terms of how we operate and how we work." (UK9)

Despite not being a legislative requirement at present (June 2017), the main rationale for the introduction of the new SORP was similarly authority-driven in RoI (albeit it was acknowledged that the ROI sector was less developed with respect to SORP-compliant reporting):

> "I think it's probably a bit different when you are dealing with the Republic than when you are dealing with some of the other jurisdictions. We are probably coming from further back in terms of our maturity ... I think it is probably a bigger jump for some of the charities [in RoI]. The changes that you are referring to ... some of the charities are between the two SORP documents. A lot of the organisations [in RoI] wouldn't have complied with the original SORP and you are seeing them jump from a very basic set of accounts to something which is very complicated and detailed ... So, I think that is more of a change. I think they might not feel like it at the moment but the charities are going to see that it [the SORP] is the benchmark now, and it's something you are going to have to comply with." (RoI3)

The use of this type of authoritative justification was even stronger in RoI than the actual reference to regulatory requirements in the UK. The motivation and pressures of internal management also played an important role. It was planned that the changes would be implemented centrally and top-down from the finance department for the vast majority of the interviewed charities in both jurisdictions. This made the role and authority of internal management particularly important, something that was recognised throughout the organisation. From a rationalisation point of view, many of the sub-strategies identified from the interviews referred to managerial arguments, such as the importance of effective decision-making and effective planning, efficient use of resources, and the necessity to increase people's skills and training. In these, tensions became apparent between the new SORP requirements being seen: as mere compliance reporting on the one hand; or, more productively, as catalysts with the potential to improve focus and decision making within, and better reporting by the charity, on the other. For instance:

> "It will be interesting to see what this change [the SORP provision on performance (including impact) measurement and reporting] does really; because if the process is the same as the one of a compliance document,

we will think about it within these time scales … that doesn't necessarily indicate how we are going to think about impact in the long term and how we are going to set these objectives. If you see the accounts being an intrinsic part of the board's oversight strategy, then I think that it should lead to a slightly different way of how you approach the reporting and how that process is managed." (UK1)

and,

"I think it [more detailed information to be provided on reserves] is a good idea because if you just look at a set of accounts and you see a very high reserve you think 'God you're a charity and what are you doing with all this money?' If it's a massive amount, you would think 'well why aren't you spending this money, why is it sitting there?' So to have a clear break-down is a very good idea and so the reader can see exactly why it's there." (RoI9)

As indicated, the third most employed strategy was narrativisation (slightly over 15% of strategies in both jurisdictions; identified as NAR1 in **Table 5.2**). As mentioned in **Chapter 2**, recent 'scandals' (such as those involving organisations like Kids Company in the UK, and Rehab and the Central Remedial Clinic in RoI)[4] (see also Hind, 2017 and the literature discussed previously in **Chapter 4**) fostered a number of narratives and comparisons based on behaviours that were largely seen as undermining trust and damaging the sector (and had to be eliminated from the sector). In relation to this thrust, stories were often used to justify SORP changes as emanating from external pressures and to emphasise the necessity for greater accountability and transparency as perceived to be demanded by society and the media. This was particularly the case for NAR1 arguments (i.e. legitimation via narrativisation) in RoI, which often referenced scandals as exemplars of behaviour to avoid.

---

[4] For further information on Kids Company see, for instance, http://www.bbc.co.uk/news/uk-33788415; for the Rehab case, see http://www.irishtimes.com/opinion/rehab-recovery-may-offer-some-solace-for-console-1.2711477; for Central Remedial Clinic see, for instance, http://www.irishtimes.com/news/ireland/irish-news/central-remedial-clinic-will-not-pursue-ex-chief-over-741-000-severance-package-1.2714126.

Table 5.2   **Total Counts of Legitimation Strategies**

Strategy Type	Code	UK Counts and Frequency	RoI Counts and Frequency
Authorisation	AUT1	445	417
		33.9%	37.3%
	AUT2	53	46
		4.0%	4.1%
Rationalisation	RAT1	286	210
		21.8%	18.8%
	RAT2	82	93
		6.2%	8.3%
Normalisation	NOR1	60	44
		4.6%	3.9%
	NOR2	24	22
		1.8%	2.0%
Moralisation	MOR1	62	39
		4.7%	3.5%
	MOR2	4	7
		0.3%	0.6%
Narrativisation	NAR1	206	174
		15.7%	15.5%
	NAR2	49	35
		3.7%	3.1%
Pathos	PAT1	34	26
		2.6%	2.3%
	PAT2	9	6
		0.7%	0.5%
Number of arguments	TOTAL 1	1,093 (83.2% of total)	910 (81.3% of total)
	TOTAL 2	221 (16.8% of total)	209 (18.7% of total)
	Overall total	1,314	1,119

Delegitimating the FRS 102 Statement of Recommended Practice in the United Kingdom and Republic of Ireland

Rationalisation was, although at a much lower base (6.2% in the UK and 8.3% in RoI; **Table 5.2**), the main strategy used to delegitimate the implementation of the FRS 102 SORP (Charity Commission and OSCR, 2014a). Criticisms were usually specific and linked to aspects of the implementation process or of the new standards to be introduced (especially in the case of RAT2 with respect to the financial statements; see the next subsection for more details). When speaking about the increased number of comparative columns in the SOFA, a fairly common remark was:

> "It's just so ridiculous. You can't force people to put all this detail on the face of the SOFA." (UK4)

In RoI, speaking about the criterion of income recognition going from "virtually certain" to "probable":[5]

> "For me the principles are all prudent, so I wasn't sure how to interpret that actually. I have always gone for the virtually certain in my thinking, particularly around how you estimate funding from the public because working with the history of our funding, we are very heavily supported by [name of the Foundation], the Foundation we were founded by at the start." (RoI8)

Delegitimation via rationalisation was followed (in terms of frequency) by criticisms based on authorisation (4% in the UK, 4.1% in RoI; **Table 5.2**) and narrativisation (3.7% in the UK, 3.1% in RoI) arguments. All the other strategies, although present, played a very minor role in undermining the changes. The rationalisation arguments mainly mirrored, although with negative nuances in this case, those first used to justify the implementation of the changes (for example, effective planning, resources, skills and education). Effective decision-making and the presence (or absence) of appropriate resources (representing in total more than 90% of the RAT2 arguments used in each jurisdiction – detail not shown in the tables), in particular, were seen as both justifying the introduction of the FRS 102 SORP (Charity Commission and OSCR, 2014a) and, in other instances, expressing caveats (delegitimation) relating to the changes. This was especially the case for changes related to the financial statements.

---

[5] FRS 102 SORP indicates that income should be recognised when the charity's entitlement to the economic benefit is probable (i.e. when there is sufficient certainty of receipt). Previous SORP versions indicated the recognition of this same entitlement to be reported only when it was 'virtually certain', suggesting a previously more conservative interpretation.

For instance, most interviewees were particularly critical of the change in the criterion of income recognition (from certain to probable) and of the new requirement of accounting for unrealised gains and losses on investment assets.[6] These two changes, in particular, were often delegitimated not only in terms of rationalisation, but also through the use of normalisation strategies, on the basis that charities are not private-sector businesses aimed at making profit. As far as delegitimation via authorisation is concerned, legal and regulatory requirements were often used to criticise some of the new SORP's provisions. Again, in most cases the criticism was related to FRS 102 (FRC, 2013), which was seen as not always fitting charity reporting needs. For example:

> "From FRS, that would be the one big thing I have found confusing in the SORP, recognising income that was almost certain. At the moment we defer, so we don't recognise the income until it is actually received you know what I mean, well you would recognise it and you would defer it. And now the SORP seems to say completely the opposite, that you don't defer, so maybe you accrue your costs, it's one thing I got quite confused on. What's the definition of probable?" (RoI9)

In the context of delegitimation, aspects of the new SORP's alignment with FRS 102 (FRC, 2013) often emerged as representing a negative regulative, or externally imposed, constraint (AUT2). This was especially so in RoI, where the aspects of FRS 102 included in the new FRS 102 SORP (Charity Commission and OSCR, 2014a) were frequently perceived as unhelpful mimetic behaviours, with pressures seen as emanating from other jurisdictions. Interestingly, such perceptions were often combined with negative views relating to professionally driven practice aspects of the FRS 102 SORP (NOR2). Overall, however, notwithstanding the above criticisms, interviewees in both jurisdictions seemed keen to be seen as understanding and committed to complying with it, thus only providing marginal delegitimation arguments. Also, it is notable that when interviewees legitimated FRS 102-related SORP changes (as was more often the case), the combination of authorisation and normalisation was frequently used (in a positive manner).

---

[6] SORP 2005 allowed charities to present both realised and unrealised investment gains and losses as an item within 'other gains and losses' after striking a total for 'net incoming/ outgoing resources'. The FRS 102 SORP requires changes in the value of financial instruments measured at fair value to be taken through profit and loss. Gains and losses on investments are now shown before striking a total for 'net income/expenditure'.

Table 5.3   **Areas of the FRS 102 Statement of Recommended Practice Spoken About**

Areas of Change	UK Total Counts and Frequency	RoI Total Counts and Frequency
Trustees' Annual Report (TAR)	261	236
	47.6%	48.0%
Financial Statements	204	160
	37.2%	32.5%
Annual Report	83	96
	15.1%	19.5%
Total	548	492
	100%	100%

A closer look at the FRS 102 Statement of Recommended Practice and its documents

As indicated in the methodology section of this chapter, the questions that the charity interviewees were asked focused not only on the FRS 102 SORP (Charity Commission and OSCR, 2014a) as a unitary document (referred to here, and in **Table 5.3**, as the 'annual report'), but also specifically on the TAR and the financial statements. Turning the attention to the different elements of the SORP, the area most often talked about was the TAR, followed by the financial statements. This was similar in each jurisdiction (47.6% and 32.2% in the UK, 48% and 32.5% in RoI; **Table 5.3**). Many interviewees also referred to the overall annual report in their assessment of the changes, although this was less frequent (15.1% in the UK and 19.5% in RoI; **Table 5.3**). Within the TAR, particular emphasis was given to the measurement of performance (including impact): indeed, in the UK, in about 38% of the times when the interviewees were referring to the TAR, they were doing so by discussing performance (including impact) reporting; the same was true in 30% of the times in RoI.

As was the case overall, and with respect to the internal legitimation of FRS 102 SORP for each of the three areas (TAR, financial statements and annual report) and in both jurisdictions, the most used legitimation strategy was authorisation (data not shown in tables), followed by rationalisation and narrativisation. It is interesting to note (and perhaps understandable in terms of the mission focus of charities) that for the TAR, moralisation arguments (favouring accountability and transparency towards both donors and beneficiaries, and principles of good administration) were relatively more used than when referring to the more technical financial statements or the annual report as a whole (in each jurisdiction). For instance, in the UK, with reference to performance (including impact) reporting:

> "The operations team are devising advanced means of tracking their impact but whether they would do that for their own benefit or whether it's being driven by the SORP ... I think there is generally much more of a move towards social returns on investments and those kinds of things, transparency and impact evaluation. [...] It's very interesting and I think it's worthwhile." (UK6)

As discussed in **Chapter 3**, the FRS 102 SORP (Charity Commission and OSCR, 2014a) requires charities to provide a narrative explanation in the TAR as far as the remuneration policy for senior staff is concerned. Charities must also disclose information about the numbers of staff paid £60,000 or more in the reporting period, together with details of the aggregate pay of their 'key management personnel' or senior management. In RoI, when discussing the disclosure of top management's pay:

> "We do the bandings and we try to describe what is going on. We have to give the exact number for the CEO's pay and where it comes from. It has to be done, there is a public demand for this. ... If you are responsible for £50 million a year of public funds and 2,500 people and providing quality services to thousands of service users, you must be paid a professional salary, but it is about transparency." (RoI4)

Normalisation strategies (NOR1), if used, mainly appeared in relation to comments on the financial statements in the UK, while in RoI these arguments were mainly found in the discussion of the annual report. In the UK, more personal engagement (a sub-strategy coded as part of pathos / PAT1) was identified when discussing the overall annual report. This was also the case when reference was made to the SORP's history and development in the organisation, a feature much less evident in the RoI interviews. A fairly typical pathos argument (showing the commitment of people working in the sector) was:

> "I think it's a positive thing that you would disclose how you arrive at your senior management pay. I think there's the risk that you pay too little, but then people wouldn't come into this sector if they were only in it for the money!" (UK6)

Looking in more detail into the legitimation arguments used for each SORP area (TAR, financial statements and annual report), authorisation-based ideas, such as pressures coming from mimetic behaviours, internal manage-ment and new regulation, were, in each case, the main justifications given for the introduction of the FRS 102 SORP (Charity Commission and OSCR, 2014a), although the sub-strategies did not occur in that same order of fre-quency for each area of change. This was observed in both the UK and RoI interviews, with the importance of taking into consideration another source of authority (external stakeholders) being particularly emphasised as a rea-son to follow the new SORP requirements in RoI. A similar picture emerged with rationalisation strategies, where the main arguments (or sub-strategies) used stressed the importance of the SORP in supporting efficient and effec-tive planning/decision-making processes, and the value of having sufficient resources and skills for the introduction of the SORP changes (although, also here, the order of frequency for these sub-strategies was different across areas of change). As indicated, the third most used strategy in all areas and in both jurisdictions was narrativisation: stories about the past relating to the organisation and the sector were often used to explain the implementation of the SORP and its new changes.

While the legitimation of the different areas of the SORP was shaped in a similar fashion, if we look at the way these areas were delegitimated, some differences emerge between the jurisdictions. In the UK, where the SORP is compulsory, the TAR, as well as the overall SORP, was mainly delegiti-mated on the basis of authorisation (AUT2, referencing mainly the role of external mimetic pressures, regulation and media), while the financial statements were delegitimated mainly on the basis of rationalisation strate-gies (RAT2). In contrast, in RoI both the TAR and the financial statements were mainly delegitimated on the basis of rationalisation arguments, while the existence and implementation of the SORP-based annual report were criticised mostly on the basis of authorisation. Interestingly, in both the UK and RoI, delegitimation based on authorisation did not only concern the pressures coming from inside the sector (and leading to the implemen-tation of changes not always appropriate for the specific organisation) or from regulations and internal management (which were identified in this study as the main authorisation sub-strategies), but also from unhelpful (and inappropriate) pressures emanating from the media. As a result of recent scandals, in particular, a strong pressure from media outlets was often exerted, perceived as forcing charities towards greater information provision and transparency, even when it was not particularly helpful. For instance:

> "We have to handle this one [salary disclosure] very carefully ... there is a huge public trust put on charities because it is public money. I am giving you my pounds to spend on saving people not to do this, but the flip side

of that is to show appreciation … I think it is so important but difficult because there are so many factors about salary … I think of the danger that it becomes if it is just picked by individuals and journalists – that is where I think is can become sort of troublesome." (UK5)

"As far as SORP is concerned, ignoring the technical changes, providing additional disclosure is a good thing … But I think then you come to the practicalities of applying it and the practical exercise of what does it actually mean. There are a few areas where there will be an uncomfortable response from journalists and the public, and maybe some unintended consequences, particularly in relation to fair value within the FRS requirements." (RoI6)

In addition, in relation to the media, the most controversial point that emerged concerned the appropriateness of disclosing the top management's pay in the TAR. Many interviewees felt that this was not necessary and could negatively impact on managers' morale. However, this seemed to be a topic on which the media focused and – it was perceived – often exploited to create news. Perhaps because of its more technical nature, a different picture emerged with respect to the financial statements, which, in terms of authorisation strategies, were delegitimated in both jurisdictions mainly through criticisms relating to FRS 102 (FRC, 2013) requirements. In particular, these were often seen as not always mirroring the charities' actual needs (reference was made, for instance, to the case of holiday pay, unrealised gains on investment assets and income recognition – see previous discussion and **Chapter 3** for more details). In these same areas, pressures from external stakeholders were also sometimes seen as problematic or, at least, not always appropriate.

When the criticism was based on rationalisation, the same arguments (effective planning, resources and skills) used to justify the changes were also deployed to highlight the shortcomings of some of the new systems and the lack of resources to make them run adequately. The scarcity of resources and appropriate skills (especially for those charities mainly relying on volunteers' work) were particularly recurrent topics in both jurisdictions. In the UK, when discussing the TAR and the financial statements, the interviewees also mentioned the lack of an appropriate culture within their organisation. Resistance and attachment to the old ways of measuring and disclosing, in particular, were seen as problematic and potentially hampering the effective implementation of the FRS 102 SORP (Charity Commission and OSCR, 2014a).

Finally, as in the case of positive legitimation, the interviewees' accounts to delegitimate change were often accompanied by the use of stories and narratives to back up their opinion. These were, however, considerably less present than in the case of legitimating arguments.

5.4 Legitimating the FRS 102 Statement of Recommended Practice: A Discussion

The results of the empirical investigation presented in this chapter showed, perhaps surprisingly, largely similar results for the UK and RoI. In both jurisdictions, charities' accountants tended to interpret and talk about the implementation of the new FRS 102 SORP (Charity Commission and OSCR, 2014a) using comparable arguments, regardless of this being mandatory in the UK and only best practice in RoI. This finding may be partly due to the common culture and views that the UK and RoI share in terms of the role charities play in society, as well as their management and accounting practices. In general, previous literature has shown the importance national culture may have in influencing the interpretation and legitimation of accounting practices (with reference to the public sector, in particular, see Hyndman *et al.*, 2014). According to previous studies, both the UK and RoI could be classified as part of the Anglo-Saxon system (Hood, 1995; Meyer and Hammerschmid, 2010). It is, however, also important to remember that the study specifically focused on larger charities (with incomes of over £5 million or €6 million – see also **Appendix 1**). Because of auditing and comparability requirements, large charities may tend to adopt, voluntarily, stricter and more rigorous forms of reporting and disclosure, especially when organisations are part of larger networks or international 'brands'. International mimetic pressures and professional standards play, in this case, an important role in increasing the uniformity of accounting practices and reporting, regardless of the actual legal and mandatory power these may have in a specific jurisdiction. The results found in the UK and RoI would perhaps display a very different pattern in countries characterised by more legalistic and bureaucratic traditions (Hyndman *et al.*, 2014).

In each jurisdiction, legitimation via authorisation was the most important strategy used, followed by rationalisation arguments. As discussed earlier, Liu *et al.* (2016) reported the importance of financial resources, international experience and charismatic leadership in the early stages of a process of change in the charity sector. Although previous research did not focus specifically on accounting practices, it is interesting to see that rational arguments (such as the importance of financial resources to implement change) and authorisation ones (especially the pressure coming from international comparisons and benchmarking) were both identified as relevant also in our study. The interviewees, however, used fewer pathos strategies (and sub-strategies), such as arguments highlighting personal commitment and charisma during the process of change.

In the study presented in this chapter, the sources of authority were not necessarily seen as something particularly negative or to be fought against (AUT2 arguments being, indeed, only marginal). In terms of formal regulation, the UK has a longer and more formalised history in the charity sector, with international accounting standards being recognised as valid. The Charity Commission for England and Wales was first established in 1853 and then restructured and renamed as a non-ministerial government department in 2007; similarly, OSCR was founded at the end of 2003 and in Northern Ireland a Charity Commission was created under the Charities Act (Northern Ireland) 2008. RoI only recently established a national statutory regulator for charitable organisations, with the Irish Charities Regulator being active as an independent authority from October 2014 (under the Charities Act 2009). However, the RoI sector, and in particular the charity accountants interviewed in this study, perceived the compulsory adoption of the SORP as almost inevitable (and, largely, something to be welcomed). The accountants, as key actors involved in the changes, were already aware of the FRS 102 SORP (Charity Commission and OSCR, 2014a) and saw it as a 'new source of authority', regardless of its formal enforcement not yet having been ratified.

While the role of authorisation strategies seems to be largely in line with former studies in the public sector (Hyndman and Liguori, 2016a and 2016b), when comparing the results of this research with previous literature in different sectors, some differences emerge. For instance, normalisation arguments were used by the charities' interviewees less than those in the public sector. Given that this study was dealing with accounting changes, which have long-standing established frameworks of reporting developed and supported by professional associations, this may be surprising. Normalisation arguments mainly dealt with the comparison with other sectors' practices and references to the professions and their standards. Unlike the public sector (Hyndman and Liguori, 2016a and 2016b), charities seemed to recognise and defend their own systems of ideas and specificities (and to justify long-standing differences). They did not appear to compare themselves with, or borrow their principles from, the private sector, at least not to the same extent as is the case in the public sector (Hyndman and Lapsley, 2016).

The results also highlighted a greater use of moralisation arguments in charities when compared to the public sector (Hyndman and Liguori, 2016a and 2016b). The wider use of references to the importance of transparency and accountability, also in response to external events and scandals, is somehow comparable with previous literature in the private sector where accounting was seen as a possible means to increase transparency and reassure the public (Covaleski *et al.*, 2003; O'Dwyer *et al.*, 2011). Although charities do not pursue profit, they seem to be sensitive to the importance of moral themes, transparency and stakeholders' involvement. This is possibly because they strongly rely on donations and volunteering and, thus, recognise the importance of the public, and pay particular attention to the way information is perceived and interpreted once disclosed (this echoing the findings highlighted by legitimacy theory studies). It is also worth remembering that moralisation strategies were mainly used with regards to the TAR. For this area of the SORP, the interviewees commented, in particular, on their organisation's mission and social role, rather than merely accounting issues.

Similar to previous public sector research, pathos had limited presence in the charities' interviewees' comments. Although research in both the charity and the private sectors has shown that pathos arguments (such as personal commitment to change, leadership, patriotism or philanthropy, etc.) may have a part to play at the beginning of the change process in order to motivate and push the implementation of new practices (Green 2004 Liu *et al.*, 2016), this does not seem to be the case here to any significant degree. At the time of the interviews, the use of the FRS 102 SORP (Charity Commission and OSCR, 2014a) was a future event; however, the accountants involved did not appear to demonstrate a particular personal attachment to the change. This possibly unexpected result regarding pathos may be due to the specific area of change (accounting), which was perceived as 'technical' and incapable of eliciting a strong emotional response.

Finally, fewer stories (i.e. narrativisation strategies) were used overall in this study when compared to similar public sector studies (Hyndman and Liguori, 2016b and 2016c). This could be explained by the fact that previous literature focused on accounting reforms that had already taken place and for which the key actors had a number of examples to rely on to justify their actions and views. On the contrary, at the time of the interviews (September 2015–March 2016), the FRS 102 SORP (Charity Commission and OSCR, 2014a) was largely in the process of being implemented. Thus, no stories based on actual use were available, and, as a consequence, the limited stories and examples that were given were aimed at foreseeing (or predicting) possible impacts and consequences.

Looking at the specific areas of the FRS 102 SORP (Charity Commission and OSCR, 2014a) (i.e. TAR, financial statements and annual report) and the way the charity accountants talked about them in the UK, normalisation strategies were mainly used with reference to the financial statements (the most technical and standard-driven area). However, in RoI normalisation was mostly used when speaking about the overall annual report. As, at the time of the interviews, the SORP was not mandatory in RoI, the interviewees tended to see the whole document as linked to professional standards and as a code of conduct, rather than only as a possible piece of future regulation. Interestingly, the overall annual report was legitimated on the basis of pathos arguments relatively more in the UK than in the RoI (notwithstanding the fact that this legitimation strategy was not overly used). This may have been particularly influenced by the consultation process that took place across the UK from 2009. Both large and small charities, and their accountants, were directly involved by the Charity Commission and OSCR through roundtables and questionnaires in order to provide input in steering the development of what eventually emerged as the FRS 102 SORP (Charity Commission, 2009; Connolly *et al.*, 2013; Charity Commission and OSCR, 2014a). This was the largest consultation process ever undertaken in relation to any iteration of the charities SORP (over a period in excess of 30 years) and is likely to have influenced the perceptions of the UK accountants, who felt they could actually participate in shaping the SORP and its contents. In RoI, however, such extensive consultation processes did not take place, and only a report generated by the UK consultation was disseminated across the sector.

Finally, as indicated earlier, delegitimation strategies were only marginally used in both jurisdictions. In the UK, the TAR and the annual report were mainly delegitimated on the basis of authorisation, while the financial statements, perhaps unsurprisingly, were mostly delegitimated via rational arguments. This latter aspect is the area of the SORP that most mirrors professional accounting standards and, to an extent, private sector accounting requirements. As noted above, the interviewees were particularly critical about this aspect and their arguments (mainly against the impact of FRS 102 (FRC, 2013) on the SORP) relied on rational bases, such as the lack of actual improvement in the decision-making process, the potential information overload and the lack of an adequate organisational culture. In RoI, both the TAR and the financial statements were mainly delegitimated in terms of rationalisation, while, interestingly, the overall annual report was mainly criticised on the basis of authorisation arguments. This could be explained by the perception that some of the RoI accountants had of the FRS 102 SORP (Charity Commission and OSCR, 2014a) as a document 'imposed' upon them by external pressures, rather than as a document supportive of more appropriate accountability and better decision making. It is once again worth remembering, however, that the new SORP was mostly seen and talked about in positive terms and, overall, there was very little delegitimation of its contents (this representing overall only 16.8% of the total arguments in the UK and 18.7% in RoI; **Table 5.2**). As highlighted before, the most contentious change was the influence of some specific technical aspects of FRS 102 on the SORP (these often seen as inappropriate to the charity context).

5.5   Implications: Legitimation and the FRS 102 Statement of Recommended Practice

This chapter presents the results of an empirical investigation of large charities in the UK and RoI as regards the implementation of the FRS 102 SORP (Charity Commission and OSCR, 2014a). The chapter explores the way accountants in charities understand, interpret and legitimate (or delegitimate) the new changes required. As discussed, both in the UK and RoI, accountants largely saw the FRS 102 SORP (Charity Commission and OSCR, 2014a) in positive terms, using very little delegitimating language to talk about it. While the criticisms were mainly related to the impact of FRS 102 (FRC, 2013) on the SORP, with aspects of FRS 102 seen as solely relevant to private-sector settings and unlikely to improve decision making and reporting in charities, the vast majority of the interviewees viewed the increased information and discursive disclosures required in the TAR in positive terms.

The evidence from this research suggests that enforcement by formal regulation is not always necessary for a new practice to be legitimated. Indeed, in RoI, where the SORP is presently only best practice, accountants saw and talked about the changes in a fashion similar to their counterparts in the UK, where the FRS 102 SORP (Charity Commission and OSCR, 2014a) is mandatory. Other factors, such as mimetic behaviours and international comparisons, appear to play a major role in the homogenisation and acceptance of charities' reporting standards. Direct participation, consultations and discussions, moreover, played a central role in shaping ideas and increasing the accountants' commitment and pathos towards the FRS 102 SORP (Charity Commission and OSCR, 2014a) in the UK. This is something that was less to the fore in RoI.

The presence of positive legitimation (principally expressed on both authoritative and rational bases), as well as some evidence of personal commitment of those involved in the implementation of the FRS 102 SORP (Charity Commission and OSCR, 2014a), will likely affect the actual embedding of these changes in charity accounting and reporting. The way and the extent its new contents and requirements are understood and legitimated (as useful rather than imposed) will influence the accountants' perceptions of why the changes should be (rather than should not be) implemented and how this should unfold. However, if the positive response shown by the interviewees is promising in terms of acceptance and potential impact of the new SORP, some caveats also need to be raised. Charities seem to perceive their sector as autonomous and do not appear automatically willing to adopt private sector standards and systems if these are not deemed consistent with the charity's needs and mission. This was at the basis of much of the criticism of the FRS 102 SORP provisions (Charity Commission and OSCR, 2014a) relating to financial statements. Consistently, specific charity-designed changes, such as the increased transparency of the TAR and performance (including impact) reporting, were perceived as most welcome.

While the evolution of the SORP over time can be considered as a steady and helpful development both in the UK and RoI in terms of accounting and reporting by charities, the legislators (and regulators) in both jurisdictions should carefully consider the findings in this research before planning future changes.

From a practice and managerial perspective, the FRS 102 SORP (Charity Commission and OSCR, 2014a) seems to have been accepted and positively welcomed. The accountants, as the key actors involved in its implementation, will now have the task of sharing and communicating the new contents across their organisations. This process should aim to strengthen the acceptance of SORP practices also at other organisational levels and widen the participation of different (including non-accountant) employees. These latter individuals, in particular, will be essential to collect and improve some of the information required by the TAR and to develop performance (including impact) disclosure further. In a similar vein, future studies on the topic are needed to explore the actual implementation of the FRS 102 SORP requirements (Charity Commission and OSCR, 2014a) and its effect on charities and on the perceptions of different stakeholders (such as internal management, donors and beneficiaries).

Chapter 6

Performance Reporting: An Investigation

This chapter begins by reviewing the concept of performance, and its various components, in the context of not-for-profit organisations (NFPOs) generally, and charities specifically (**Section 6.1**). In particular, key elements of the performance process, including impact/outcome, efficiency and effectiveness are considered. Reasons as to why it is important to measure performance are then explored, including that it can form the basis for discharging accountability and provide essential information to improve management planning and control systems (**Section 6.2**).

Next, some of the potential difficulties in designing performance management systems in charities are examined in the context of: setting objectives; differing organisational levels (alignment); avoiding a ritualistic approach; measuring quality; providing a basis for comparison; reliability of the information; and measuring what is important (**Section 6.3**). These first three sections, coupled with the material presented in **Chapters 2, 3** and **4**, provide a framework to understand the empirical work presented later in the chapter relating to the current state of charity performance reporting (**Sections 6.4–6.6**).

Utilising a checklist developed to capture the number of charities disclosing performance accountability information in the Trustees' Annual Report (TAR)[1] and annual review (if one is published) (see **Section 6.4**), **Sections 6.5** and **6.6** report the number of charities disclosing financial and operational managerial accountability information respectively, with significant differences identified (at the 1% and 5% levels) between UK and RoI charities in the reporting of such information in the TAR. Examples of the disclosure of financial and operational managerial accountability information from the TARs and annual reviews of UK and RoI charities are also provided.

---

[1] In this book, the term 'annual report' is used to refer to the TAR and financial statements. This research, while recognising the importance of traditional financial statements, focuses on information contained in the TAR (i.e. excluding the financial statements). The term 'financial statements' is used in this context to include the statement of financial activities, balance sheet, statement of cash flows and related notes.

6.1   What is Performance?

After considering performance as a production process more generally, this section examines the elements of impact/outcome, efficiency and effectiveness in more detail.

Production Model

With both business enterprises and charities, and NFPOs in general, there is a consensus regarding the importance of measuring and reporting performance, both from an accountability and a managerial decision-making perspective. However, a major difference between a charity and a business enterprise is that of entity purpose, i.e. a business has a profit objective while a charity does not. In the case of charities (and, indeed, any other NFP or public sector organisation), it is common to view performance in terms of a production process, with performance often being judged in terms of efficiency and effectiveness. Details of the elements of a range of production-process models relating to the operation of an NFPO are presented in **Table 6.1**.

Table 6.1   **Elements of the Production Process in a Not-for-profit Organisation**

Brace et al. (1980)	American Accounting Association (1989)	Carter et al. (1992)	Connolly and Hyndman (2003)	The W. K. Kellogg Foundation (2004)	Connolly and Dhanani (2009)	Breckell et al. (2011)
Input	Cost and Input	Input	Input	Resources/Input	Input	
Process		Process	Process	Activities		
Output	Output	Output	Output	Output	Output	Output
Result	Outcome	Outcome	Outcome/ Result	Outcome/Impact	Result/Impact	Outcome/ Impact

While there are no standardised definitions for the terms input, activities (processes), output and impact/outcome, the following explanation may aid understanding. Input is the resources used in providing a service (for example, expenditure incurred and number of staff). Processes represent the activities carried out by an organisation (for example, number of visits made, number of cancer research projects funded). Output is the actual goods or services produced for consumption (for example, number of children fed, number of cancer research projects completed). Impact (or outcome) is concerned with the long-term effect of an organisation's activities on both individual beneficiaries and at a societal level (for example, change in the level of education, overall level of satisfaction with the services provided). While these stages of the 'production process' are represented as being distinct (see **Table 6.1**), in reality there may be some blurring at the edges. Difficulties, for example, may arise in distinguishing between an output and an outcome or impact in certain circumstances. Notwithstanding this, the disclosure of such information is reported later in this chapter (see **Table 6.3** and **Section 6.6**).

In businesses, both the input and the output can usually be measured in financial terms. Furthermore, because the overall objective is profitability, then profitability – the difference between input (expenses) and output (revenues) – is useful (albeit not perfect) for evaluating performance. With charities, there is no corresponding monetary measure of output and no profit objective; therefore the 'profit' (or surplus) figure does not have the same meaning. However, such a number may indicate whether the organisation has lived within its means and, in most cases, it would seem reasonable for charities to seek a small surplus to support existing activities and future plans; albeit reporting large surpluses may raise questions, especially in the minds of potential donors. With less focus on 'profit' or 'surplus', coupled with charities often having multiple, non-financial objectives, it may be difficult to measure output and therefore to evaluate performance.

Impact and Outcome

Debate as to distinctions between impact and outcome has occurred (Breckell *et al.*, 2011). For example, in the logic model/framework (The W. K. Kellogg Foundation, 2004), outcome is defined as long-term effects that are individual, while impact is considered in terms of consequences that are long-term and society-wide. It is perhaps likely that in many cases distinctions between the outcome at the individual level and impact at a societal level may be somewhat arbitrary, particularly given that outcome at an individual level is often part of wider societal change. In other studies, these definitional machinations are somewhat by-passed by using the terms synonymously and interchangeably with one another (Connolly and Hyndman, 2003). In this book, for convenience, the terms are used in this way.

Notwithstanding such reflections, it is clear that the term 'impact' (or 'outcome') has, of late, gained particular prominence and usage. For larger funders (and particularly those commissioning public services) information on impact/outcome and impact-/outcome-based effectiveness is demanded as a basis for the targeting of resources at proven solutions to social problems (Lumley *et al.*, 2011). In addition, the UK government has highlighted the importance of focusing on societal impact/outcome in government decision-making and, in particular, when funding non-government organisations in the delivery of social programmes (HM Treasury, 2011).

Moreover, the UK government has also funded a cross-sector group known as 'Inspiring Impact', which seeks to encourage and support good practice in reporting on impact/outcome (Lumley *et al.*, 2011) and has developed a *Code of Good Impact Practice* (Inspiring Impact, 2013). Interestingly, as was highlighted in **Chapter 3**, the extant SORP (Charity Commission and OSCR, 2014a) refers to, and defines, impact (a term not used in the earlier previous versions of SORP) when discussing the reporting of 'Achievements and performance' (see **Chapter 3**, **Section 3.4**) as part of the TAR.

Efficiency and Effectiveness

Given this production process, it can be argued that the two key criteria for judging performance are efficiency (the ratio of output to input – for example, expenses, or the amount of output per unit of input) and effectiveness (the relationship between an organisation's output, or impact/outcome, and its objectives). An example of an efficiency measure for a charity might be the cost (an input) per child fed (an output), or the number of cases handled (an output) per employee (an input). A measure of effectiveness could be the number of children fed versus the planned number, or the decrease in blindness in a particular area versus the planned decrease as a result of a particular intervention. Often these criteria are used in a comparative, rather than an absolute sense. For example, it is not normally said that an organisation is 90% efficient, but rather that it is more (or less) efficient than a comparable organisation, or that it is more (or less) efficient than it was last year, or that it is more (or less) efficient than budgeted for.

A representation of a performance model that brings together the elements of the production process and relates them to the two key performance criteria (efficiency and effectiveness) is shown in **Figure 6.1**. This model will be used in relation to the empirical analysis presented later in the chapter.

Figure 6.1 **The Production Model**

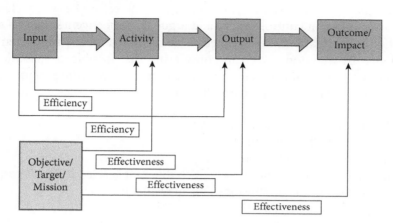

6.2 Why is it Important to Measure Performance?

Two main reasons for measuring performance in a charity are, first, that it can form the basis for discharging accountability by the charity (and build connections with key stakeholders, which can support the establishment of external legitimacy) and, secondly, it can provide essential information to improve management planning and control systems within the organisation. These issues are often linked. Indeed, it has been argued in the public sector that the external pressure provided by the need to disclose performance information frequently encourages a focus on performance by management, and provides a catalyst for performance improvement (Eden and Hyndman, 1999). Similar claims are relevant to the charity sector.

As was discussed in detail in **Chapter 2**, accountability involves explaining what has been, or is being, done and what has been planned. In discharging such accountability, two main types of information are important: financial information (often contained in traditional financial statements); and wider performance information (often of a non-financial nature and relating to the efficiency and effectiveness of the charity). Indeed, it is argued that the external reporting of performance information by charities can provide a visibility to the activities and achievements of the organisation, enabling informed discussion (and decision making) on the part of stakeholders.

In terms of planning and control (and decision making), the importance and potential roles in establishing performance targets in operating a system of planning and control in a NFPO are emphasised by Anthony and Young (2002). They describe a statement of targets (or objectives) as a key element in the management control system and argue that effectiveness can be measured only if actual output is related to targets. This idea is supported and developed by Mayston (1985) in considering the possible contribution of NFP performance indicators in the public sector. Among the potential roles highlighted by Mayston for such indicators are to:

- clarify the organisation's objectives;
- evaluate the final outcome;
- indicate performance standards;
- indicate the effectiveness with which different service activities contribute to each of the dimensions of achievement;
- trigger further investigation and possible remedial action; and
- indicate areas of potential cost savings.

These roles would support the planning and control system outlined in **Figure 6.2**. While it is accepted that extensive judgement in making decisions in charities is inevitable (especially where objectives are not clear-cut and there is considerable uncertainty about cause-and-effect relationships), the provision of quantified performance targets and performance measures can highlight:

- the actual achievements versus targets;
- when diagnostic interventions are necessary; and
- how the performance of the organisation has changed over time.

Discussions on the basis of such information are frequently an indicator of good management.

The potential benefits of developing links between the use of performance information in the planning and control system of a charity and the discharge of performance accountability by a charity are unmistakable. While a focus on performance measures and performance targets in planning and control systems of charities would stress the importance of objectives and targets in supporting management as they make decisions, such objectives and targets could also provide a platform for the discharge of performance accountability by charities. Hyndman and Anderson (1997, p. 46), in reviewing the use of performance information in external reporting and internal planning in the public sector, argue that "a well-developed set of objectives and targets can provide a valuable basis for the discharge of accountability."

Similar comments can be made with respect to charities, suggesting that a clearly articulated and performance-focused planning and control framework would support the discharge of accountability. These themes emerge consistently in discussions on management and reporting systems in charities (Charities Aid Foundation, 2001; Charity Commission, 2004a, 2004b).

Figure 6.2   **Conventional planning and control system**

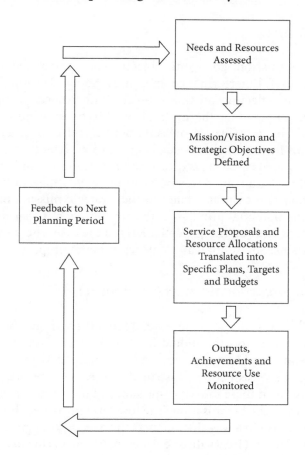

6.3   Difficulties in Designing Performance Management Systems in Charities

Although the need to develop appropriate performance measures in charities is well founded (Connolly and Dhanani, 2009; Nevill and Lumley, 2011; Charity Commission and OSCR, 2014a; McConville, 2017), there are considerable difficulties in designing an information system which provides such information. These are examined below under the following headings: setting objectives; differing organisational levels (alignment); avoiding a ritualistic approach; measuring quality; basis of comparison; reliability of the information; and measuring the important. A consideration of these difficulties may help to focus attention on the key issues to be addressed by the system designer, and provide the basis for a better understanding of the empirical work in this research report.

Setting Objectives

In many cases mission, goals and objectives are so vaguely drafted that they inhibit useful performance measures being developed. Williams (1985, p. 3), in reflecting on this problem with respect to public-sector organisations, argues that the drafting of objectives is the most difficult part of the whole performance-measurement exercise: "I never cease to be amazed at how little thought is usually given to it." However, without clear objectives an organisation lacks direction. It is tempting (and in some cases unavoidable) to define objectives in terms of activity measures rather than outcome (impact) measures related to the strategic mission of the organisation. Yet the potential problem with this approach is that more activity is not necessarily a good thing, particularly in the case where more activity, and more expense, does not lead to more, or better, impact/outcome.

Differing Organisational Levels (Alignment)

If at all possible, it would seem appropriate that there should be measures of performance at each organisational level in a charity. At the lower levels these may tend to be more specific and technical. It is important for the alignment of the measurement system that there is a proper relationship established between these low-level measures of performance and the high-level objectives of the organisation. The low-level measures should motivate managers to behave in a way that furthers the overall strategic mission of the organisation. Carter (1989) distinguishes between performance measures being used as either 'dials' or 'tin-openers'. Implicit in the use of performance measures as dials is the assumption that standards of performance are unambiguous. With tin-openers, there is the assumption that performance is a contestable notion (or difficult to measure in any objective or agreed way). At the lower levels in the organisation it is more likely that the measures used will be more akin to dials, while the higher-level measures will tend to resemble tin-openers.

Establishing tight alignment between the high-level and low-level measures is often a very challenging (if not impossible) task in many charities because of multiple (and frequently competing) organisational goals, multiple stakeholder influences and unclear input-output relationships. If this is the case, loose alignment is perhaps a more achievable ambition. Throughout the process, it must be realised that the most important performance measures are those that are related to the high-level objectives of the organisation. Low-level measures should be developed by reference to already developed high-level measures. The development of high-level measures requires much thought and experimentation (and debate/discussion), because it is often at this level in the organisation that there is the greatest vagueness about objectives. Indeed, at this level, what is measured is strongly influenced by strategic priorities that may change, particularly as the external environment with which the charity interacts changes.

Avoiding a Ritualistic Approach

While setting objectives is critical to the development of a performance measurement system, there is a danger that defining goals and objectives, and setting targets and reporting performance against them, will degenerate into a formal ceremony that has little impact on the behaviour of managers and does nothing to improve the efficiency, effectiveness and accountability of charities. Thompson (1995) warned that unless care is taken in developing useful systems (that are frequently refreshed), there is a possibility of the whole performance-measurement exercise lapsing into a senseless ritual, which, sooner or later, would be abandoned as cost-ineffective. As Sharifi and Bovaird (1995) argue in referring to public-sector organisations, there is a temptation, especially when forced by external pressures directed towards inappropriate external legitimation, that the whole process can degenerate into the production of 'symbols' in a ritualistic manner that has little to do with better management decision-making or enhanced accountability. Similar concerns could be expressed with respect to charities.

Measuring Quality

In charities, as is often the case in other NFPOs, there is a danger that quantity (possibly being easier to measure), rather than quality (possibly being more difficult to measure), will be overemphasised in performance-measurement systems. However, measures of performance which do not address the question of quality may be misleading (especially where the quality of service provision is critical and variations in it frequently occur – a situation that often arises in charity-service provision). Quality can, in certain circumstances, be measured in terms of freedom from error.

How many are correct? How many have passed? In other circumstances (and usually the case with higher-level measures) user surveys, professional judgement or peer-group review may be needed to assess quality. These approaches introduce the dimension of subjectivity. Overall, a focus on quality needs to be deliberately built in to the performance-measurement system, and carefully managed.

Basis of Comparison

Measures of performance are normally relative rather than absolute, therefore some basis of comparison is needed. The most usual evaluations require: comparisons with previous years, comparisons with similar organisations, and comparisons of actual with target. To make these comparisons meaningful there is a need, wherever possible, to match like with like. When this is not possible, it is important to interpret the measures in the light of any differences that exist. One area of particular difficulty is with the allocation of joint costs (needed to derive measures of efficiency). The unscrambling of these costs, often on a fairly arbitrary basis, may make it difficult to compare measures between charities (or between charities and other organisations providing similar services). External influences may also make comparisons difficult. Differences in socio-economic variables regarding populations from various geographic areas may render comparisons of performance meaningless unless interpreted in the light of such differences.

Reliability of the Information

It has been argued in a number of influential publications (Accounting Standards Board, 1999) that accounting information should possess qualities such as relevance, objectivity, understandability, reliability and timeliness. Some of these characteristics pull in opposite directions and trade-offs are often required; for example, the price of improved relevance may be less objectivity, or the most reliable results may not be the timeliest. Because of this, managers must exercise judgement in the selection of appropriate performance measures. A particularly important issue relating to the use (and reporting) of performance measures is that of the reliability of the information, described by Pendlebury *et al.* (1994) as the most significant technical problem.

The reliability of a performance measure rests on the faithfulness with which it represents what it purports to represent (possibly indicated by the extent to which it is verifiable and neutral (Financial Accounting Standards Board, 1980)). For this reason, Mayston (1985) has argued a case for bringing to bear similar disciplines on the external reporting of performance measures that are imposed on financial accounting information, i.e. disclosure requirements, external auditing and standard-setting after consultation with interested parties. However, there are clear cost–benefit issues that have to be considered (Hedley *et al.*, 2010; Hyndman and McConville, 2017). It is possible that if there is no requirement for verification of the performance numbers reported by a charity, then there may be a temptation to present performance in a manner which is perceived as more acceptable to the reader (for example, by exaggerating performance in a positive manner, regardless of its accuracy).

Measuring the Important

High-level performance measures (related to impact/outcome) are often the most difficult to establish, because, among other things, many costs and benefits arise over the long term, difficulties exist regarding the separation of the impact of environmental factors from programme input and output, and it is particularly difficult to capture the quality dimensions (Hedley *et al.*, 2010; Nevill and Lumley, 2011). These factors encourage a concentration on low-level measures which are significantly removed from the crucial strategic issues, and where the measurement and data-capture difficulties exist to a much lesser extent. This may result in the production of a plethora of low-level performance measures but a scarcity of vital measures that reflect the most important impact/outcome. Notwithstanding the profound difficulties of measuring impact/outcome, a lack of attempt to do this (no matter how contestable the resulting measures may be) can significantly undermine the strategic focus of the charity and weaken the discharge of accountability.

6.4   Research Method

This research employs a mixture of quantitative and qualitative research methods to address the research objectives (see **Chapter 1, Section 1.4**), and this section presents the research methods adopted to analyse the discharge of performance accountability (including impact reporting) by UK and RoI charities. While recognising the importance of traditional financial statements, this research focuses on the disclosure of financial and operational managerial accountability information contained in the TAR and annual review (if one is published). While all forms of data reaching the public domain can be considered to be part of the performance accountability discharge function, these two channels were chosen as suitable units of analysis because they are within direct managerial control

(Guthrie and Parker, 1989), and also because they have a level of formality that goes beyond a marketing/publicity type document.

Moreover, each reflects a specific characteristic. The annual report is a statutory document, often seen as the official accountability document, the content of which is regulated and subject to independent monitoring. The annual review is a voluntary form of communication with external stakeholders which many charities prepare alongside their annual report as a means of both marketing the charity and discharging accountability to external stakeholders. It is frequently written in less formal language and includes a higher proportion of stories, photographs and figures.

Utilising the classification of charities in terms of what they (primarily) do and who they (primarily) help forms part of the Advanced Search features available on the Charity Commission website.[2] The following five broad categories of charitable activities were developed:

1. Medical/health/sickness;
2. Medical research;
3. Overseas aid/famine relief;
4. Animal welfare; and
5. Wider social objects (children/poverty/social welfare).

To identify the performance information made available publicly to charity stakeholders, 25 UK and 25 RoI charities were selected and their most recent annual reports and annual reviews (if one was published) were obtained from their website. In order to obtain a sample of UK charities, the Advanced Search features available on the Charity Commission website were used to select five large charities based upon total income from each of the above five categories. As a similar search facility is not available for RoI charities, this sample was drawn from the Boardmatch (2013) *Charity 100 Index*. However, while 25 RoI charities were selected, as it was only possible to obtain three RoI 'animal welfare' charities due to the number of such organisations represented on the index, additional charities from categories 1. and 2. above were selected (see **Table 6.2**). Of the 50 charities selected, which include those 21 organisations from which representatives were interviewed (see **Chapter 5**), 20 (UK – 16; RoI – 4) prepared a separate annual review (or equivalent) document (see **Table 6.2**).

---

[2] See http://apps.charitycommission.gov.uk/ShowCharity/RegisterOfCharities/AdvancedSearch. aspx.

Table 6.2   **Document Content Analysis Sample**

	Medical/ Health/ Sickness	Medical Research	Overseas Aid/ Famine Relief	Animal Welfare	Wider Social Objects	Annual Report	Annual Review
UK	5	5	5	5	5	25	16
RoI	6	6	5	3	5	25	4
Total	11	11	10	8	10	50	20

Drawing upon the accountability framework discussed in **Chapter 2**, the requirements of the FRS 102 SORP (Charity Commission and OSCR, 2014a) with respect to the TAR (see **Chapter 3, Section 3.4**) and the production model discussed above (see **Figure 6.1**), together with the accountability classification system developed by Taylor and Rosair (2000) and Brody (2001), accountability may be discharged by charities in terms of their fiduciary and managerial accountability (see **Table 6.3**). Fiduciary accountability (which focuses on issues relating to financial accountability and is typically discharged through the medium of audited financial statements) emphasises probity, compliance, control and good governance to assure organisational stakeholders that the funds, assets and future of the organisation are safeguarded (Taylor and Rosair, 2000; Brody, 2001). In this regard, it is analogous to the stewardship function that charity financial accounting fulfils, whereby there is confirmation and, in turn, confidence that the funds and assets of the organisation are not misappropriated.

Managerial accountability (which focuses on performance accountability but includes aspects of financial accountability – see below), on the other hand, refers to managerial effectiveness and the organisation's impact on society (i.e. organisational performance and success). Based on the premise that charities should provide a review of their financial position and the impact that organisations have had on societal development, managerial accountability can be separated into managerial success in financial and operational terms (see **Table 6.3**).

Table 6.3   **Accountability Disclosures:**
                Fiduciary and Managerial Accountability

Themes of Accountability	Associated Disclosure Items
Fiduciary accountability emphasises probity, compliance, control and good governance, to assure organisational stakeholders that the funds, assets and future of the organisation are safeguarded.	• Organisation structure, including managerial structures and how key decisions are made; • Trustee selection, appointment induction and training policies; • Reserves policy; • Financial investment policy; and • Risk management statement.
Financial managerial accountability addresses organisational performance in financial terms, that is, managerial success at generating and using funds. To enhance performance accountability, information disclosures include: • comparison of actual performance with targets; • objectives, previous year results or competitor organisations; • explanations/justifications for activities and performance; and • future intentions and information.	• Financial position/stability (income, expenditure and surplus/deficit levels); • Financial performance of investments and reserves policies; • Fundraising efficiency; and • Overall organisational efficiency.
Operational managerial accountability addresses performance in terms of the impact of the organisation on society. To enhance performance accountability, information similar to that stated above applies.	• Organisational aims and objectives; • Organisational activities; and • Direct charitable activities (input, with separate attention to volunteers, output, impact/outcome, efficiency and effectiveness).

While acknowledging the importance of fiduciary accountability information, as this chapter focuses on performance (including impact) reporting, it examines the disclosure of financial and operational managerial accountability information (see **Sections 6.5** and **6.6**).

To analyse the relevant data from the charity annual reports[3] and annual reviews, this research employed content analysis. This is a technique that enables researchers to codify qualitative information in anecdotal and literary form into previously determined categories in order to derive and understand the presentation and reporting patterns (Abbott and Monsen, 1979). Identifying the text or material to be examined, and determining what categories researchers will collect information about, are therefore critical attributes of content analysis. Moreover, how to collect the information (i.e. how best to code and/or count the various types of disclosure) is important.

Based upon the accountability themes and disclosures presented in **Table 6.3**, a checklist was developed (see **Appendix 4**) to, *inter alia*, capture performance accountability disclosures. In terms of 'how' the data was collected, the checklist was tested on a small sample of organisations on a number of occasions and revised accordingly to enable the collection of a complete, objective and reliable source of data that: (i) captured all the disclosures provided in the TAR and annual review that could be classified as performance accountability disclosures; and (ii) produced an objective and reliable final coding instrument. Definitions and rules were developed for classifying the highlighted copy information in order to reduce the impact of subjectivity. The rules included: information presented in more than one way was only counted once (in its most detailed form); when there was an efficiency target and the actual achievement of efficiency was given, this was counted as a measure of efficiency only; and when there was a quality target and the actual achievement of quality was given, this was counted as a measure of effectiveness. This approach ensured that, as far as possible, terms were being used in the same manner for each charity.

The next two sections (**Sections 6.5** and **6.6**) report the disclosure of financial and operational managerial accountability information respectively, with examples of the disclosure of such information from the TARs and annual reviews of UK and RoI charities also being provided.[4] The number of charities providing financial managerial accountability information is presented in **Table 6.4**, with operational managerial accountability information being shown in **Table 6.5**. As discussed in **Chapter 3 (Section 3.2)**, while compliance with the charities SORP has been effectively mandatory for large UK charities for a number of years, in contrast it has been only (and remains at the time of writing – June 2017) best practice for RoI charities. Given this variance, chi-square tests

---

[3]   As indicated previously, this research, while recognising the importance of traditional financial statements, focuses on information contained in the TAR.

[4]   As the FRS 102 SORP (Charity Commission and OSCR, 2014a) is effective for accounting periods beginning on or after 1 January 2015, due to the timing of this research the illustrative disclosures pre-date the publication of the FRS 102 SORP.

were carried out to identify if there were differences in the number of UK and RoI charities reporting financial and operational managerial accountability information, with significant differences (at the 1% and 5% levels) between UK and RoI charities in the reporting of such information in the TAR indicated in **Tables 6.4** and **6.5** and discussed in the relevant sections.

6.5   Financial Managerial Accountability

Table 6.3 indicates that financial managerial accountability considers managerial performance in relation to generating funds and using them appropriately to secure the future of the organisation and to optimise its impact. The Charity Commission and OSCR (2014a) explain that the aim of disclosing such information should be to enable readers to understand how the numerical parts of a charity's accounts relate to its organisational structure and activities. In the TAR, charities should therefore provide a review of their income, expenditure and surplus/deficit (see **Table 6.4**, items (a)–(f)), together with an analysis of the efficiency with which charitable funds have been utilised (see **Table 6.4**, items (g)–(i)). Moreover, for those organisations engaged in fundraising, financial performance is measurable in terms of fundraising efficiency and return on investment/turnover (i.e. the efficiency with which public funds have been raised) (see **Table 6.4**, items (j)–(l)).

Thus, as illustrated in **Table 6.4** (and the checklist provided in **Appendix 4**), the disclosure of 12 items of financial managerial accountability information was collected and collated under the following three sub-headings: financial (items (a)–(f)); organisational efficiency (items (g)–(i)); and fundraising efficiency (items (j)–(l)). Details of the number of UK and RoI charities disclosing this information in the TARs and annual reviews are provided in **Table 6.4** and discussed below, with significant differences (at the 1% and 5% levels) between the number of UK and RoI charities reporting each information item in the TAR indicated. Examples of the disclosure of financial managerial accountability information are also provided (see **Exhibits 6.1–6.16**).[5]

---

[5]   As the FRS 102 SORP (Charity Commission and OSCR, 2014a) is effective for accounting periods beginning on or after 1 January 2015, due to the timing of this research the illustrative disclosures pre-date the publication of the FRS 102 SORP.

Table 6.4 **Financial Managerial Accountability**

	United Kingdom		Republic of Ireland		Total	
	Trustees' Annual Report (n = 25)	Annual Review (n = 16)	Trustees' Annual Report (n = 25)	Annual Review (n = 4)	Trustees' Annual Report (n = 50)	Annual Review (n = 20)[6]
Financial:						
(a) General discussion	20 (80%)	7 (44%)	16 (64%)	1 (25%)	36 (72%)	8 (40%)
(b) Income by source	22 (88%)	11 (69%)	12 (48%)	2 (50%)	34 (68%)^^	13 (65%)
(c) Expenditure by activity	19 (76%)	11 (69%)	9 (36%)	2 (50%)	28 (56%)^	13 (65%)
(d) Income review	25 (100%)	3 (19%)	16 (64%)	0 (0%)	41 (82%)^^	3 (15%)
(e) Expenditure review	20 (80%)	3 (19%)	14 (56%)	1 (25%)	34 (68%)	4 (20%)
(f) Trading activities	11 (46%)	3 (19%)	1 (4%)	0 (0%)	12 (25%)^	3 (15%)
Average – Financial	*20 (78%)*	*6 (40%)*	*11 (45%)*	*1 (25%)*	*31 (62%)*	*7 (37%)*
Organisational efficiency:						
(g) General discussion	3 (12%)	0 (0%)	1 (4%)	1 (25%)	4 (8%)	1 (5%)
(h) Management and administration costs	11 (44%)	7 (44%)	6 (24%)	1 (25%)	17 (34%)	8 (40%)
(i) Spend on charitable activities	17 (68%)	8 (50%)	8 (32%)	2 (50%)	25 (50%)	10 (50%)
Average – Organisational efficiency	*10 (41%)*	*5 (31%)*	*5 (20%)*	*1 (33%)*	*15 (31%)*	*6 (32%)*
Fundraising efficiency:						
(j) General discussion	4 (16%)	1 (6%)	1 (4%)	1 (25%)	5 (10%)	2 (10%)
(k) Spend on fundraising	16 (64%)	9 (56%)	7 (28%)	1 (25%)	23 (46%)	10 (50%)
(l) Voluntary income	20 (80%)	10 (63%)	8 (32%)	1 (25%)	28 (56%)^^	11 (55%)
Average – Fundraising efficiency	*13 (53%)*	*7 (42%)*	*5 (21%)*	*1 (25%)*	*19 (37%)*	*8 (38%)*
Average – Overall	*16 (63%)*	*6 (38%)*	*8 (33%)*	*1 (27%)*	*24 (48%)*	*7 (36%)*

^ Difference in disclosure between UK and RoI charities in the TAR significant at the 1% level.
^^ Difference in disclosure between UK and RoI charities in the TAR significant at the 5% level.

Before examining the disclosure of the financial managerial accountability items individually, it is important to note that, overall, the number (percentage) of UK charities disclosing this information in the TAR was greater than RoI charities for each of the 12 items (see **Table 6.4**). A similar trend emerges with respect to the annual reviews, with the percentage of UK charities disclosing this information being greater for eight items

---

[6] Given the small number of RoI charities producing an annual review, chi-square tests were not carried out to identify if there were significant differences in the number of UK and RoI charities reporting financial managerial accountability information in their annual reviews.

((a), (b), (c), (d), (f), (h), (k) and (l)), and the same for one item ((i) – 50%). However, it should be noted that with respect to the annual reviews, a meaningful comparison is difficult as only four RoI charities (compared with 16 UK charities) published an annual review. These findings are consistent with previous research (for example, Connolly and Hyndman, 2001, 2004 (see **Chapter 4**)) and may be due to the charities SORP effectively being mandatory for large UK charities for a number of years, while in contrast it has been only (and remains at the time of writing – June 2017) best practice for RoI charities.

Financial

As discussed above, six items (see **Table 6.4**, items (a)–(f)) capture the disclosure of information relating to the 'Financial' aspect of Financial Managerial Accountability. Each of these is now discussed in turn.

(a) General discussion   Of the 50 TARs examined, 36 (72%) (UK – 20 (80%); RoI – 16 (64%)) provided a general discussion of the organisation's financial position and performance. While not shown in **Table 6.4**, 18 (36%) (UK – 9 (36%); RoI – 9 (36%)) included a comparison with the previous year(s) and three (UK – 2 (8%); RoI – 1 (4%)) outlined the challenges faced by the organisation. An example of such a disclosure is provided in **Exhibit 6.1**.

Exhibit 6.1   **Financial Position and Performance Discussion (1)**

Financial review.

Financial performance continued to improve in 2014/15, with an increase in net funds of £5.8m, which feeds through to the balance sheet. However, the key achievement of a small operational surplus of £0.7m was against the backcloth of reducing income.

Economic conditions continue to be difficult and we have responded to that environment, continuing to improve our financial strength. There were good savings in the cost of delivering and supporting our services to enable us to continue and develop our work for vulnerable children and young people. We have targeted reserves to invest in fundraising, develop our brand and ensure our infrastructure is resilient in supporting and safely engaging with young people and staff.

We highlighted last year the continuing pressure on local authorities' funds and a possible reduction in our income. That has been the case in 2014/15. Funding was down £9.0m to £147.1m, particularly for our Children's Centres and Family Support services, Youth and Leaving Care services. However, income was up for our Schools and Fostering services. By looking at effective ways of working, and controlling overheads, we were able to provide all our services to children and young people with lower support costs, helping achieve our operational surplus.

The amazing work of our supporters and volunteers helps provide the donations, gifts and legacies to support our work. In 2014/15 income from donations and gifts was down slightly on the previous year. Legacies tend to fluctuate, and were also down. To create the environment where voluntary income can grow it was agreed to make investment in fundraising and brand awareness. That strategic investment started in December 2014, and already, by the end of March 2015 the initial target of 6,000 new regular donors had been achieved. However, the income takes time to come through, and as the investment shows in the cost of fundraising, the results for 2014/15 are not directly comparable to the previous year.

Source: Action for Children (UK), *Annual Report 2014/15*. Available at www.actionforchildren.org.uk/media/4394/annual-report-2015.pdf

Of the 20 annual reviews available, eight (40%) (UK – 7 (44%); RoI – 1 (25%)) included a general discussion of the organisation's financial position and performance. An example of such a disclosure is provided in **Exhibit 6.2**. One (UK) charity presented information graphically (not shown in **Table 6.4**).

Exhibit 6.2   **Financial Position and Performance Discussion (2)**

Where does our money come from?

Funding to support the programmes we deliver comes from a wide variety of sources: voluntary donations, trading income, investment income, governments, institutional donors and other public authorities.

Total income available for our development, humanitarian and campaign programmes grew by £15.7 million over the last financial year.

This was made possible through particularly strong performance in our efforts to secure institutional donor income; a rise in income secured from major givers; and our continued efforts to ensure we recruit and retain a broad base of people who give regularly to Oxfam through direct debits.

What do we spend our money on?

In 2014/15 we spent £298.4 million on charitable activities undertaken in three interconnected ways: development, humanitarian and campaign programmes. Most of our programme spending in 2014/15 was allocated to our development work (54%). We spent 11% more on charitable activities in 2014/15 than we did in 2013/14. This was due in large part to the unprecedented number of humanitarian emergencies that we responded to across West Africa, South Sudan and the Middle East; as well as significant increases in our development and rehabilitation programmes in Pakistan and the Philippines.

Being accountable for the impact of our work

Oxfam is committed to ensuring that in all that we do we are accountable to those with whom we work. We:

- Report data on the numbers of people and communities reached by our programmes
- Complete review exercises to understand – and speak about – our outcome achievements as well as our challenges, and how we deal with them
- Undertake evaluations to assess our overall strategies, test the core assumptions about how Oxfam contributes to social change and assess our effectiveness in different contexts, and
- Consult with key stakeholders to gather their insights and assessments about our overall efforts.

Source: Oxfam (UK), *Annual Report & Accounts 2014/2015*. Available at www.oxfam.org.uk/what-we-do/about-us/plans-reports-and-policies/plans-reports-and-policies-archive

(b) Income by Source   Thirty-four (68%) charities (UK – 22 (88%); RoI – 12 (48%)) provided details of the source of their income in their TAR, with 24 (48%) (UK – 14 (56%); RoI – 10 (40%)) providing this information graphically (not shown in **Table 6.4**). An example is provided in **Exhibit 6.3**

(with **Exhibit 6.12** illustrating a combined analysis of income and expenditure by source). Sixteen (32%) charities (UK – 3 (12%); RoI – 13 (52%)) did not discuss their income by source (not shown in **Table 6.4**). The difference in disclosure levels between UK and RoI charities is significant at the 5% level.

Exhibit 6.3　**Income by Source (1)**

Income

ActionAid Ireland receives its income from the following sources – Child & Community Sponsorship, Irish Aid, Revenue tax reclaim, Appeals and Bank Interest.

In 2014 the total Income for Action Aid Ireland was €3,300,155 compared with €2,909,910 for 2013, an increase of 13.4%. Excluding the one off Donation of €500,000 for the work in the Philippines, the income in fact decreased by 3.8%. That reduction is accounted for by a reduction in Child Sponsorship income and the Irish Aid grant partially offset by increases in the remaining income streams. Recent changes to the operation of the tax relief scheme on donations to charities that took effect from January 2014 on all qualifying donations significantly simplified the administration of the scheme and was the primary reason for the increased income in that scheme in 2014 (12.9%).

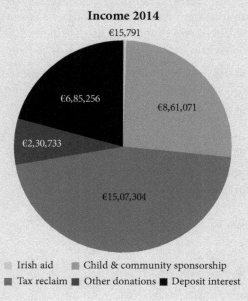

Income 2014

- Irish aid
- Child & community sponsorship
- Tax reclaim
- Other donations
- Deposit interest

Irish Aid

A grant of €861,071 was received from Irish aid in 2014, which was a decrease of 1.9% from the previous year in line with similar reductions to all Programme grant Partner Organisations funded by Irish Aid. This represents the Year 3 funding of a 5 year programme with Irish Aid in 4 countries – Kenya, Malawi, Nepal and Vietnam.

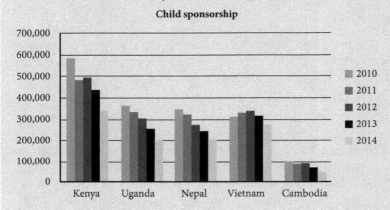

Child sponsorship

Child & Community Sponsorship decreased from €1,668,413 in 2013 to €1,507,304 in 2014. This was a decrease of 9.7% on 2013 which was disappointing. Recruitment of new supporters is still a challenge despite the apparent improvement in the Irish economy, however a significant fundraising investment will be made in the first half of 2015 in respect of new Child Sponsors and a new Village Sponsorship programme.

Source: ActionAid (RoI), *Directors Report and Accounts 2015*. Available at www. actionaid.ie/wp-content/uploads/2016/10/Annual-Audited-Accounts-2015.pdf

Of the 20 annual reviews available, 13 (65%) (UK – 11 (69%); RoI – 2 (50%)) provided details of the charity's income by source, with this information typically being presented graphically. An example of such a disclosure is provided in **Exhibit 6.4**.

Exhibit 6.4   **Income by Source (2)**

YOUR MONEY IS SAVING LIVES

Research is cancer's ultimate enemy. With your support, our scientists are making more breakthroughs to improve the way we prevent, diagnose and treat the disease.

We fund more than 4,000 world-class scientists, doctors and nurses across the UK. Their work deepens our understanding of cancer and finds new ways to tackle it.

We receive no funding from the Government for our research. Our life-saving work relies entirely on your support. Every single pound raised really does count.

More than nine out of 10 donations we receive are for less than £10, proving that small amounts make a big difference. Whatever the size of your donation, we will put your money to the best possible use in our fight to beat cancer sooner.

80p
For every £1 donated, over 80p is used to beat cancer. The rest is used to raise funds for the future.

OUR INCOME
£621m

Income from charitable activities
£89 million: This includes money from our company Cancer Research Technology, which develops new treatments, and ploughs the profits back into our research.

Income from our fundraising activities
£169 million: More than a third of our research is funded by legacies.

£122 million: Over one million donors give us regular donations which help us plan vital research into the future.

£91 million: This includes £75 million from our shops and £16 million from the trading aspect of our events, including merchandise sales and registration fees.

£63 million: Events like Race for Life are a key part of our fundraising.

£41 million: Our corporate partnerships raised millions for our work. And over 900 local fundraising groups raised £14 million in their communities.

£36 million: This includes major giving and appeals which raise money for key projects, including the construction of the Crick.

Other income
£10 million: This mainly consists of income from our investments.

Source: Cancer Research UK, *Annual Review 2014/15*. Available at http://www.cancerresearchuk.org/sites/default/files/cruk_annual_review_2014_15.pdf

(c) Expenditure by Activity   Twenty-eight (56%) charities (UK – 19 (76%); RoI – 9 (36%)) disclosed their expenditure on the basis of the organisation's different activities in their TAR, with 22 (UK – 13 (52%); RoI – 9 (36%)) depicting this information graphically (not shown in **Table 6.4**) (see **Exhibit 6.5**) The difference in disclosure levels between UK and RoI charities is significant at the 1% level.

Exhibit 6.5   **Expenditure by Activity (1)**

Expenditure

In 2014 €2.5m was spent in respect of our overseas programmes. The cost of generating voluntary income was €444,599 in 2014. This figure represents 18% of Voluntary income in 2014. It is a priority for ActionAid Ireland to control costs and to ensure that best value is obtained from any expenditure to promote and support the work of ActionAid Ireland.

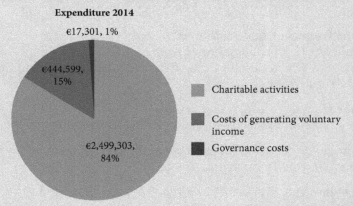

Expenditure on Charitable Activities includes €223,535 spent before the year end on the re-housing building programme in the hurricane devastated area of the Philippines. This was funded by the extremely generous donation of €500,000 referred to earlier, and the balance will be used to complete the project in early 2015.

Source: ActionAid (RoI), *Directors Report and Accounts 2015*. Available at http://www.actionaid.ie/wp-content/uploads/2016/10/Annual-Audited-Accounts-2015.pdf

Of the 20 annual reviews available, 13 (65%) (UK – 11 (69%); RoI – 2 (50%)) analysed the charity's expenditure by activity, with this narrative information in all but one instance being supplemented graphically. An example of this is provided in **Exhibit 6.6**.

Exhibit 6.6   **Expenditure by Activity (2)**

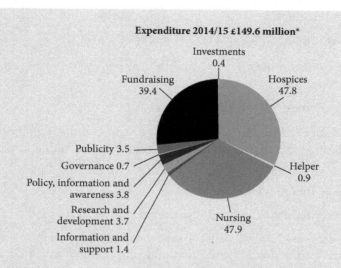

Expenditure 2014/15 £149.6 million*

- Investments 0.4
- Fundraising 39.4
- Hospices 47.8
- Publicity 3.5
- Governance 0.7
- Policy, information and awareness 3.8
- Research and development 3.7
- Information and support 1.4
- Helper 0.9
- Nursing 47.9

*Excludes retail activities.

Source: Marie Curie (UK), *Impact Report 2014/15*. Available at http://www.mariecurie.org.uk/globalassets/media/documents/who-we-are/vision-and-strategic-plan/marie-curie-impact-report-2014-2015.pdf

(d) Income review   Each of the UK charities (100%), and 16 (64%) RoI charities, discussed their income for the year under review in their TAR, with examples of such disclosures being provided in **Exhibits 6.3** and **6.7**; 29 charities (UK – 20 (80%); RoI – 9 (36%)) included prior year comparisons (not shown in **Table 6.4**). The difference in disclosure levels between UK and RoI charities is significant at the 5% level.

Exhibit 6.7   **Income Review (1)**

Where Our Income Came From

It has been a successful year with total income[1] of £621 million. Our income comes mainly from fundraising activities, royalties, EU grants and investment income.

INCOME FROM ROYALTIES AND GRANTS

This income (£89 million) includes royalty income of £66 million generated by Cancer Research Technology, from treatments based on earlier innovations, as well as EU grants received by our 'in-house' research institutes.

INCOME FROM FUNDRAISING ACTIVITIES

Income from fundraising (£522 million) is split into trading and voluntary activities.

Trading income (£91 million)

This includes £75 million generated by our shops and £16 million from the trading aspect of events (including merchandise sales and registration fees). We have a network of 579 shops across the UK.

Voluntary income (£431 million)

The main voluntary fundraising areas are:

- **Legacies** (£169 million) – Legacies continue to perform strongly, with income from notifications and wills at historically high levels.
- **Direct giving** (£122 million) – This includes regular gifts from over a million people, demonstrating that small donations really do add up. More than nine out of 10 of the donations we receive are less than £10.
- **Events** (£63 million) – Over 550,000 Race for Life participants raised £42 million of sponsorship income. Pretty Muddy, our obstacle course event, launched nationally and outperformed our initial expectations. 53,000 Dryathletes gave up alcohol in January, raising over £5 million, and Stand Up to Cancer returned to UK TV screens raising £9 million of donations. Our portfolio of other sporting events and challenges continues to grow.
- **Partnerships and volunteer fundraising** (£41 million) – Over 900 local fundraising groups brought together thousands of volunteers and supporters to raise £14 million in their communities. Individual supporters also raised funds in their local communities, contributing a further £9 million.
- **Other voluntary activities** (£36 million) – We have a range of major giving appeals including 'Create The Change' which is raising funds for the construction of the Crick. We received a major contribution to the appeal of $25 million from HSBC.

We continue to develop other initiatives to diversify the sources of our income. For example, we launched Cancer Research UK Kids & Teens in 2015, a new campaign dedicated to raising money for research into cancers affecting children and young people.

INCOME FROM OTHER AREAS

This income (£10 million) mainly consists of investment income of £6 million.

[1] Before exceptional item.

TOTAL INCOME (£M)

£621m

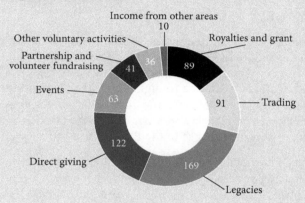

Source: Cancer Research UK, *Annual Report and Accounts 2014/15*. Available at http://www.cancerresearchuk.org/sites/default/files/cruk_annual_report_and_accounts_2014_15.pdf

Three (15%) (UK) charities provided an analysis of their income in their annual review, with two including comparatives (not shown in **Table 6.4**). None of the four RoI charities preparing an annual review provided this analysis. An example is provided in **Exhibit 6.8**.

Exhibit 6.8 **Income Review (2)**

The charity's incoming resources increased by £1.1 million (0.7%) to £155.9 million. Income from the NHS for our hospices was unchanged while income for Marie Curie Nurses increased by £0.4 million. Our fundraising income increased by 1.1% and retail sales by 3.5%.

Source: Marie Curie (UK), *Impact and achievements 2014/15*. Available at http://www.mariecurie.org.uk/globalassets/media/documents/who-we-are/vision-and-strategic-plan/marie-curie-impact-report-2014-2015.pdf

(e) Expenditure review   Thirty-four (68%) charities (UK – 20 (80%); RoI – 14 (56%)) provided an overall assessment in their TAR of their expenditure, with 19 (38%) (UK – 13 (52%); RoI – 6 (24%)) providing comparative figures and two (4%) (UK – 1 (4%); RoI – 1 (4%)) illustrating this information graphically (not shown in **Table 6.4**). Examples of such disclosures are provided in **Exhibits 6.5** and **6.9**.

Exhibit 6.9   **Expenditure Review**

EXPENDITURE

The Statement of Financial Activities (SOFA) shows the analysis of charitable activities split between development, humanitarian, and campaigning and advocacy. Total spending on charitable activities, at £298.4m, is 11% higher than last year, due to higher restricted expenditure, both in our overseas development work and humanitarian responses; notably our Ebola response in Liberia and Sierra Leone, the crisis in South Sudan, and Typhoon Haiyan response in the Philippines.

Unrestricted charitable spend reduced by 7%, due to a combination of factors: securing restricted funding to cover spend; insecurity in certain countries making programme implementation challenging; delayed programme implementation, for which funds have been earmarked for 2015/16.

Further analysis of charitable activity expenditure, showing the operational activities undertaken by Oxfam and those undertaken by partners through grants from Oxfam, is given in Note 3c to the accounts. The table below shows the proportion of charitable expenditure on each charitable activity.

	2011/12	2012/13	2013/14	2014/15
Development	47%	45%	49%	50%
Humanitarian	39%	41%	35%	35%
Campaigning and advocacy	5%	6%	7%	6%
Total	91%	92%	91%	91%
Support costs	9%	8%	9%	9%
	100%	100%	100%	100%
Total charitable expenditure	£286.4m	£290.0m	£268.9m	£298.4m

Source: Oxfam (UK), *Annual Report & Accounts 2014/15*. Available at http://www.oxfam.org.uk/what-we-do/about-us/plans-reports-and-policies/plans-reports-and-policies-archive.

Four annual reviews (20%) (UK – 3 (19%); RoI – 1 (25%)) included a review of the charity's expenditure, with one (6%) (UK) including comparative figures and one (6%) (UK) presenting the information graphically (not shown in **Table 6.4**).

(f) Trading activities   Of the 48 charities that undertook trading activities, only 12 (25%) (UK – 11 (46%); RoI – 1 (4%)) discussed these separately in their TAR. The difference in disclosure levels between UK and RoI charities is significant at the 1% level. An example of a review of trading activities is provided in **Exhibit 6.10**.

Exhibit 6.10   **Trading Activities**

Commercial activities

The financial activities of Barnardo's subsidiary companies are summarised in note 3 to the accounts. In total, the subsidiaries generated net income of £5.6m (2014: £6.3m) with all of the subsidiaries contributing to the surplus. The net income from each subsidiary is gift aided to Barnardo's.

Barnardo Trading Limited generated a profit of £871,000 during the year (2014: £618,000) from its mail order, publishing and retail activities. Barnardo's total retail and trading activities (including the sale of donated goods in Barnardo's shops, which is accounted for as part of the charity's activities) produced a profit of £11.3m (2014: £10.1m).

Barnardo's Development Limited's principal activity is the development and sale of properties that are surplus to Barnardo's operational requirements. The company generated a profit of £3,864,000 during the year (2014: £4,807,000), largely from the sale of properties built and sold on its site in Barkingside, Essex. The sales programme continues with further sales expected in 2015–16.

Source: Barnardo's (UK), *Annual Report and Accounts 2015*. Available at http://www.barnardos.org.uk/annual-report-2015.pdf

Each of the 20 charities publishing an annual review undertook trading activities, with only three in total (15%) (UK – 19%) providing an analysis of their trading activities in their annual review.

Organisational Efficiency

As discussed above, three items (see **Table 6.4**, items (g)–(i)) capture the disclosure of information relating to the 'Organisational efficiency' aspect of financial managerial accountability. Each of these is now discussed in turn.

(g) General discussion   With respect to financial managerial accountability, only four (8%) charities (UK – 3 (12%); RoI – 1 (4%)) provided a general discussion of their organisational efficiency during the period in their TAR. This is illustrated in **Exhibit 6.11**.

Exhibit 6.11   **Organisational Efficiency Discussion**

Financial Review

SUMMARY

Transforming the RNLI into a truly sustainable, complete lifesaving service (encompassing both rescue and prevention work) will have a significant financial impact, and this can clearly be seen in our 2015 results. Total expenditure has increased by £16.2M, in line with our plans, as we improve all aspects of what we do to save lives at sea. Income is around the same level as last year, as expected, with a fall in donations matched by an increase in legacies. We have spent the latter half of the year reviewing and improving our fundraising methods to retain the trust of our supporters, in light of the criticism that the charity sector has received. Capital expenditure has reduced by £13.4M with the completion of the All-weather Lifeboat Centre in early 2015, but still remains high at £51.3M as we continue to improve our lifeboat fleet. Our overall investments have reduced as planned by £16.6M, but we remain in a healthy financial position, with free reserves within the range prescribed by the Trustees at 11 months' worth of charitable expenditure. This is 1 month more than last year, largely due to an increase in the legacy accrual from accounting changes this year to the Charity SORP, and 1 month better than we planned, mainly due to delays in capital expenditure.

Source: RNLI (UK), *RNLI Annual Report and Accounts 2015*. Available at https://rnli.org/about-us/how-the-rnli-is-run/annual-report-and-accounts.

Surprisingly, given the trend with regards to the majority of the other disclosure items, none of the UK charities publishing an annual review presented a general discussion of their organisational efficiency in their annual review, and only one (25%) RoI charity did so.

(h) Management and administration costs Seventeen (34%) charities (UK – 11 (44%); RoI – 6 (24%)) discussed their management and administration costs in their TAR, with 12 (UK – 7 (28%); RoI – 5 (20%), illustrating the information graphically and three (UK – 2 (8%); RoI – 1 (4%)) calculating these costs as a percentage of total expenditure (not shown in **Table 6.4**). **Exhibit 6.12** illustrates an analysis of income and expenditure, with the latter distinguishing between direct, governance and fundraising expenditure.

Exhibit 6.12   **Management and Administration Costs**

Financial Review		
	2014	
	€m	**%**
Mix of income		
Grant income	11.38	58%
Fundraising income	6.37	32%
Rental income	1.34	7%
Other income	0.51	3%
	19.60	100%
Mix of expenditure		
Direct charitable activities costs	17.10	89%
Governance and support costs	0.32	2%
Fundraising and events costs	1.88	9%
Operational expenditure	19.30	100%
Fundraising cost to income ratio		
Fundraising income	6.37	
Fundraising costs	1.88	
	4.49	70%

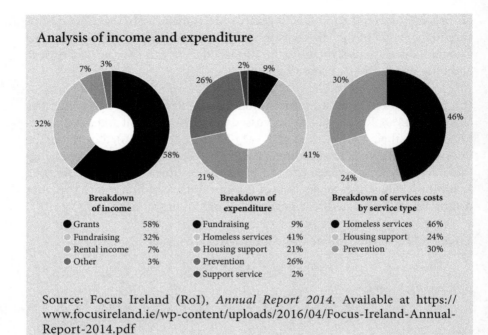

Analysis of income and expenditure

Breakdown of income		Breakdown of expenditure		Breakdown of services costs by service type	
● Grants	58%	● Fundraising	9%	● Homeless services	46%
● Fundraising	32%	● Homeless services	41%	● Housing support	24%
● Rental income	7%	● Housing support	21%	● Prevention	30%
● Other	3%	● Prevention	26%		
		● Support service	2%		

Source: Focus Ireland (RoI), *Annual Report 2014*. Available at https://www.focusireland.ie/wp-content/uploads/2016/04/Focus-Ireland-Annual-Report-2014.pdf

Eight (40%) charities (UK – 7 (44%); RoI – 1 (25%)) provided an analysis of their management and administration costs in their annual review, with four (20%) (UK – 25%) charities presenting information graphically (not shown in **Table 6.4**) (similar to that shown in **Exhibit 6.12**).

(i) Spend on charitable activities   Twenty-five (50%) charities (UK – 17 (68%); RoI – 8 (32%)) discussed their spend on charitable activities in their TAR. An example is presented in **Exhibit 6.13**. While not shown in **Table 6.4**, 14 (28%) (UK – 9 (36%); RoI – 5 (20%)) presented the information graphically, four (8%) (UK – 16%) included comparative figures and three (6%) (UK – 1 (4%); RoI – 2 (8%)) presented these costs as a percentage of total expenditure.

Exhibit 6.13   **Spend on Charitable Activities**

Fundraising

The Fundraising Office was set up in 2000 with the sole purpose of raising funds to make Temple Street a better place. Since it was established it has raised more than €40million for the hospital, with €32million already invested.

This amazing achievement is all thanks to our wonderful army of supporters, fundraisers, ambassadors and network of volunteers. These people work tirelessly to ensure that our little patients get the care and treatment they deserve.

Here is a snapshot of some of the amazing transformations that have been made possible thanks to fundraised money...

Life-Saving Equipment
(€13.4million invested since 2000)

- MRI Scanner - €2million
- CT Scanner - €1.3million
- Tandem Mass Spectrometer - €500k
- Patient Entertainment System (Top Flat) - €160k
- Neurosurgery Equipment (SonoWand invite, Stealth Station, OPMI Pentero) - €2million

Patient and Parental Support
(€2.9million invested since 2000)
Pet Therapy - €5k annually
Sibling Clubs - €4k annually
Bereavement Counselling - €13k annually
Home Away from Home, Fontenoy Street – €1 million

Source: Temple Street Children's University Hospital (RoI), *Annual Report & Accounts 2014*. Available at http://www.cuh.ie/wp-content/uploads/2015/09/Temple-Street-Annual-Report-2014.pdf

Ten (50%) charities (UK – 8 (50%); RoI – 2 (50%)) discussed their spend on charitable activities in their annual review. Although not shown in **Table 6.4**, 8 (40%) (UK – 6 (38%); RoI – 2 (50%)) presented the information graphically and one (5%) (UK – 6%) displayed these costs as a percentage of total costs.

Fundraising Efficiency

As discussed above, three items (see **Table 6.4**, items (j)–(l)) capture the disclosure of information relating to the 'Financial efficiency' aspect of financial managerial accountability. Each of these is now discussed in turn.

(j) General discussion Five (10%) charities (UK – 4 (16%); RoI – 1 (4%)) evaluated their fundraising efficiency in their TAR. An example is presented in **Exhibit 6.14**. One charity (2%) (RoI – 4%) presented a ratio of fundraising return to investment and one (2%) (UK – 4%) included prior year comparatives (not shown in **Table 6.4**).

Exhibit 6.14   **Fundraising Efficiency Discussion**

Fundraising review

Total voluntary income for 2014/15 amounted to £64.6million (2014: £71.7million), a decrease of £7million against 2013/14. This is due to the level of income from legacies in the year. We are pleased to have achieved this against the background of the current economic difficulties that we all face. Gifts in kind included in voluntary income amount to £0.3million (2014: £0.3million) for pro bono work from various firms of lawyers and £0.2million (2014: £0.2million) for advertising. There is also £3.1million (2014: £3million) of lottery and statutory grants within income from charitable activities which is actively supported by our fundraising team.

On 1 April 2009, RNIB and Action entered into an association agreement. Under the terms of that agreement RNIB has taken over the responsibility for the fundraising operation of Action in return for a grant. The grant in 2014/15 amounted to £5.5million (2014: £8.4million). The net proceeds of this fundraising activity have been restricted within these financial statements for the benefit of Action. The fall year-on-year is due to the adoption of a Group free reserves policy to ensure we use our resources as effectively as possible to support blind and partially sighted people.

On 1 July 2014, RNIB and RNIB Charity entered into an association agreement. Under the terms of that agreement RNIB has responsibility for the fundraising operation of RNIB Charity in return for a grant. The grant in 2014/15 amounted to £10.4million. The net proceeds of this fundraising activity have been restricted within these financial statements for the benefit of RNIB Charity.

Fundraising costs for 2014/15 amounted to £20.7million (2014: £15.7million). The fundraising costs are net of an internal recharge in the sum of £4.7million (2014: £5.2million) for costs incurred in raising public awareness about matters relating to sight loss. These costs have been included within the costs of 'Charitable activities'. The increase from last year is due to the reduction in the allocation to raising awareness, work on a new CRM system and investment in medium- to long-term income.

Our investment in fundraising is vital to sustaining our income and our ability to plan and fund direct services, but we remain focused on driving efficiencies and reducing our costs.

RNIB is a member of the Fundraising Standards Board (FRSB) scheme, the body of self-regulation of fundraising in the UK, and as a member we adhere to the highest standards of good practice. RNIB is also a member of the Institute of Fundraising and adheres to contemporary best practice codes of fundraising.

Source: RNIB (UK), *RNIB Group Annual Report and Financial Statements 2014/15*. Available at http://www.rnib.org.uk/sites/default/files/RNIB_AR_2015%20Interactive.pdf

Two (10%) charities (UK – 1 (6%); RoI – 1 (25%)) discussed their fundraising efficiency in their annual review, with each calculating a ratio of fundraising return to investment.

(k) Spend on fundraising Twenty-three (46%) charities (UK – 16 (64%); RoI – 7 (28%)) provided an analysis of their spend on fundraising in their TAR. Twelve (24%) (UK – 8 (32%); RoI – 4 (16%)) illustrated the information graphically, three (6%) (UK – 12%) included a comparison with other organisations and three (6%) (UK – 1 (4%); RoI – 2 (8%)) presented a ratio of these costs to total expenditure (not shown in **Table 6.4**). An analysis and discussion of fundraising income and costs is included in **Exhibit 6.15**.

Exhibit 6.15 **Spend on Fundraising**

TRUSTEES' REPORT – STRATEGIC REPORT

FINANCIAL REVIEW

	2015 £m	2014 £m	Change %
Total income[1]	621	590	5.3
Fundraising income	522	490	6.5
Income from royalties and grants	89	95	(6.3)
Total spend on charitable activities	464	414	12.1
Managed cash and investments	307	282	8.9

[1] Before exceptional items.

OVERVIEW

We are pleased to report an increase in total income to £621 million (2014: £590 million). This includes a record performance by our fundraising team and stable income from our Cancer Research Technology licensing portfolio.

Our charitable expenditure increased by 12% to £464 million (2014: £414 million) with significant uplifts in cancer research of £393 million (2014: £358 million), information and policy outreach of £30 million (2014: £21 million) and further contributions to the Crick construction of £41 million (2014: £35 million).

Fundraising growth, alongside managed cash and investments of £307 million, provide a strong platform from which we can continue to grow our charitable expenditure including our remaining capital contributions to the construction of the Crick.

Fundraising income and costs

	2015 Voluntary £m	2015 Trading £m	2015 Total £m
Income	431	91	522
Costs	104	73	177
Net contribution from fundraising activities	327	18	345

Income from fundraising increased by 7% to £522 million (2014: £490 million). Our main income stream continues to be from legacies, which grew 4% due to increases in the underlying value of individual legacies. Income raised for the Crick appeal ('Create The Change') was £27 million (2014: £8 million), including a $25 million donation from HSBC.

The costs of generating funds has increased to £177 million (2014: £160 million) due to the new legacies strategy, continued investment in brand advertising, the growth of new shops and re-fit of existing shops, as well as increased investment in fundraising innovations such as Stand Up to Cancer.

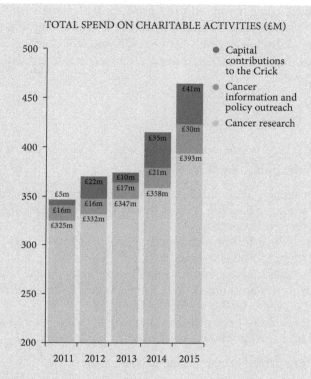

TOTAL SPEND ON CHARITABLE ACTIVITIES (£M)

Income from royalties and grants

Income from royalties and grants decreased by 6% to £89 million (2014: £95 million) of which £66 million was generated by Cancer Research Technology Ltd's licensing portfolio (2014: £68 million).

Source: Cancer Research UK, *Annual Report and Accounts 2014/15*. Available at http://www.cancerresearchuk.org/sites/default/files/cruk_annual_report_and_accounts_2014_15.pdf

Ten (50%) charities (UK – 9 (56%); RoI – 1 (25%)) provided an analysis of their spend on fundraising in their annual review; 8 (40%) (UK – 7 (44%); RoI – 1 (25%)) illustrated the information graphically and one (5%) (UK – 6%) presented a ratio of these costs to total costs (not shown in **Table 6.4**).

(l) Voluntary income Twenty-eight (56%) charities (UK – 20 (80%); RoI – 8 (32%)) discussed their voluntary income in the context of fundraising efficiency. While not shown in **Table 6.4**, 14 (28%) (UK – 9 (36%); RoI – 5 (20%)) illustrated the information graphically, nine (18%) (UK – 8 (32%); RoI – 1

(4%)) included a comparison with the previous year and two (4%) (UK – 1 (4%); RoI – 1 (4%)) presented voluntary income as a percentage of total income. The difference in disclosure levels between UK and RoI charities is significant at the 5% level. **Exhibit 6.16** illustrates a disclosure statement with regards to voluntary income.

Exhibit 6.16   **Voluntary Income**

Thanks to the public for their support

An unprecedented rise in demand for our services resulted in an increased need for funding. We are grateful that the public responded with such generosity in 2014.

- The response to our Christmas appeal was unprecedented, with more than €1,500,000 raised.
- People climbed mountains, held sleep outs, organised school events, ran marathons, baked cakes, recorded CDs and helped us to raise over €400,000 in the community.
- We continue to be grateful to people who have left a lifetime gift of a legacy, from whom we received over €415,000.

For every €1 spent on fundraising, we raise €4 more.

Source: Focus Ireland (RoI), *Annual Report 2014*. Available at https://www.focusireland.ie/wp-content/uploads/2016/04/Focus-Ireland-Annual-Report-2014.pdf

Eleven (55%) charities (UK – 10 (63%); RoI – 1 (25%)) discussed their voluntary income in the context of fundraising efficiency in their annual review; while not shown in **Table 6.4**, nine (45%) (UK – 56%) illustrated the information graphically and one (5%) (RoI – 25%) included a comparison with the previous year.

Having addressed the reporting of financial managerial accountability information, the next section focuses on operational managerial accountability information.

6.6   Operational Managerial Accountability

Table 6.3 indicates that operational managerial accountability addresses performance in terms of the impact of the organisation on society.

The Charity Commission and OSCR (2014a) explain that the aim of disclosing such information should enable readers to understand the aims and objectives set by the charity and the main strategies and activities undertaken to achieve them. Accordingly, charities should explain the charity's objectives and the significant activities undertaken in pursuit of the achievement of those objectives (see **Table 6.5**, items (a)–(c)). In addition, the TAR should provide a review of activities and assess actual performance against objectives to enable readers to understand and assess the achievements of the organisation, together with the effect on beneficiaries (see **Table 6.5**, items (d)–(g)). Furthermore, as discussed in **Section 6.1** (and illustrated in **Figure 6.1**), performance may be viewed in terms of a production model that includes organisational input, output, impact/outcome, efficiency and effectiveness, with future target information being required to subsequently assess effectiveness (see **Table 6.5**, items (h)–(m)). Ní Ógáin *et al.* (2012) suggest that an organisation should also provide details of lessons learned (see **Table 6.5**, item (n)).

Thus, as illustrated in **Table 6.5** (and the checklist provided in **Appendix 4**), the disclosure of 14 operational managerial accountability information items was collected and collated under the following two sub-headings: general (items (a)–(g)); and performance (items (h)–(n)). For the purposes of this research, items (h)–(m) were classified as being: monetary (for example, value of grants awarded); non-monetary (for example, number of cases handled per employee); quality (for example, customer satisfaction levels); and/or were presented graphically. Details of the number of UK and RoI charities disclosing operational managerial accountability information in the TARs and annual reviews are provided in **Table 6.5** and discussed below, with significant differences (at the 1% and 5% levels) between the number of UK and RoI charities reporting each information item in the TAR indicated. Examples of the disclosure of operational managerial accountability information are also provided (see **Exhibits 6.17–6.38**).[7]

---

[7] Given the small number of RoI charities producing an annual review, chi-square tests were not carried out to identify if there were significant differences in the number of UK and RoI charities reporting operational managerial accountability information in their annual reviews.

Table 6.5   **Operational Managerial Accountability Disclosures**

	United Kingdom		Republic of Ireland		Total	
	Trustees' Annual Report (n = 25)	Annual Review (n = 16)	Trustees' Annual Report (n = 25)	Annual Review (n = 4)	Trustees' Annual Report (n = 50)	Annual Review (n = 20)[7]
General:						
(a) Aims and objectives	25 (100%)	16 (100%)	24 (96%)	4 (100%)	49 (98%)	20 (100%)
(b) What activities does the organisation carry out to achieve its aims?	24 (96%)	15 (94%)	25 (100%)	4 (100%)	49 (98%)	19 (95%)
(c) What resources does the charity use to make these activities happen?	23 (92%)	12 (75%)	18 (72%)	4 (100%)	41 (82%)	16 (80%)
(d) Achievements by objective	21 (84%)	14 (88%)	20 (80%)	4 (100%)	41 (82%)	18 (90%)
(e) Who benefits from the charity's work?	21 (84%)	14 (88%)	19 (76%)	4 (100%)	40 (80%)	18 (90%)
(f) How does the charity respond to beneficiary needs?	10 (40%)	4 (25%)	8 (32%)	0 (0%)	18 (36%)	4 (20%)
(g) How do beneficiaries influence the charity's development?	7 (28%)	7 (44%)	12 (48%)	1 (25%)	19 (38%)	8 (40%)
Average – General	*19 (75%)*	*12 (73%)*	*18 (72%)*	*3 (75%)*	*37 (73%)*	*15 (74%)*
Performance:						
(h) Input	6 (24%)	0 (0%)	2 (8%)	1 (25%)	8 (16%)	1 (5%)
(i) Output	20 (80%)	8 (50%)	11 (44%)	3 (75%)	31 (62%)^^	11 (55%)
(j) Impact/outcome	23 (92%)	16 (100%)	20 (80%)	4 (100%)	43 (86%)^^	20 (100%)
(k) Efficiency	6 (24%)	9 (56%)	5 (20%)	1 (25%)	11 (22%)	10 (50%)
(l) Effectiveness	8 (32%)	1 (6%)	0 (0%)	0 (0%)	8 (16%)^	1 (5%)
(m) Future target information	11 (44%)	2 (13%)	6 (24%)	1 (25%)	17 (34%)	3 (15%)
(n) Lessons learned	4 (16%)	3 (19%)	2 (8%)	0 (0%)	6 (12%)	3 (15%)
Average – Performance	*11 (45%)*	*6 (35%)*	*7 (26%)*	*1 (36%)*	*18 (35%)*	*7 (35%)*
Average – Overall	*15 (60%)*	*9 (54%)*	*12 (49%)*	*2 (55%)*	*27 (54%)*	*11 (54%)*

^ Difference in disclosure between UK and RoI charities in the TAR significant at the 1% level.
^^ Difference in disclosure between UK and RoI charities in the TAR significant at the 5% level.

Before examining the disclosure of the operational managerial accountability items individually, it is important to note that, overall, the average percentage of UK and RoI charities disclosing operational managerial accountability information in both TARs and annual reviews was 54%. While arguably relatively low, with just over half of the surveyed charities providing such information, it compares favourably with the average percentages of 48% and 36% for UK and RoI charities disclosing financial managerial accountability information in TARs and annual reviews, respectively (see **Table 6.4**).

With respect to the percentage of UK and RoI charities disclosing operational managerial accountability items in TARs, the level of disclosure was greater for 12 of the 14 items in the UK TARs, with only items (b) and (g) being higher for RoI charities. Moreover, UK charities were more likely to disclose each of the performance information items (h)–(n) in their TAR than RoI charities, with the difference being significant at either the 1% or 5% level in three cases (items (i) output, (j) impact/outcome and (l) effectiveness). These findings are consistent with those for financial managerial accountability information and previous research (for example, Connolly and Hyndman, 2001, 2004 (see **Chapter 4**)), and may be due to the charities SORP effectively being mandatory for large UK charities for a number of years, while in contrast it has been only (and remains at the time of writing – June 2017) best practice for RoI charities. With respect to the annual reviews, a meaningful comparison is difficult as only four RoI charities (compared with 16 UK charities) published an annual review.

General

As discussed above, seven items (see **Table 6.5**, items (a)–(g)) capture the disclosure of information relating to the 'General' aspect of Operational Managerial Accountability. Each of these is now discussed in turn.

(a) Aims and objectives It is important that organisations explain why they exist and the changes they seek. All but one (RoI) of the charities provided details of their aims and objectives in their TAR, with the information typically being presented as a single overarching mission or vision with more detailed objectives (see **Exhibit 6.17**). Each of the charities publishing a separate annual review provided details of their aims and objectives in this document.

Exhibit 6.17   **Aims and Objectives**

About Focus Ireland

Mission

Focus Ireland aims to advance the rights of people out-of-home to live in a place they can call home through quality services, research and advocacy.

Vision

Focus Ireland believes that everyone has the right to a place they can call home.

Objectives

Focus Ireland's objectives are to:

- respond to the needs of people out-of-home and those at risk of becoming homeless, through a range of appropriate high-quality services
- provide emergency, transitional and long-term accommodation for people out-of-home
- campaign and lobby for the rights of people out-of-home and the prevention of homelessness.

Source: Focus Ireland (RoI), *Annual Report 2014.* Available at https://www.focusireland.ie/wp-content/uploads/2016/04/Focus-Ireland-Annual-Report-2014.pdf

(b) What activities does the organisation carry out to achieve its aims?
All but one (UK) of the charities described the activities undertaken to achieve their objectives in their TAR (see **Exhibit 6.18**); one (RoI) charity illustrated this graphically (not shown in **Table 6.5**).

Exhibit 6.18   **Activities Undertaken to Achieve Objectives (1)**

Our Services and Activities

In line with our mission to support and promote independence, dignity and enhanced quality of life for people with disabilities or reduced mobility, Irish Wheelchair Association provides the full range of services that enable people to live in their own home and community. Maximum independence, with freedom of choice and the best possible quality of life, is the goal and the role of IWA is to support each individual in making that possible. Services provided by IWA include:

- **Assisted Living Service:** Person-centred, individually-tailored and practical support whereby skilled personal assistants work directly with people with disabilities in their own homes and communities. In 2015, we delivered 1.17 million hours of Assisted Living on a daily basis to 1,962 adults and children across Ireland.
- **IWA at Home:** Our newest service provides superior quality home support services to clients with disabilities and reduced mobility. This social enterprise utilises IWA's extensive knowledge and expertise to address a growing demand for community-based support, while at the same time generating essential income that the charity can re-invest to help deliver its objectives.

- **Community Supports:** Through our network of 57 Resource and Outreach Centres around Ireland, we provide education and recreation facilities as well as essential personal supports to individuals of all age groups in their community. These services include rehabilitative training, a range of youth activities and 'Youth Cafés'. In 2015, we provided over 90,000 days of service to 1,954 people through our Centres and in doing so benefited not just individual service users but also their families and carers who enjoyed some much-valued respite.
- **Holiday and Respite Services:** We provide accessible and supported holidays and short breaks through our dedicated holiday centres in Roscommon, Kilkenny and Dublin. In 2015, we provided almost 8,000 bed-nights directly through our holiday centres and, in addition, we also facilitated a wide range of independent accessible holidays at destinations chosen by the individual.
- **Transport:** Our nationwide fleet of 120 accessible buses provide essential transport services and are a vital support for all our services as well as for a wide range of voluntary social and sports activities.
- **Motoring:** We promote independence for people with disabilities through motoring advice, assessment and tuition. In 2015, we provided 2,770 lessons and assessments to 351 students through our national network of Driving Centres. IWA is also a Department of Transport approved agency for the issue of Disabled Drivers' Parking Permits.
- **Independent and supported living services:** IWA is a Department of Environment approved housing provider with various models of support to facilitate independent living.
- **Sports:** IWA-Sport is the national governing body for wheelchair sport, supporting high-performance athletes nationally and internationally as well as encouraging wide participation in sports for children and adults across all age groups and activity levels.
- **Access:** IWA is an established expert on environmental access. We act as an advisor to Government and the National Standards Authority of Ireland (NSAI) on building regulations as well as an advisor to national transport providers.
- **Information Services and Advocacy:** IWA provides a wide range of information services to our 20,000 members and to the general public. IWA acts as an effective voice for positive change on key disability issues.

Source: Irish Wheelchair Association (RoI), *Annual Financial Statements for the year ended 31 December 2015*. Available at https://www.iwa.ie/downloads/information/publications/financial-statements/0685-WEB-IWA-2015-Financial-Accounts.pdf

All but one (UK) of the charities described the activities undertaken to achieve their objectives in their annual review (see **Exhibit 6.19**); one (UK) charity illustrated this graphically (not shown in **Table 6.5**).

Exhibit 6.19   **Activities Undertaken to Achieve Objectives (2)**

Child sexual exploitation

Our CSE services worked with 3,200 people last year.

Child sexual exploitation (CSE) is a form of child abuse, with far-reaching effects on a child's physical and mental health, education and training, relationships and family. We have been working to prevent and protect children from CSE for more than 20 years.

Our aim

Our aim is that all children, whatever their background, behaviour or situation, are free from sexual exploitation.

Our work

In 2014–15, several high-profile inquiries highlighted the failure of key agencies to protect children from sexual exploitation. Our own internal research shows that our CSE services experience extremely high demand as professional and public awareness increases.

Our CSE services worked with 3,200 people in 2014–15, an increase from 2,100 in 2013–14 and 1,800 in 2012–13. Of these, 19 per cent were boys, 17 per cent were from black and minority ethnic communities and 20 per cent were looked after children. Our other services worked with an additional 300 people who were at risk of or had experienced CSE.

We opened 11 new services this year and now work from over 40 locations across the UK.

Our CSE workers use a model of assertive outreach to engage with young people who are most at risk. Wherever we work, there is always high demand, and we believe that many more children and young people are not receiving the support that they need.

Our 'Four A's' model of Access, Attention, Assertive outreach and Advocacy underpins how we engage and work with vulnerable children.

We work with children in a structured yet flexible, holistic, trusting and personalised way. We help them to identify and expand the range of choices open to them, and gradually rebuild their lives.

Source: Barnardo's (UK), *Impact Report 2015*. Available at www.barnardos.org. uk/impact-report-2015.pdf

(c) What resources does the charity use to make these activities happen?
Forty-one (82%) of the charities (UK – 23 (92%); RoI – 18 (72%)) surveyed outlined the resources used in undertaking their activities. While this was typically explained narratively (see **Exhibit 6.20**), two charities (4%) (UK – 1 (4%); RoI – 1 (4%)) also illustrated this graphically (not shown in **Table 6.5**). Sixteen (80%) of the charities (UK – 12 (75%); RoI – 4 (100%)) publishing a separate annual review discussed the resources used in undertaking their activities.

Exhibit 6.20   **Resources Used in Undertaking Activities**

Review of the year's activities and future plans

During 2014/15, we spent a total of £21.0m (2013/14: £23.8m) on developing communities. We delivered:

- more than 17.2 million people reached in 46 countries through 328 partners, as we tackled poverty and injustice through long-term country strategies and development projects
- the identification of the following core competencies in which Tearfund has particular expertise: church envisioning and mobilisation, and national advocacy (process expertise); water, sanitation and hygiene, food security, livelihoods and resilience (sectoral expertise)

Source: Tearfund (UK) *Annual Report and Financial Statements 2014/15*. Available at http://www.tearfund.org/~/media/files/main_site/about_us/financial_reports_2015.pdf

(d) Achievements by objective Forty-one (82%) of the charities (UK – 21 (84%); RoI – 20 (80%)) surveyed linked the discussion of their achievements during the period under review to their objectives, with two RoI charities (8%) depicting this graphically and one UK charity (4%) comparing this to targets (not shown in **Table 6.5**). Eighteen (90%) of the charities (UK – 14 (88%); RoI – 4 (100%)) publishing a separate annual review discussed their achievements in the context of their objectives. **Exhibit 6.21** illustrates the disclosure of achievements by objective.

Exhibit 6.21 **Achievements by Objective**

Progress against our 2014/17 strategic objectives.

1. Improving costs and efficiency.

Balancing budgets and driving forward effective change that puts full focus on delivering more evidence-based early action services.

In the past year, working in a climate of welfare reform and political uncertainty in the run up to the general election, improving costs and efficiency has been necessary to mitigate the risk severe government budget cuts place on delivering vital services for vulnerable children and families.

In response to local authorities looking to new ways of working to reconcile severely reduced budgets, we have been streamlining our delivery. We have substantially reduced our costs and improved efficiency by implementing a number of structural changes – integrating teams, reducing overheads, balancing budget.

Doing more with less is the new reality unless we substantially increase income from diversified sources to counter steep decline in statutory funding. With demand for front-line services on the increase and further budget cuts ahead, our challenge over the next five years will be to continue to become more effective and efficient across all our activities.

This year, data from across more than 650 local services reveals that despite cuts, we continue to deliver a real and lasting difference for children and families across the UK:

- We have continued to find new ways of making children safer.
- We have continued to deliver effective help as early as possible.
- We have succeeded in finding new ways of meeting children's needs.

2. Investing to support income generation.

In response to declining statutory funding, we are investing in new ways of funding early action services that nip problems in the bud.

We are currently working at a local and national level to develop early action funding products to generate greater support from the public and the business community.

Social investment is a key response. Evaluation of the first Social Impact Bond (SIB) for the children's sector to fund front-line youth intervention services in Essex, together with a further initiative in Manchester for children in care, is providing the platform to expand social investment delivery.

Fundraising also plays its part. In its second year, our Giant Wiggle event (in partnership with 'The Very Hungry Caterpillar' by world famous author, Eric Carle), continued to raise vital funds and engaged over 54,000 young families. Byte Night, now in its 18th year, is ranked within the top 20 UK mass participation events.

Over the course of our strategy leading up to our 150th anniversary, we will continue to invest in brand and digital to improve income generation and deliver our ambitious goals. To set the platform, our new user-centric, multi-device website was launched in May 2015.

Source: Action for Children (UK), *Annual Report* 2014/15. Available at https://www.actionforchildren.org.uk/media/4394/annual-report-2015.pdf

(e) Who benefits from the charity's work? Forty (80%) charities (UK – 21 (84%); RoI – 19 (76%)) provided details of those who benefited from their work. An illustrative disclosure is presented in **Exhibit 6.22**. Nine charities (18%) (UK – 5 (20%); RoI – 4 (100%)) provided a numerical/monetary analysis and seven (14%) (UK – 2 (8%); RoI – 5 (20%)) presented this information graphically (not shown in **Table 6.5**).

Exhibit 6.22 **Beneficiaries**

Key highlights from 2014

During 2014, a total of 11,378 children and parents benefited from Barnardos services, an increase on 2013 (8,980). This growth can largely be attributed to three areas of Barnardos work; a 21 per cent increase in the uptake of Barnardos prevention and early intervention services for children and families, the Partnership with Parents (PwP) programme and the ongoing roll out of Roots of Empathy in schools.

Table 1:   **Total work with children and parents**

	Children's Services	Roots of Empathy	GAL	Total
Children	3,977	1,960	821	6,758
Parents	3,136	NA	NA	3,136
Other Carers	167	NA	NA	167
Sub-total	**7,280**	**1,960**	**821**	**10,061**
Prevention and Early Intervention service users	1,317	NA	NA	1,317
Total	**8,597**	**1,960**	**821**	**11,378**

Source: Barnardos (RoI), *Annual Report and Financial Statements 2014.* Available at https://www.barnardos.ie/assets/files/Annual%20Reviews/2014_annual_review.pdf

Eighteen (90%) of the charities (UK – 14 (88%); RoI – 4 (100%)) provided details of those who benefited from their work in their annual review; three (15%) (UK – 19%) provided numerical information and two (10%) (UK – 13%) presented this information graphically.

(f) How does the charity respond to beneficiary needs? Eighteen (36%) charities (UK – 10 (40%); RoI – 8 (32%)) provided details of how they had responded to beneficiary needs in their TAR (see **Exhibit 6.23**). This was typically presented as a narrative review of the services provided, together with a description of how staff/volunteers had responded to beneficiary needs during the period.

Exhibit 6.23   **Responding to Beneficiary Needs**

As part of Focus Ireland's commitment to developing and delivering services of the highest standard, the advocacy team undertakes an annual programme of evaluations to assess the quality and outcomes of

Focus Ireland services. During 2014, the following evaluation work
was undertaken:

- An evaluation of the Therapeutic Service was completed by Mark
  Ward, Trinity College Dublin.
- An evaluation of Focus Ireland and the Peter McVerry Trust's
  'Support to Home' service was conducted by TSA Consultancy.
- Evaluations of the Cork and Limerick Prison In-Reach services
  were completed by Dr Kiran Sarma, NUI Galway.
- Work on the Advice and Information Services by Ciara Murray
  and Sandra Velthuis was completed in 2014, and this report will
  be published in 2015.
- An internal review of Focus Ireland's Housing Management Pilot
  Project in Dublin and Waterford was conducted.
- An Annual Report on Services Statistics for 2013 was presented to
  the Board.
- A number of papers based on this work were published in the
  European Journal of Homelessness.

Source: Focus Ireland (RoI), *Annual Report 2014*. Available at https://www.
focusireland.ie/wp-content/uploads/2016/04/Focus-Ireland-Annual-
Report-2014.pdf

Four (20%) (UK – 25%) charities outlined how they had responded to beneficiary needs in their annual review. This was typically presented as a narrative review of the services provided, including a description of how staff/
volunteers had responded to beneficiary needs during the period.

(g) How do beneficiaries influence the charity's development? Nineteen
(38%) charities provided details in their TAR of how beneficiaries influenced the charity's development. This was typically facilitated through surveys and other feedback mechanisms, and is illustrated in **Exhibit 6.24**. In
contrast to the other items (excluding item (b)), the percentage of RoI
charities disclosing this information in their TAR was greater than UK
charities.

Exhibit 6.24   **Beneficiary Voice (1)**

Customer engagement

We ensured that Focus Ireland provided a voice for its customers. One
of our tenants spoke on TV news at the launch of our Annual Report,
and a family who are homeless spoke when President Higgins visited

our housing development in George's Hill in September. A mother also spoke movingly on the RTÉ 1 Sean O'Rourke show about the terrible impact of homelessness. We also arranged many print media interviews with customers. This included the landmark *Irish Times* piece on 'Dublin's Homeless Children', carried out in partnership with the award-winning reporter Kitty Holland (see Homeless Children, *Irish Times* report).

Source: Focus Ireland (RoI), *Annual Report 2014*. Available at https://www.focusireland.ie/wp-content/uploads/2016/04/Focus-Ireland-Annual-Report-2014.pdf

Eight (40%) charities (UK – 7 (44%); RoI – 1 (25%)) provided details in their annual review of beneficiary involvement, with this typically being facilitated through various feedback mechanisms (see **Exhibit 6.25**).

Exhibit 6.25   **Beneficiary Voice (2)**

We believe that 'good enough' isn't good enough and that we should be leading the way in providing outstanding care for those living with a terminal illness and their families.

So every year we carry out a survey of our patients and their carers, and we use the results to develop our care and research.

We regularly consult with our Expert Voices Group, made up of people who have been affected by terminal illness, on our new initiatives and policies.

Every year Marie Curie's services are examined across three key areas: patient experience, patient safety and clinical effectiveness.

So how did we do this year?

92% of our patients rated our hospice and nursing services as very good (the highest rating).

98.5% of our patients said they were likely to recommend the service to friends and family.

See our Quality Account Report 2014/15 at mariecurie.org.uk/quality

Source: Marie Curie (UK), *Impact and achievements 2014/15*. Available at https://www.mariecurie.org.uk/globalassets/media/documents/who-we-are/vision-and-strategic-plan/marie-curie-impact-report-2014-2015.pdf

Performance

As discussed above, seven items (see **Table 6.5**, items (h)–(n)) capture the disclosure of information relating to the 'Performance' aspect of Operational Managerial Accountability. Each of these is now discussed in turn.

(h) Input This represents the resources used in providing the charity's service(s) (for example, sources of income, expenditure incurred, number of staff or volunteers, including hours). Eight (16%) charities (UK – 6 (24%); RoI – 2 (8%)) provided input information in the narrative section of their TAR; two (4%) (UK – 8%) provided monetary information and six (12%) (UK – 4 (16%); RoI – 2 (8%)) non-monetary (not shown in **Table 6.5**). One (5%) (RoI – 25%) charity provided details in its annual review of the resources used in providing its services. **Exhibit 6.26** illustrates the type of input information provided.

Exhibit 6.26   **Input**

> Over **2,100** nurses worked night and day, in people's homes across the UK, providing hands-on care and vital emotional support to **31,589** people.
>
> They helped give people with a terminal illness the choice to stay in the comfort of their own home for as long as possible – a place they want to be, surrounded by their loved ones.
>
> All told, our nurses spent **1.2 million hours** providing high-quality care for people living with a terminal illness.
>
> **"The emotional support the nurses give me is almost the most important part. They make me feel safe."** Julie M, who was cared for by Marie Curie Nurses.
>
> Source: Marie Curie (UK), *Impact and achievements 2014/15*. Available at https://www.mariecurie.org.uk/globalassets/media/documents/who-we-are/vision-and-strategic-plan/marie-curie-impact-report-2014-2015.pdf

(i) Output This information represents the actual goods and services produced (for example, number of tests/inspections, number of people assisted or trained); it does not measure impact upon clients or problems (Anthony and Young (2002) – 'process measures'). Thirty-one (62%) charities (UK – 20 (80%); RoI – 11 (44%)) disclosed output information in their TAR, with the difference in disclosure levels between UK and RoI charities being significant at the 5% level. While not shown in **Table 6.5**, the details were non-monetary in the majority of instances; five (10%) (UK – 3 (12%); RoI – 2 (8%)) organisations presented output information graphically. An example of the disclosure of output information in charity TARs is presented in **Exhibit 6.27**.

Exhibit 6.27   **Output (1)**

> Driving tuition remains a critical IWA service. In 2015, **IWA conducted 513 Assessments and delivered 2,770 driving lessons to 351 students** via our 10 Driving Centres around the country. The impact of this service is evident in the numbers of people with disabilities whose lives have been transformed by being able to drive – a skill which can enable them to secure employment, build relationships, or enjoy a regular social life.
>
> Source: Irish Wheelchair Association (RoI) *Annual Report 2015*. Available at https://www.iwa.ie/downloads/information/publications/annual-reports/0630-WEB-IWA-Annual-report-2015.pdf

Eleven (55%) charities (UK – 8 (50%); RoI – 3 (75%)) disclosed output information in their annual review. While not shown in **Table 6.5**, the details were non-monetary in the majority of instances; two (10%) (UK – 1 (6%); RoI – 1 (25%)) organisations presented output information graphically. Examples of the disclosure of output information in charity annual reviews are presented in **Exhibits 6.28** and **6.29**.

Exhibit 6.28   **Output (2)**

> **Great news from Battambang, Cambodia**
>
> One of the most rewarding experiences of being a child sponsor is when the community you are supporting becomes sustainable thanks to your support. In 2014, there was a cause for celebration as Action-Aid completed its eight year development plan in Battambang, Cambodia leaving behind a strong local community now able to manage its own continued development.
>
> **What difference has been made?**
>
> - **12,465 community members** were trained on basic healthcare and **2,462 people were vaccinated**

- **2,185 children** who were out of the school, now have access to quality education and child labour has dramatically decreased.
- **326 farmers** who were struggling to feed their children increased their incomes through organic farming and seed banking
- A further **686 families** were able to increase their crop production through irrigation projects
- **Three rice banks** were established and managed by 9 community committees to ensure quality seeds for local farmers
- Domestic violence has **decreased from 60% of households in 2010 to 10% in 2014**
- **5 maternity facilities** are now running and have serviced 639 families and 18 midwives were trained
- **18 women** from various local villages in Battambang have committed to lead local networks to further development in their community

In the last 5 years ActionAid Ireland has celebrated the sustainability of four communities in Africa and Asia.

2010:	Malindi, Kenya
	Mandera, Kenya
2012:	Baitadi, Nepal
2014:	Battambang, Cambodia

Source: ActionAid (RoI), *Directors' Report and Accounts 2015.* Available at http://www.actionaid.ie/wp-content/uploads/2016/10/Annual-Audited-Accounts-2015.pdf

Exhibit 6.29   **Output (3)**

Our hospices provide specialist medical care and emotional support in a friendly, welcoming environment, giving people with a terminal illness the best possible quality of life.

In 2014/15, we cared for **8,465 people** in our nine hospices across the UK.

That includes **3,326** people staying in the hospices as in-patients and **5,139** who visited us for other services, including physiotherapy, medical care and wellbeing sessions.

Source: Marie Curie (UK), *Impact and achievements 2014/15.* Available at https://www.mariecurie.org.uk/globalassets/media/documents/who-we-are/vision-and-strategic-plan/marie-curie-impact-report-2014-2015.pdf

(j) Impact/Outcome This type of information relates to the short-term difference that an activity makes to those the organisation is trying to help (for example, change in level of awareness/education, user/customer satisfaction, personal stories). Forty-three (86%) of the charities (UK – 23 (92%); RoI – 20 (80%)) surveyed presented details of the impact/outcome of their activities. The information provided was usually non-monetary and focused on the quality of the services provided. An example of the disclosure of impact/outcome information in charity TARs is presented in **Exhibit 6.30**.

Exhibit 6.30   **Impact/Outcome (1)**

Examples of Impact

1. Afghanistan
Ghulam used to be one of the poorest people in his village. Now, he runs his own dairy business, including a cheese shop which helps other villagers earn a living – all thanks to a heifer which one of Tearfund's partners gave him. He gave its first calf to benefit another family.

2. India
Naina would have been sold into abuse had it not been for Tearfund partner EHA raising awareness of trafficking locally. Her parents were able to foil an attempt to traffic Naina and she is now safely home and receiving trauma support and livelihoods training to build a positive future back home.

3. Malawi
Volunteer Mother Buddies working with vulnerable pregnant women in rural communities in Malawi have helped reduce mother-to-child transmission of HIV from fourteen per cent down to less than two per cent in these areas. More than 6,000 pregnant women have benefited so far, as well as 60,000 other people with improvements in other health areas.

4. Syria
Tearfund helped 32,628 people affected by the conflict in Syria in 2014/15, providing education, trauma care, winter supplies, food and hygiene packages, and help with accommodation costs.

5. Tanzania
Since a Tearfund partner introduced Anna to conservation farming techniques, her crop yield has vastly improved, and her income from the sale of vegetables has increased from an average 17,000 Tanzanian Shillings to 125,000 per week, enabling her to send all eight of her children to school, without any outside help.

6. Rwanda
Over the last ten years, Tearfund partners in Rwanda have helped set up 11,127 selfhelp groups, opening up access to affordable financial services for 222,540 households – or more than 1.1 million people – giving them the means to overcome extreme poverty.

7. Colombia
Tearfund partner Red Viva has been providing food packages and medical care for the remote Wayuu tribe, supporting 743 people, as they face a crippling drought.

8. Brazil
After severe flooding hit northern Brazil, Tearfund partner Asas do Socorro assisted hard-to-reach communities along the Rio Madeira. Some 400 families received food and clothing parcels, 740 people benefited from water filters and more than 400 people received medical care.

Source: Tearfund (UK) *Annual Report and Financial Statements 2014/15*. Available at http://www.tearfund.org/~/media/files/main_site/about_us/financial_reports_2015.pdf

Each of the charities publishing an annual review discussed the impact/outcome of their activities in this document. The information provided was usually non-monetary and focused on the quality of the services provided. Examples of the disclosure of impact/outcome information in charity annual reviews are presented in **Exhibits 6.31** and **6.32**.

Exhibit 6.31   **Impact/Outcome (2)**

Employment, training and skills

We provided training and support to over 4,600 young people last year.

We work in partnership with employers, schools, colleges, and other charities to ensure young people receive support that has a real and lasting impact on their lives.

In 2014–15 we provided training and support to over 4,600 young people aged 16–24.

Examples of positive outcomes for these young people include:

- Of 330 young people starting our Employability Fund provision in Scotland, 188 (57 per cent) achieved an accredited qualification and 180 (55 per cent) progressed into employment.
- Of 197 leavers from our Study Programme, 143 young people (73 per cent) achieved a positive progression (employment or further training).
- Of the 74 referrals to our Work Programme in the Midlands, 71 young people progressed into employment (96 per cent), of whom 52 sustained paid employment for over six months (70 per cent of referrals).

"Barnardo's has done so much for me – helping me to get a job and live independently – and with their help I'm making the very most of life. Josh, participant, PHASE 2"

We provide a range of employment, training and skills services. Our PHASE 2 – South East project, for example, provided support to young people to develop skills to achieve and maintain sustained employment. The project, financed by the European Social Fund, focused on increasing confidence, resilience, and self-esteem through employment, work experience, volunteering, educational opportunities and qualifications.

Source: Barnardo's (UK), *Impact Report 2015*. Available at http://www.barnardos.org.uk/impact-report-2015.pdf

Exhibit 6.32   **Impact/Outcome (3)**

Delivering early action.

3.1 Taking action to grow up safe.

We recognise when children are at risk and view safeguarding as fundamental in all our services. We not only protect children, we seek to equip them with safety skills that build up their resilience to deal with exploitation and abuse in its many guises.

Our annual safeguarding review involves independent review of our case records and multiple discussions with front-line practitioners and managers. We also continually ask ourselves if we can make children safer so that we improve. The review confirmed that Action for

Children's safeguarding practice and governance arrangements are strong, improving outcomes for children and young people.

We succeeded in the majority of our cases in reducing risk of abuse, neglect, suicide, self-harm and domestic abuse within the home.

98% reduced risk of suicide.
96% kept safe at home or within the family network.
95% indicators of neglect are addressed.

2014/15 data from all Action for Children services across the UK.

We also know that public services are more and more stretched as a result of rising need and declining finance. In the light of this, our Safeguarding Board, chaired by our Chief Executive, has taken steps to ensure that all staff can escalate concerns whenever they believe a child is not safe.

Source: Action for Children (UK), *Impact Report 2015*. Available at https://www.actionforchildren.org.uk/media/3686/impactreport2015full.pdf

(k) Efficiency This type of information indicates the relationship between input and output (for example, cost per person assisted, number of cases handled per employee). Eleven (22%) charities (UK – 6 (24%); RoI – 5 (20%)) provided information on efficiency in their TAR. The information disclosed being primarily monetary (see **Exhibit 6.33**).

Exhibit 6.33   **Efficiency (1)**

In 2014

89% of every Euro received

was spent directly on our services to combat and prevent homelessness.

Source: Focus Ireland (RoI), *Annual Report 2014*. Available at https://www.focusireland.ie/wp-content/uploads/2016/04/Focus-Ireland-Annual-Report-2014.pdf

Ten (50%) charities (UK – 9 (56%); RoI – 1 (25%)) provided information on efficiency in their annual review. This was primarily monetary, with two (UK) charities presenting the details graphically (not shown in **Table 6.5**) (see **Exhibit 6.34**).

Exhibit 6.34   **Efficiency (2)**

A brief look at our finances

In 2014/15...

We spent £20.8 million to raise £65.8 million – a three-to-one return on investment.

For every £1 we receive we spend 81p on supporting people with sight loss. The rest is used to raise further funds and on running costs.

The RNIB group of charities focused expenditure on the following areas of work:

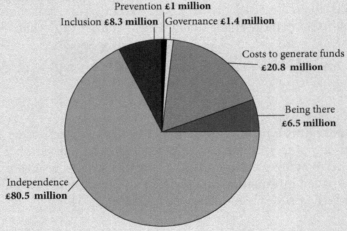

Total expenditure £118.6m

Source: RNIB (UK), *Annual Review 2014/15*. Available at http://www.rnib.org.uk/sites/default/files/APDF-RES091502_Annual%20Review%202015.pdf

(l) Effectiveness This represents the relationship between output and objectives (for example, actual number of operations versus the operations planned). Eight (16%) charities (UK – 32%) disclosed effectiveness information in their TAR; this was primarily non-monetary. **Exhibit 6.35** illustrates the disclosure of effectiveness information (including the provision of future target information (item (m)). The difference in disclosure levels between UK and RoI charities is significant at the 1% level.

Exhibit 6.35   **Effectiveness**

Strategic Report

In last year's Annual Report, we said that during 2014/15 we would aim to:

- continue responding to typhoon Haiyan in the Philippines, helping communities to rebuild, recover and strengthen their resilience to future disasters
- respond to the heightened humanitarian needs in South Sudan arising from renewed political instability and conflict
- scale up our response to the crisis in Central African Republic
- monitor the security situation and humanitarian needs in Afghanistan as international troops withdraw
- respond to smaller-scale or low-profile disasters, developing and resourcing partners as well as providing emergency funds, either from our own internal sources or via the newly established Start Fund. We aim to continue to support the ongoing development of the Start Network, of which Tearfund is a member, and its disbursement of two substantial UK government grants.
- continue to work with the other members of the Integral Alliance to capture learning from the response in the Philippines and further strengthen our collaboration

In 2014/15 we spent a total of £25.5m (2013/14: £24.4m) responding to disasters.
We delivered:

- emergency relief to 236,000 people in the Philippines, providing shelter, rebuilding livelihoods and strengthening the resilience of communities through protecting children, supporting water and sanitation, and disaster risk reduction
- emergency relief to more than 95,000 people affected by conflict in South Sudan. Tearfund treated more than 51,150 malnourished mothers and children under five. More than 18,000 displaced people were provided with mosquito nets, blankets and tarpaulin to protect them from the heavy rains and 25,000 people have been provided with clean water. Some 24,000 people, most of them displaced, have been able to plant crops as Tearfund provided seeds and tools.

- food distributions, food security and water and sanitation programmes in the Central African Republic, reaching 100,000 people in Lobaye and Ombella M'poko. We also carried out peacebuilding and trauma care initiatives.
- the successful withdrawal of our operational programme from Afghanistan. We made the decision to continue to support Tearfund's long-term partners, thus resolving issues linked to accessing insecure locations and managing projects remotely.
- support for Tearfund partners responding to multiple smaller-scale and low-profile emergencies in countries including Afghanistan, Bangladesh, the DRC, Malawi, Mozambique, Pakistan and Mali – using both internal emergency funds and via the Start Fund. The Start Fund has been set up to respond to forgotten disasters.
- active involvement in the Start Network, helping it to secure two multi-million pound grants which were shared between a cross section of Start Network members. Start Build has been established to develop local partner capacity and enhance humanitarian response systems globally and locally.
- participation in a review in the Philippines in January 2015 with the other members of the Integral Alliance, confirming the added value of responding collaboratively to disasters, and pooling funds and partner relationships to increase impact

We learnt:

- the added benefits of working through networks such as the Integral Alliance and the Start Network in disaster response, to pool knowledge and funding and to maximise coordination and impact
- the importance of pursuing contingency and preparedness plans for disaster response at the country and local level in advance of a disaster
- the importance of drawing on the knowledge of local partners when responding to disasters, as highlighted in a collaborative report, *Missed opportunities*, that we co-commissioned

In 2015/16, we aim to:

- **Large-scale disasters and complex political emergencies**
  respond quickly and effectively to new largescale disasters (such as Nepal) including complex political emergencies (such as Democratic Republic of Congo). We will also capture learning, for

example by conducting real time reviews of existing responses to ensure we adapt to the changing needs of affected people and apply the lessons learnt to future responses.

- **Small-scale disasters**
respond to an increased number of small-scale disasters by identifying Disaster Priority Countries where we will position local partners intentionally and develop their skills and strengths to ensure high-quality responses, linking them to international humanitarian funding streams, national government and others networks of responders
- **Strategic alliances**
deepen our collaboration with the Integral Alliance and Start Network so that our disaster responses have greater impact on the people worst hit. Our aim is that by strengthening these strategic alliances, we help ensure funding reaches the most vulnerable people and we commit to support the reform of the humanitarian system for the benefit of people affected by disaster.

Source: Tearfund (UK) *Annual Report and Financial Statements 2014/15*. Available at http://www.tearfund.org/~/media/files/main_site/about_us/financial_reports_2015.pdf

Only one (5%) (UK – 6%) charity provided effectiveness information in their annual review.

(m) Future target information In relation to managerial accountability disclosures, charities should provide additional comparative information, such as information pertaining to the previous year, to enable stakeholders to place the results in context. Although comparison of performance between charities is believed to encourage an improvement in organisational performance, it can be misleading because charity ratios may differ significantly between organisations, being based on actual activities and areas of need rather than on managerial effectiveness. As such, framing the performance of an organisation within its own context is valuable for both the readers and the organisation. Moreover, in accordance with Jackson's (1982) and Patton's (1992) definitions of accountability, and as recommended by the Charity Commission and OSCR (2014 a) in relation to disclosures about deficit levels, charities should not only report on their actions and performance, but also provide justifications and explanations for these actions and performance, together with their intentions for the future. This latter information should include a time frame and be more than a 'bland' statement. Seventeen (34%) charities (UK – 11 (44%); RoI – 6 (24%)) presented future target information in their TAR; this was non-monetary in all but one instance (not shown in **Table 6.5**). Examples of the disclosure of future target information are presented in **Exhibits 6.35–6.37**.

Exhibit 6.36   **Future Target Information (1)**

Thanks for supporting our new retail outlet

We opened our first Beloved shop in Malahide and have received more support than we had imagined from clothes donors and shoppers. We'd like to thank our amazing volunteers who worked tirelessly to help us set up the shop and make it the success that it is. We hope to open a further two stores in 2015, again, thanks for your support.

Source: Focus Ireland (RoI), *Annual Report 2014*. Available at https://www.focusireland.ie/wp-content/uploads/2016/04/Focus-Ireland-Annual-Report-2014.pdf

Exhibit 6.37   **Future Target Information (2)**

OXFAM STRATEGIC PLAN 2013–19: 'THE POWER OF PEOPLE AGAINST POVERTY'

External Change Goals: Six Goals to Change the World

Goal 1: Active citizens
By 2019: More women, young people and other poor and marginalised people will exercise civil and political rights to influence decision making by engaging with governments and by holding governments and businesses accountable.

Goal 2: Advancing gender justice
By 2019: More poor and marginalised women will claim and advance their rights through the engagement and leadership of women and their organisations and violence against women will be significantly less socially acceptable and prevalent.

Goal 3: Saving lives, now and in the future
By 2019: By reducing the impact of natural disasters, fewer men, women and children will die or suffer illness, insecurity and deprivation. Those most at risk will have exercised their right to have clean water, food and sanitation and other fundamental needs met, to be free from violence and coercion, and to take control of their own lives.

Goal 4: Sustainable food
By 2019: More people who live in rural poverty will enjoy greater food security, income, prosperity and resilience through significantly more equitable, sustainable food systems.

Goal 5: Fair sharing of natural resources
By 2019: The world's most marginalised people will be significantly more prosperous and resilient, despite rising competition for land, water, food and energy sources and stresses caused by a changing climate.

Goal 6: Financing for development and universal essential services
By 2019: There will be higher quality and quantity of financial flows that target poverty and inequality, and empower citizens, especially women, to hold governments, donors and the private sector to account concerning how revenue is raised and spent. More women, men, girls and boys will exercise their right to universal quality health and education services, making them full participants in their communities and strengthening the economic, social and democratic fabric of their societies.

Enabling Change Goals: Six Goals to Change the Way we Work

Goal 1: Creating a worldwide influencing network
By 2019: There will be profound and lasting changes in the lives of people living with poverty and injustice as a result of a worldwide influencing network united by a common vision for change, that will demonstrably amplify our impact, bolster our international influence and support progressive movements at all levels.

Goal 2: Programme quality, monitoring, evaluation and learning (MEL)
By 2019: Oxfam will be able to demonstrate that it has created a culture of evidence-based learning and innovation that has contributed to progressive improvement of programme quality and increased our accountability and our capacity to achieve transformational change in people's lives.

Goal 3: Strengthening accountability
By 2019: Oxfam will be able to demonstrate that our commitment to strengthened accountability contributes to greater impact.

Goal 4: Investing in people
By 2019: Oxfam will be an agile, flexible network of organisations with skilled and motivated staff and volunteers delivering the change goals.

Goal 5: Cost effectiveness
By 2019: Throughout the period of the Strategic Plan, Oxfam will be cost effective in all aspects of its work. Savings released by cost-effectiveness measures will be reinvested in the achievement of the Strategic Plan goals.

Goal 6: Income strategies
By 2019: A step-change in investment, fundraising and cooperation among affiliates will secure €100 million – €300 million more than our forecast income, and position us to match our future ambitions to significantly increase the scale and impact of Oxfam's work.

Source: Oxfam (UK), *Annual Report & Accounts 2013/14.* Available http://www. oxfamannualreport.org.uk/wp-content/uploads/2014/07/ARA_web.pdf

Three (15%) charities (UK – 2 (13%); RoI – 1 (25%)) presented future target information in their annual review, with it being primarily non-monetary in nature (not shown in **Table 6.5**).

(n) Lessons learned Six (12%) charities (UK – 4 (16%); RoI – 2 (8%)) described how the organisation had improved or changed as a result of its experiences. Three (15%) (UK – 19%) charities described how the organisation had improved or changed from its experiences in their annual review. **Exhibit 6.38** illustrates the disclosure of this type of information.

Exhibit 6.38   **Lessons Learned**

Cost saving initiative: Due to the amount of waste following the discharge of a patient, Laura Keogh put a cost saving initiative in place to try and guard against overstocking of certain patient supplies (i.e. nappies, nappy bags, suction catheters etc). Since this initiative has commenced there has been a marked improvement, and a heightened awareness amongst staff regarding the cost of supplies.

Source: Temple Street Children's University Hospital (RoI), *Annual Report and Accounts 2014.* Available at http://www.cuh.ie/wp-content/uploads/2015/09/ Temple-Street-Annual-Report-2014.pdf

6.7   Implications For Performance and Impact Reporting

Drawing upon the accountability framework discussed in **Chapter 2**, the requirements of the FRS 102 SORP (Charity Commission and OSCR, 2014a)

with respect to the TAR (**Chapter 3, Section 3.4**) and the production model discussed in **Section 6.1 (Figure 6.1)**, accountability may be discharged by charities in terms of their fiduciary and managerial accountability (see **Table 6.3**) (Taylor and Rosair, 2000; Brody, 2001). While fiduciary accountability is analogous to the stewardship function that financial accounting fulfils, managerial accountability addresses organisational performance and success (and can be separated into managerial success in financial and operational terms (**Table 6.3**)). This chapter focuses upon the concept of performance in NFPOs and, after considering issues associated with its measurement from a theoretical perspective (**Sections 6.1–6.3**), the findings from the analysis of UK and RoI TARs and annual reviews with respect to the current state of charity managerial accountability are presented (**Sections 6.4–6.6**).

After discussing the results with respect to the disclosure of financial and operational managerial accountability information, this section considers their broader implications.

Financial Managerial Accountability Information

Overall   The disclosure of the 12 items of financial managerial accountability information was collected and collated under the following three sub-headings: financial; organisational efficiency; and fundraising efficiency (**Table 6.4**). Overall, the average percentage disclosure level in UK and RoI TARs of financial managerial accountability information was 48%, compared with 36% in the annual reviews. This is perhaps surprising, as it might be expected that such information would be more prevalent in annual reviews, which are generally less-formal, shorter and pithier publications than annual reports and include a greater proportion of performance-related information (disclosures viewed by donors as of greatest importance) (Connolly and Hyndman, 2013). This perhaps indicates that annual reports remain an important communication mechanism. Moreover, it is interesting that while, on average, UK and RoI charities were more likely to disclose financial information in the TAR (compared with the annual review) (62% versus 37%), the opposite was the case with regards to organisational efficiency and fundraising efficiency information (31% versus 32%, and 37% versus 38%), albeit to a lesser extent compared with financial information and only marginally so; in addition, the relatively small number of annual reviews has to be borne in mind when interpreting the results.

TARs versus Annual Reviews   Comparing the percentage disclosure levels for the 12 items utilised to capture the discharge of financial managerial accountability (**Table 6.4**, items (a)–(l)) in the UK and RoI TARs with that in the annual reviews, a higher percentage of charities disclosed seven of the items (items (a), (b), (d), (e), (f), (g) and (l)) in the TAR, of which five represent the financial aspect of financial managerial accountability (items (a), (b), (d), (e) and (f)). The percentage disclosure levels were the same for two items (items (i) and (k)) and higher in the annual reviews for three items (items (c), (h) and (k)), one in each of the financial, organisational efficiency and fundraising efficiency sub-headings. Although again, the relatively small number of annual reviews has to be borne in mind when interpreting the results.

UK TARs versus RoI TARs   With respect to the extent of disclosure of the 12 financial managerial accountability items in UK TARs compared with that in RoI TARs, a higher percentage of UK charities disclosed each of the items in the TAR (**Table 6.4**). Moreover, the difference between UK and RoI charities was significant at either the 1% or 5% level in five cases (items (b) Income by source, (c) Expenditure by activity, (d) Income review, (e) Expenditure review and (l) Voluntary income), of which four related to the financial subheading (items (b), (c), (d) and (e)). These findings are consistent with previous research (for example, Connolly and Hyndman, 2001, 2004 (see **Chapter 4**)), and are perhaps to be expected given that the charities SORP has effectively been mandatory for large UK charities for a number of years, while in contrast it has been only (and remains at the time of writing – June 2017) best practice for RoI charities.

UK Annual Reviews versus RoI Annual Reviews   In relation to the disclosure of financial managerial accountability items in the annual reviews (**Table 6.4**), a higher percentage of UK charities compared to RoI charities provided eight of the items (items (a), (b), (c), (d), (f), (h), (k) and (l)), with the disclosure of one (item (i)) being the same (50%). While admittedly on the basis of disclosure in one (out of four available) annual review, the level of disclosure in percentage terms was greater for three items (items (e), (g) and (j)) in RoI documents.

Operational Managerial Accountability Information

Operational managerial accountability addresses performance in terms of the impact of the organisation on society. As illustrated in **Table 6.5**, the disclosure of the 14 items ((a)–(n)) of operational managerial accountability information was collected and collated under the two sub-headings 'general' and 'performance'. The former (items (a)–(g)) incorporates the provision of information that enables readers to understand the aims and objectives set by the charity and the main strategies and activities undertaken to achieve them. Accordingly, on the basis of arguments consistently appearing in both recent iterations of the charities SORP and broader sector-wide debates and discussions, charities should explain their objectives, together with an explanation and review of the significant activities undertaken in pursuit of the achievement of those objectives. Performance information (items (h)–(n)) includes an analysis of organisational input, output, impact/outcome, efficiency and effectiveness, with future target information being required to subsequently assess effectiveness.

Overall   The average percentage of UK and RoI charities disclosing operational managerial accountability information in both TARs and annual reviews was 54%. While arguably relatively low, with just over half of the surveyed charities providing such information, it compares favourably with the average percentage of 48% and 36% for UK and RoI charities in TARs and annual reviews respectively for financial managerial accountability information (**Section 6.5** and **Table 6.4**). Moreover, it is interesting, and perhaps encouraging, that a higher percentage of charities disclose this information since it addresses performance in terms of the impact of the organisation on society. Furthermore, it is noteworthy that in both the TARs and annual reviews a higher percentage of charities disclosed general information (**Table 6.5**, items (a)–(g)) than performance information (73% versus 54% in both documents).

TARs versus Annual Reviews   Comparing the percentage of UK and RoI charities disclosing the 14 items utilised to capture the discharge of operational managerial accountability (**Table 6.5**, items (a)–(n)) in TARs with that in annual reviews, a higher percentage provided the information in the TARs with respect to seven of the items (items (b), (c), (f), (h), (i), (l) and (m)), of which four represent the performance aspect of operational managerial accountability (items (h), (i), (l) and (m)). The percentage disclosure levels were also higher in the annual reviews for seven items (items (a), (d), (e), (g), (j), (k) and (n)), of which four fell under the 'general' category (items (a), (d), (e) and (g)).

UK TARs versus RoI TARs   With respect to the extent of disclosure of the operational managerial accountability items in UK TARs compared with that in RoI TARs, a higher percentage of UK charities disclosed 12 of the 14 items, with only items (b) and (g) being higher for RoI charities. Moreover, a higher percentage of UK charities provided performance information items ((h)–(n)) compared with RoI charities, with the difference in the level of disclosure being significant at either the 1% or 5% level in three cases (items (i) Output, (j) Impact/Outcome and (l) Effectiveness).

UK Annual Reviews versus RoI Annual Reviews   In relation to the disclosure of operational managerial accountability items in the annual reviews, a higher percentage of RoI charities compared with UK charities provided seven of the items (items (b), (c), (d), (e), (h), (i) and (m)), with the disclosure of two items ((a) and (j)) being the same (100%). A meaningful comparison is difficult, though, as there are only four RoI annual reviews included in the sample (compared with 16 UK annual reviews).

Broader Implications

Previous charity accounting research (see **Chapter 4**) has indicated that performance information (largely referred to as 'managerial accountability information' in this chapter) is important to users of charity accounts, and is recognised as such by providers of information, but is not widely disclosed by charities. However, the difficulties of developing useful performance measurement and performance reporting systems by charities have been stressed. While these difficulties may provide some explanation for limited reporting, other factors may have an impact. These include the desire or willingness of charities to report, the cost of reporting and the possible repercussions of highlighting poor performance.

However, a lack of disclosure undermines accountability. In addition, limited external reporting might indicate that performance information is unavailable internally to management, which may weaken their ability to plan and control effectively. Moreover, it has been argued by some that managers in both charities and, more widely, NFPOs may prefer limited performance reporting because they seek to avoid accountability. While these arguments ignore the commitment and professionalism of charity managers, they do provide a persuasive case for the development and use of more substantial charity performance measurement and performance reporting systems.

To encourage the development and use of performance information, in particular with respect to reporting by charities via annual reports and annual reviews as a basis for meeting the information needs of key external stakeholders, it would seem appropriate that guidance relating to managerial accountability information should be provided by those concerned with the administration and control of the charity sector, both in the UK and RoI. This may include the Charity Commission in England and Wales, the Charity Commission for Northern Ireland, OSCR and the Charities Regulatory Authority in RoI. In particular, and with respect to RoI, given the relative scarcity of the reporting of performance information in this jurisdiction, and the less established regulatory framework and focus on the sector, moves to provide steering in this direction would seem especially apposite here.

As highlighted earlier in this chapter, an important issue relating to the external publication of managerial accountability information is its reliability. If no verification of the performance numbers reported by a charity is required, then there may be a temptation to present performance in a manner which is perceived as more acceptable to the reader, for example by exaggerating good performance, regardless of its accuracy. Given that external parties may use externally reported performance information to make judgements and decisions regarding a charity, there is a case for some degree of independent verification (perhaps similar to that which is imposed on financial accounting information, i.e. disclosure requirements, external auditing and standard setting after consultation with interested parties). It should be noted that the managerial accountability information analysed in this research has not been subject to independent verification (as is the case with such information reported by the vast majority of NFPOs), although, with some charities, there is evidence that attempts have been made to provide stakeholders with the basis of the performance information (for example, how it is collected) as it is reported (Hyndman and McConville, 2016).

Finally, it is possible that differences in the extent of the reporting of managerial accountability information by charities may be affected by the type of charities reporting. For example, some charities may have greater incentive to produce such information (for example, charities operating on the fringe of the public sector), while other charities are demand-led and may encounter greater difficulty in providing such information (for example, disaster relief charities). A different 'mix' of charities in the UK and RoI could possibly provide an explanation of differences in the disclosure of managerial accountability information.

Chapter 7

Conclusions

Notwithstanding the fact that drawing a precise boundary of what constitutes the charity sector is problematic, it is clear that such a sector is large and growing both in the UK and the RoI (and elsewhere). Given that charities exist to fulfil specific socially beneficial objects, and do so by spending money provided by third parties (including individual donors, institutional funders and the government) who normally receive no direct economic benefit to themselves, this is a sector in which the fact and perception of accountability is important. Set against this context, this book examined how charity reporting (and accountability) has evolved over time and is likely to evolve in the future. Key aspects of this, which were examined empirically in the book, include: the increasing importance afforded to performance (including impact) reporting; and, at a time of significant accounting change, how modifications to required accounting and reporting practices are interpreted and legitimated by key stakeholders.

In terms of structure, this chapter begins by reviewing two of the main themes of the book relating to the evolution of the charities Statement of Recommended Practice (SORP) and the linked issues of accountability and performance reporting (**Section 7.1**). It then summarises the key findings from the empirical analysis in **Chapters 5** and **6** (**Section 7.2**), before making suggestions for policy, practice and further research (**Section 7.3**) and finally presenting some concluding comments (**Section 7.4**).

7.1 Some Main Themes

Evolution of Charity Reporting

Charities have an accountability obligation towards those outside their immediate management, and the annual report, consisting of a trustees' annual report (TAR) and financial statements, is a key medium through which this accountability can be, and is, discharged. In considering this, two key questions emerge: to whom is a charity accountable and what form should that account take? Within this book, it is contended that external stakeholders, particularly donors and funders, have legitimate information needs and often must primarily rely on external communications (such as the annual report) to meet those needs. Moreover, it is claimed that while information disclosed in the financial statements may be of importance to such stakeholders, other wider information, particularly relating to performance, is of paramount importance in discharging accountability. Good accounting and reporting, as an important aspect of a wider accountability framework, can lead to greater confidence in the sector, and greater confidence in the sector can lead to a willingness by third parties (including individual donors, institutional funders and government) to increase funding.

In the early 1980s, Bird and Morgan-Jones (1981) identified significant failings in charity accounting which, if left unchecked, had the potential to undermine faith in the sector. This initiated a process that led to the development of a SORP for accounting by charities in 1988 and its subsequent revision in a number of later iterations. Over time, various stakeholders provided input to this process (auditors, the accounting profession, donors and the government), and (in tandem with the development of a more rigid regulatory framework) what has emerged is a significantly different accounting regime for charities. As detailed in **Chapter 3**, the first charities SORP (SORP 1988) largely applied existing commercially based standards to charities. Yet while it was groundbreaking in its existence and in some of its suggestions, the impact of the SORP was described as marginal, as compliance with it was entirely voluntary (Charity Commission, 2009). Over time, it became generally accepted that the sector's poor response to implementing the SORP necessitated the development of a more rigid regulatory framework to ensure proper accountability in the sector. A key element of this more rigid framework was the further development of the SORP.

From 1990, responsibility for preparing the SORP passed to the SORP Committee of the Charity Commission for England and Wales (and in 2006, the Office of the Scottish Charity Regulator (OSCR) joined them in creating a joint SORP-making body). Subsequent iterations of the SORP were issued: SORP 1995 (Charity Commission, 1995), SORP 2000 (Charity Commission, 2000), SORP 2005 (Charity Commission, 2005) and, most recently, the FRS 102 SORP (Charity Commission and OSCR, 2014a), which applies to all charities for reporting periods starting on or after 1 January 2015. Over these various iterations, the SORP has evolved massively, with the FRS 102 SORP being unrecognisable from its early predecessors (particularly SORP 1988). For example: the name has changed (to an 'Accounting and Reporting' rather than purely an 'Accounting' SORP); a much greater emphasis is now placed on the TAR (and, in particular, on the need for performance and governance reporting); and it has become much more charity specific (for example, with the Statement of Financial Activities (SOFA) replacing the income and expenditure statement, and in relation to the terminology which it uses, as terms like 'restricted funds' and 'designated funds' have no meaning in the business sector). As a consequence, the SORP has lengthened considerably, from 30 pages in 1988 to 193 pages in the FRS 102 SORP. At the time of writing (June 2017), all charities in the UK that prepare accounts on the accruals basis to give a true and fair view must follow the FRS 102 SORP (regardless of their size or constitution); in RoI, the FRS 102 SORP represents recommended best practice.

Overall, this SORP-development process, resulting in the current FRS 102 SORP (Charity Commission and OSCR, 2014a) has: attempted to reflect best and appropriate financial accounting practice; gained greater stakeholder input in its development over time; and highlighted the need for increasing focus on communicating 'accounts', or stories, of what charities are doing (or plan to do). It has the potential to provide the basis for a better-managed, more accountable and healthier charity sector in the UK and RoI. The degree to which this occurs will, to an extent, be a function of whether charities themselves embrace and internally legitimate (or justify) the SORP (and, in particular, the changes included in the latest iteration), and embed the required practices in their daily routines and regular reporting. The widespread adoption of appropriate accounting and reporting practices (as reflected in the SORP), and the ongoing renewal of such, has the potential to provide a basis for greater confidence in the control processes within charities and result in a more accountable and trusted charity sector.

Need for Better Accountability and Better Performance Information

Issues such as governance and accountability often become central in discussions regarding the development of the charity sector, albeit these terms have a range of meanings and can be seen as overlapping. Good governance and good accountability are viewed as key foundations for the growth and health of the sector. Charity governance can be viewed as relating to the distribution of rights and responsibilities among, and within, various stakeholder groups. This involves the ways in which these groups are accountable to one another, and also embraces ideas relating to how a charity sets its goals and objectives and devises strategies to achieve them. This combines the conception of governance as a set of relationships between stakeholders, with the idea of governance ensuring the organisation is effectively run in terms of attaining its objectives (defined, in this case, as meeting the needs for which the organisation was created which, for charities, will have a beneficiary or society-at-large focus). In addition, it recognises the importance of groups other than the board of trustees in delivering good governance in a charity.

While accountability, in its widest sense, is more than accounting (however widely accounting is defined), focusing on the information needs of stakeholders/users (a key aspect of a contemporary definition of accounting) seems clearly linked with ideas relating to accountability. Accountability involves explaining what has been, or is being done, and what has been planned. However, this concept is multifaceted. As referred to above, two main types of information are particularly important in discharging accountability: financial information, as contained in traditional financial statements; and wider performance information, often of a non-financial nature, especially relating to the efficiency and effectiveness of the charity. Arguably, the latter (performance information) is likely to be more important to many key stakeholders (including donors and beneficiaries).

Terms such as financial accountability and performance accountability have been used to highlight such distinctions in an accountability framework. Likewise, in the language of Taylor and Rosair (2000) and Brody (2001), similar, although at times overlapping ideas are found when reference is made to fiduciary and managerial accountability (terms that are explored in detail in **Chapter 6**). As used by these writers, fiduciary accountability largely equates to financial accountability (and is discharged through the medium of financial statements). On the other hand, managerial accountability largely focuses on performance accountability (although with some aspects being aligned to financial accountability). In this book, it was argued that the task of reflecting on performance, and disclosing performance (including impact) information in formal communications (such as annual reports and annual reviews), will not only lead to a more accountable charitable sector, but also has the potential to sharpen focus and improve decision making within a charity.

The direction of accountability is also an important consideration, and may (or perhaps should) influence how accountability is discharged. The need to be accountable to upward stakeholders (particularly donors and funders) may serve a charity's funding objectives by encouraging the flow of funds from financial supporters. However, despite claims to the contrary, it does not necessarily undermine, and has the potential to underpin, accountability to downward stakeholders (such as beneficiaries) as well. This is the case because donors' interests may be (or perhaps should be) aligned with those of beneficiaries. Indeed, if a charity focuses on its impact in terms of its beneficiaries (or benefit to society at large) through its actions and in its reporting, it may gain external legitimacy from its funders/donors, regulators and society at large (upward stakeholders)

(Connolly and Hyndman, 2017). However, the manner of the discharge of accountability is likely to be different depending on its direction. Many downward stakeholders (especially beneficiaries) are likely to be uninterested in (or incapable of engaging with) traditional accounting and reporting formats (and view accountability in terms of direct engagement with a charity and its services); whereas many upward stakeholders (often located at a distance from a charity's operations) depend and expect well-prepared and engaging formal communications, such as annual reports (Connolly and Hyndman, 2013).

While recognising the importance of charities developing appropriate performance measurement and performance reporting systems, it is acknowledged that many difficulties confront those tasked with designing an information system that provides such measures. Indeed, most, if not all, charity performance reporting systems are likely to be contestable and partial, and this is especially the case when attempts are made to measure and report on performance in terms of impact. Difficulties include: (i) setting clear goals and objectives; (ii) avoiding a ritualistic approach where the process of setting objectives and reporting performance has the potential to degenerate into a formal ceremony with little influence on behaviours; (iii) ensuring that the information is reliable; (iv) dealing with the complexity of organisations; (v) ensuring that quality, as well as quantity, is measured; (vi) making meaningful comparisons between measures; and (vii) co-ordinating measures so that the low-level measures help to motivate individuals to behave in a way that furthers the overall strategic mission of the organisation. An awareness of these difficulties may help to focus attention on some of the important issues to be addressed by the system designer, and support the development of appropriate and well-balanced performance-measurement systems.

7.2   Key Findings of Empirical Analysis

Legitimation and the FRS 102 SORP

In **Chapter 5**, how key charity actors (accountants in charities) involved in the introduction of the FRS 102 SORP (Charity Commission and OSCR, 2014a) understand, interpret and legitimate (justify) or delegitimate (question) the changes required (that is, the process of internal legitimation) was examined. It was argued that how, and the extent to which, this occurs will affect the ultimate influence of the SORP in changing accounting and reporting. The more such actors extensively legitimate (justify) the changes to the SORP, the more likely these will be accepted and embedded within the organisation, and the more likely positive change will occur. What is novel in this research is that it investigates individual legitimation strategies employed by charity accountants (key actors) at a time when significant changes had been announced but were not yet mandated (and, largely, not implemented). Twenty-one semi-structured interviews were conducted in large fundraising UK and RoI charities. Key findings were as follows.

- Overwhelmingly, in each jurisdiction, the majority of strategies used and identified in the interviews were legitimation strategies (over 80% in each jurisdiction). Interviewees in both jurisdictions mainly discussed the SORP changes in positive terms (legitimated or justified the changes), and rarely used delegitimation (or questioning) strategies. In other words, most charity accountants justified, and were in favour of, the FRS 102 SORP changes. This was regardless of the fact that the SORP was compulsory in the UK, but only best practice in RoI. Given this, it suggests that, over time, changes will embed in both UK and RoI charity reporting practices (and influence charity thinking). A possible explanation suggested for the jurisdictional similarities is that the reactions and perceptions reflect a common culture and shared views as to the role that charities, and charity accounting and reporting, play (or should play) in society.
- In each jurisdiction, the main legitimation strategy used was authorisation, followed by rationalisation. Perhaps surprisingly, despite the SORP not being a legislative requirement in RoI at the time of the interviews (or at the time of writing – June 2017), the main rationale for the introduction of the new SORP was perceived in RoI in a similar, authority-driven manner as in the UK (where it was mandatory). However, it is notable that when interviewees legitimated FRS 102-related SORP changes (as was, by far, the situation with the majority of the cases), the combination of authorisation and rationalisation was frequently used, which means the changes were perceived as rational and emanating from sources which possessed authority. Because of similarities between the jurisdictions, both being common-law countries and both having strong, similar professional accounting traditions, it was argued that international mimetic pressures and professional standards encourage moves towards an increasing uniformity of accounting practices and reporting, regardless of the actual legal and mandatory power these may have in a specific jurisdiction. It was suggested that the results would likely be different if such changes were recommended in countries with more legalistic and bureaucratic traditions (and where professional accounting bodies were less powerful).

- The dominance of authorisation legitimation strategies to the SORP changes among UK interviewees was suggested as being connected to the long-established, and accepted, formal regulation that the UK has (with the Charity Commission in England and Wales operating since the mid-nineteenth century). What was perhaps rather surprising was that positive authorisation strategies also dominated in RoI interviews, even though the Irish Charities Regulator only became active as an independent authority in 2014. It appears that the interviewees in RoI (charity accountants) regarded the likely designation of the SORP as mandatory as almost inevitable and, largely, something to be welcomed. This suggests that formal regulation is not always necessary for a new practice to be legitimated, with factors such as mimetic behaviours and international comparisons appearing to play an important role.
- When positive rationalisation arguments were utilised, many of the sub-strategies identified from the interviews referred to managerial arguments (such as the importance of effective decision-making). At times, in each jurisdiction, tensions were evident between the new SORP requirements, seen in terms of merely compliance reporting, and, more usefully, as mechanisms with potential to improve focus, decision making and reporting.
- Moralisation arguments were mobilised in interviewees, but only to a limited extent (and mainly with reference to the TAR changes, rather than those related to the financial statements). It is possible that, while moral issues often surface in wider discussions in the charity sector, due to the perceived 'technical' nature of many of the financial statement-related SORP changes, such strategies were referred to infrequently in this context. However, when the interviewees did use moralisation arguments, these were often in reference to the TAR-related changes contained in the SORP (for example, in respect of impact reporting or senior management pay), and often linked to sub-strategies connected to accountability and transparency towards both donors and beneficiaries, and principles of good administration. This is perhaps understandable given the mission focus of charities.
- There was very little delegitimation of the changes to charity reporting contained in the FRS 102 SORP in either jurisdiction; although, when occurring, these were often expressed in terms of questioning the rationality of the change. Such criticisms were frequently linked to aspects of FRS 102 (FRC, 2015a) relating to financial statements (for example, with respect to the more liberal policy of income recognition – changing from 'virtually certain' to 'probable'), which were seen as not being justified in the charity sector. This provides evidence that charities seem to view themselves as within an autonomous sector and are not easily

persuaded to embrace private-sector standards and systems if these are not deemed appropriate. However, despite such delegitimations, the interviewees in both jurisdictions seemed keen to be seen as understanding and committed to complying with the new SORP changes.

Performance (Including Impact) Reporting

It was argued in this book that while financial (or fiduciary) accountability is important, performance accountability (a key aspect of what is sometimes referred to as 'managerial accountability') is paramount in meeting key stakeholder information needs. In **Chapter 6**, after the concepts related to performance were examined, an empirical analysis of a matched sample of performance (including impact) disclosures by 25 large UK and RoI charities in their TARs and annual reviews was presented. This was used to ascertain the current extent of performance reporting in UK and RoI charities, and was then discussed in the context of performance accountability. Of note is the fact that as the SORP has evolved over time, the performance reporting aspects in it have developed considerably, seen most clearly by the reference to 'impact' (viewed as the 'ultimate expression of performance of a charity' – para. 1.43) in the FRS 102 SORP (Charity Commission and OSCR, 2014a). The empirical research here used content analysis and, drawing on the work of Taylor and Rosair (2000) and Brody (2001), identified the disclosure (or non-disclosure) of 26 possible items relating to the discharge of managerial accountability (which predominantly focused on performance accountability). Key findings of this empirical analysis were as follows.

- With respect to the more performance-related disclosures of managerial accountability (in **Chapter 6** referred to as 'operational managerial accountability disclosures'), the average disclosure of the 14 operational managerial disclosures was 54% in both the TARs and annual reviews (when the jurisdictions were combined). Given the importance of, and justifications of, such performance disclosures, and allowing for the fact that there are many difficulties experienced by charities in seeking to measure and report performance, the results suggest that extant charity reports do not meet the most important information needs of users. As a consequence, the relevance of such reporting can be questioned. For example, a significant proportion of charities reported no information on effectiveness and efficiency, two key criteria for judging performance. It was argued that such a lack of disclosure may disadvantage good performing charities. The publication of performance information, in cases where a charity has operated efficiently and effectively, may well increase its attraction to potential contributors.

- There was very limited use of annual reviews by RoI charities, with only 16% of RoI charities surveyed publishing such a document compared with 64% of UK charities. In previous UK-based research (Connolly and Hyndman, 2013), these documents have been found to be more engaged with by donors than more formal annual reports. Annual reviews, compared with annual reports: (i) are normally shorter, pithier publications that include some of the information in the annual report (but often in a more condensed form); (ii) are frequently written in less formal language; and (iii) often include a higher proportion of stories, photographs and diagrams. Given that they have been found to 'connect' more with individual donors, a lack of utilisation of such formats in RoI, while possibly understandable when reflecting on cost considerations, does suggest a weaker accountability regime.
- Interestingly, when comparisons are made with earlier research (see **Chapter 4**), albeit that such comparisons are difficult due to differing methodologies and frameworks, the rapid rise in the use of impact reporting (in both the UK and RoI) is clear. Despite the fact that there is no consideration of the extent or manner of reporting within individual charities in the research reported in this book, given the prominence afforded to such disclosures in the FRS 102 SORP, the significant increase in charities reporting under this heading can be viewed as noteworthy progress.
- In terms of jurisdiction, the number (and percentage) of UK charities reporting performance-related information in the TAR is higher than RoI charities. Comparing the disclosure of 14 operational managerial disclosures, the average percentage of UK charities providing such information was 60% compared with 49% for RoI charities. When the focus is on the subset of nine specific 'performance' disclosures, differences are even more marked (average: UK 45%, RoI 26%), with a greater percentage of UK charities providing each of these nine disclosures in their TARs compared with RoI charities. To an extent, this probably reflects the greater engagement of UK charities in such discussions (some of them relating to SORP developments and contact with the Charity Commission over the years) and the greater presence and push for such reporting from UK groups (such as Inspiring Impact, New Philanthropy Capital and the National Council for Voluntary Organisations). Due to the more undeveloped and less regulated sector in RoI (Breen and Carroll, 2015), such pressures have not been present to the same extent (not least because of the absence, until very recently, of a regulator).
- While limited performance reporting (as highlighted in this research) undermines accountability, and has the potential to damage confidence and trust in charities by external stakeholders (including donors/funders – key sources of funds), limited external reporting might also

indicate that performance information is unavailable internally to management, which may lessen their ability to plan and control effectively.

- With respect to financial managerial accountability disclosures (as a subset of wider managerial accountability disclosures), overall the percentage of charities disclosing the 12 items considered in this research is higher than the more performance-focussed operational managerial disclosures (average: UK 75%, RoI 72%, combined 74%). Such disclosures (although occurring in the TAR and outside of the financial statements) are largely connected to commentary and calculation relating to the key financial landscape that a charity faces. This suggests a greater willingness, and capability, to comment upon (and generate figures) relating to financial matters, albeit that such financial accountability is not central to stakeholders' needs.

7.3 Implications for Policy, Practice and Further Research

The charity sectors in the UK and RoI are large, socially engaged and pervasive. Their operations touch the lives of many people, whether as donors, beneficiaries or volunteers. They are a much-valued and trusted platform for citizen and civil society engagement, receiving formal recognition and encouragement through legislative and fiscal arrangements. This book, focusing on the UK and RoI, explored how charity accounting and reporting (and accountability) has evolved over time (and is likely to evolve going forward). Key aspects of this (which were investigated empirically) relate to: the importance, and current state, of performance (including impact) reporting; and the view that, during processes of accounting change (such as the introduction and evolution of the charities SORP), it is important to not only understand accounting technicalities but also the way they are interpreted and internally legitimated (or justified).

Implications for Policy and Practice

In terms of the internal legitimation process during the implementation of accounting changes (this considered a necessary foundation for the embedding of new or amended reporting practices), the evidence from this research suggests that although new practices can be legitimated without the authority of formal legislation, formal legislation provides valuable back-up. If changes are seen, at a minimum, as being rational and having authority, if they emerge from conversations and discussions involving key stakeholders, and if they are 'tested' prior to being launched, then it is likely that stakeholders (including charities and charity accountants) will not only shape the changes but, as a consequence, legitimate (justify) them. If done well, the processes involved in this are likely to build consensus and commitment, and have the potential to help develop pathos in those involved.

Evidence suggests that this scenario reflects how a number of the changes were developed in the context of the shaping of the FRS 102 SORP (Charity Commission and OSCR, 2014a), particularly those related to adjustments to the TAR. Conversely, if changes are imposed, and are perceived as having been 'read across' from an inappropriate setting (such as the private sector), internal legitimation is harder to achieve. Such is the case with a number of the FRS 102-related (FRC, 2015a) changes connected to financial statements contained in the new SORP. These lessons should be reflected upon by those in the UK and RoI charged with developing future changes to the SORP (or, more generally, future legislative changes in the sector).

From a practice and managerial perspective, on balance, the changes to charity reporting included in the FRS 102 SORP (Charity Commission and OSCR, 2014a) have been seen in positive terms by charities (and by charity accountants), albeit only at a time when they were just being introduced. The accountants, as key actors, will now be required to cascade the requirements (and thinking behind them) within their organisations. Not only can this reinforce the acceptance of new SORP practices at other organisational levels, but it also has the potential for these new practices to change employee behaviours within charities. Such (often non-accountant) individuals can be encouraged, for example, to collect information and reflect on possible areas for impact case studies and the provision of performance-related impact information to be reported (a new focus of the latest SORP). In addition, this has the possibility of flowing through into everyday operations and decision making within a charity and, if handled well, to contribute to a sharpening of the mission focus of the organisation. In this regard, much work needs to be done within charities, and by sector-wide support organisations in both the UK and RoI, to ensure that the benefits of having a new SORP are understood and optimised.

The performance reporting aspects of this research identify weaknesses in performance (managerial) accountability, both in the UK and, more substantially, in RoI. Such shortcomings can undermine trust and confidence in the sector, and damage reputation, which, ultimately, can impact on funding flows. Some degree of improvement over time is identified in respect of performance reporting, particularly relating to the use of impact disclosures (although direct comparisons with earlier research are difficult). To an extent, such improvements may be influenced by the increased 'messaging' of the importance of performance and a general 'spirit of the age' which has embraced the need particularly to isolate and quantify such aspects of performance as output and impact (Hyndman and McConville, 2017). In the light of a number of high-profile scandals, the issue of 'governance', of which performance systems and performance reporting are part, has come to the fore (Hyndman and McDonnell, 2009; Hind, 2017).

It could be argued that those charities with 'better' governance regimes are more likely to develop more extensive internal systems to target, measure and report performance, especially measures related to impact, effectiveness and efficiency. It may be the case that charities with better governance regimes may have more complete foundations on which to base the external reporting of performance. Yet, as this research suggests, much work has still to be done to improve such reporting as a basis for building trust and confidence. However, without the provision and promotion of specific, charity-focused guidance, possibly provided and promoted by those concerned with the administration and control of the charity sector, it is likely that progress will be slow. The involvement of the regulators (in the various jurisdictions), and of support organisations (like the Charities Aid Foundation in the UK or The Wheel in RoI) in encouraging a journey of improvement, and possibly even developing such guidance, would help. Given charities' expertise, focus and limited resource base, to expect individual charities to develop meaningful and extensive performance reporting systems without guidance is perhaps too optimistic.

Areas for Further Research

This book makes a contribution to the understanding of: (i) the evolution of the charities SORP; (ii) the role of internal legitimation in embedding accounting and reporting changes over time; and (iii) accountability (and, in particular, performance accountability) in relation to UK and RoI charities. The area, however, is still under-researched, and further work is needed.

The empirical work that is an aspect of this research focused solely on large charities in the UK and RoI. Such charities, which numerically are a small part of the entire sector in each jurisdiction, represent a large proportion of the sector's economic activity. Other research considering different sizes of organisation, different organisational forms, or charities engaged with particular causes or means of operation could identify (and explain) differences in internal legitimation and performance reporting relating to such variables.

As seen in this book (and the accompanying empirical research), the FRS 102 SORP (Charity Commission and OSCR, 2014a) has been largely welcomed by charity accountants at a time before implementation. Subsequently, these changes will be applied and, it is anticipated, will become embedded within the reporting systems. Future studies on the topic are needed to explore the actual implementation of the SORP requirements. This could examine its effect on charities and the perceptions, understanding, actions and roles of different internal stakeholders (such as key non-accountant managers, and charity accountants), subsequent to implementation.

This research identified weak accountability with respect to performance reporting, but (not being the focus of the study) did not provide evidence regarding reasons for this. Possible causes include: (i) difficulties in measuring performance; (ii) general satisfaction with existing reporting procedures; (iii) fear that some performance information may be misinterpreted; and (iv) the high cost of providing such information, money which charity managers (and possibly donors/funders) would rather spend on direct charitable activities. Qualitative research, possibly utilising interviews, might help to provide useful insights to help explain the reasons for the current level of reporting of performance information.

As also outlined in this book, the UK charity sector (especially in respect of England and Wales) has a significant history of control and regulation. This is more developed and long-standing than in many other jurisdictions, including RoI (the focus of the comparative empirical research presented in this book). The expectation is that greater maturity in control and regulation leads to greater demands from stakeholders, which in turn provide the impetus for greater accountability. Furthermore, greater control and regulation, and better accountability, may support charitable activity by reducing any information asymmetry problems that can impact detrimentally on charitable giving. These possible connections, although alluded to in this book, have not been the focus of investigation, but are certainly worthy of consideration. A mixture of quantitative and qualitative research methods might support such future investigations, with further studies possibly comparing charities (and other NFPOs) from a range of different jurisdictions. This would facilitate a more international reflection on these issues.

7.4   Concluding Comments

The charity sectors in both the UK and RoI have grown significantly over time, and are continuing to grow. They have major economic, cultural and social impact. To maintain confidence and build trust, good accounting and reporting systems are essential. Indeed, such could be viewed as necessary conditions for the health and growth of these sectors, and the continuing funding of their activities. This book contributes to the debate relating to the shape and structure of accounting and reporting by charities. Well-developed and appropriate accounting and reporting systems can help charities as they seek to discharge accountability to external stakeholders, as well as supporting internal mangers in making planning and control decisions that sharpen mission focus. Within such a framework, the importance of performance reporting and performance accountability is considerable. Charities exist for reasons other than to generate profit, and their performance can only be judged in similar terms.

It is suggested that the strength of the accounting and reporting systems used by charities is increased considerably if those responsible for their implementation and operation are convinced of the legitimacy (or justification) of the rules and norms with which they are meant to comply. Indeed, if key stakeholders engage in the process of shaping the required accounting and reporting structure, the chances of commitment to, and justification of, any emerging framework is likely to be high, as are the chances that what transpires will be viewed as appropriate.

Good accounting and reporting are essential in building confidence in the charity sector and have the potential both to increase charitable giving and improve charitable activity (as well as to reduce the likelihood of scandal). The development, adoption and constant renewal of appropriate reporting practices that meet the information needs of a range of stakeholders (including donors/funders and beneficiaries) can provide a basis for greater confidence in the control processes within charities and result in a more accountable and more trusted sector. In addition, the necessary debate surrounding this process is likely to encourage sharper reporting and more mission-centred decision-making.

Over time, the development and evolution of the charities SORP, and the processes through which this has taken place, has contributed to the narrowing of a 'relevance gap' between stakeholder information needs and information disclosed. Moreover, it has resulted in a growing commitment by charities to both the SORP-development process and the end product of this process (at present, the FRS 102 SORP). Going forward, such engagements in SORP renewal, if they continue to involve key stakeholders, and if they continue to reflect the context in which charities operate, are likely to result in an ever-more accountable charity sector. Surely this is a desire of all those with a heart for the varied, valuable and socially desirable activities with which charities engage.

Appendix 1

United Kingdom and Republic of Ireland Thresholds

The following thresholds, which are based upon those included in Appendix Three of the FRS 102 SORP (Charity Commission and OSCR, 2014a), have been updated to reflect subsequent changes up to June 2017.

Threshold for the Preparation of Accruals Accounts

Company charities, irrespective of size, must prepare accruals accounts that give a true and fair view. However, certain jurisdictions permit the trustees of smaller non-company charities to prepare their accounts on a receipts and payments basis, instead of preparing accounts on an accruals basis to give a true and fair view.

In England and Wales, the threshold at which accruals accounts must be produced by non-company charities is a gross annual income of more than £250,000.

In Scotland, the threshold at which accruals accounts must be produced by non-company charities is a gross annual income of £250,000 or more.

In Northern Ireland (NI), the threshold at which accruals accounts must be produced by non-company charities is a gross annual income of £250,000 or more.

In the Republic of Ireland (RoI), a charity with a gross annual income of €10,001 or more is required to prepare a profit and loss account (or income and expenditure account and statement of assets and liabilities) for the reporting period.

Threshold for Statutory Audit

In England and Wales, an audit is required if either the charity's gross annual income exceeds £1 million or its gross assets exceed £3.26 million and gross annual income exceeds £250,000.

In <u>Scotland</u>, an audit is required if either the charity's gross annual income is £500,000 or more, or its gross assets exceed £3.26 million and the charity has prepared accruals accounts.

In <u>NI</u>, an audit is required if the charity's gross annual income exceeds £500,000.

In <u>RoI</u>, a charity with a gross annual income of more than €100,001 is required to provide a full set of audited accounts, including directors and auditors reports for the reporting period.

Threshold for the Preparation of Consolidated (Group) Accounts

In <u>England and Wales</u>, any parent charity where the aggregate gross income of the group (i.e. the parent charity and its subsidiaries) exceeds £1 million after consolidation adjustments must prepare consolidated accounts.

In <u>Scotland</u>, any parent charity where the aggregate gross income of the group (i.e. the parent charity and its subsidiaries exceeds £500,000 after consolidation adjustments) must prepare consolidated accounts.

In <u>NI</u>, any parent charity where the aggregate gross income of the group (i.e. the parent charity and its subsidiaries) exceeds £500,000 after consolidation adjustments must prepare consolidated accounts.

In <u>RoI</u>, the only legal requirement for consolidated (group) accounts applies to parent company charities. Consolidated accounts are prepared in accordance with the Companies Acts 1963–1990 as amended by Regulation 4 of the European Communities (Companies: Group Accounts) Regulations 1992. The exemption for small and medium private companies does not apply to company charities that are classified as public companies.

Appendix 2

Examples of Trustees' Annual Reports and Financial Statements

A number of examples of SORP-compliant trustees' annual reports and financial statements are provided on the Charity Commission website (www.charitysorp.org/about-the-sorp/example-trustees-annual-reports/).

England and Wales

Arts Theatre Trust (FRS 102)

This is for a company limited by guarantee, operating a theatre and related activities with one trading subsidiary which is preparing consolidated accounts under accounting standard FRS 102.

Arts Theatre Trust (FRSSE)

This is for a company limited by guarantee, operating a theatre and related activities with one trading subsidiary which is preparing consolidated accounts under accounting standard FRSSE.

Rosanna Grant Trust (FRS 102)

This is for an unincorporated trust which has endowment invested on a total return basis and makes grants to institutions and individuals.

Rosanna Grant Trust (FRSSE)

This is for an unincorporated trust which has endowment invested on a total return basis and makes grants to institutions and individuals.

Scotland

The four examples above developed for England and Wales have been reworked by OSCR for reporting in Scotland:

1. Scottish limited company group accounts prepared under the FRS 102 SORP.
2. Scottish limited company group accounts prepared under the FRSSE SORP.
3. Almond Grant Trust: Scottish unincorporated accounts prepared under the FRS 102 SORP.
4. Almond Grant Trust: Scottish unincorporated accounts prepared under the FRSSE SORP.

Appendix 3

Interview Guide

1. Could you please tell us what your role and responsibilities are? How long have you been working in your present role? And in the organisation?
2. Are you aware of the changes that have been happening in relation to accounting, reporting and performance measurement in the charity sector over the past few years? In your opinion, how does the FRS 102 SORP differ from SORP 2005? – If limited response was given, the prompts below were used:

- *Prompts: Trustees' Annual Report*
  - *Encouragement to report on impacts (term not used in previous SORPs). Also SORP 2015 defines impact. What might this mean for the charity?*
  - *The statement concerning risk management made by larger charities is dropped (was very general) and instead larger charities are required to provide a description of the principal risks and uncertainties facing the charity and its subsidiary undertakings, as identified by the charity trustees, together with a summary of their plans and strategies for managing those risks.*
  - *The charity must explain any policy it has for holding reserves and state the amounts of those reserves and why they are held. If the trustees have decided that holding reserves is unnecessary, the report must disclose this fact and provide the reasons. (New here: relates to stating the amounts and explanation if no reserves are held.)*
  - *Larger charities must now disclose their arrangements for setting the pay and remuneration of the charity's key management personnel and any benchmarks, parameters or criteria used in setting their pay, as well as information about the transactions with trustees and de-facto trustees. Also, relate to disclosure requirement relating to number of staff paid £60,000 or more (although this was a requirement in SORP 2005 for charities requiring a statutory audit).*
- *Prompts: SOFA*
  - *The heading of 'governance costs' is dropped altogether from the SOFA in SORP 2015, with these costs being included in expenditure on 'charitable activities'. For those charities reporting on an activity basis, governance costs are now a separate component of support costs.*

- o *Treatment of gains and losses on investment asset: SORP 2005 presented both realised and unrealised investment gains and losses as an item within 'other gains and losses' after striking a total for 'net incoming/outgoing resources'. FRS 102 requires that changes in the value of financial instruments measured at fair value are taken through profit and loss. Gains and losses on investments are now shown before striking a total for 'net income / expenditure'.*
  - o *FRS 102 changes one of the three criteria for income recognition. It requires that income should be recognised when its receipt is 'probable' whereas the equivalent criterion under SORP 2005 was 'virtually certain'.*
- • *Prompts: Other*
  - o *New recommendations on impact reporting, what they mean for the organisation and the expected impacts and reactions: do you detect a changed emphasis with respect to impact in SORP 2015; if so, where has the emphasis come from; why has it arisen; and what effect has this had on your charity?*

For each major change [SORP, SOFA, non-financial measures, impact reporting]:

3. What changed? How did it change?
   - • *Prompts: processes, contents, actors, tools, behaviours, skills, etc.*
4. What was your input in the change process? Were you involved in the consultations? Could you give us examples of how the process unfolded?
   - • *Prompts: for example, through professional bodies, roundtables, etc.*
5. Why do you think this change was introduced?
   - • *Prompts: external pressures (scandals, Good Governance code, market forces/financial pressures); internal pressures (values, power, interests, leadership, etc.)*
6. How was the change promoted throughout the charity? Could you give us examples of how the process unfolded?
   - • *Prompts: people involved/supporting the change, arguments made, roundtables/workshops/meetings, etc.*
7. Was change opposed? By whom? How?
   - • *Prompts: actors involved – people opposing the change, arguments made.*
8. Do you see an adjustment in how this change has been perceived (5, 6) over time? Could you please give us some examples?
9. What results do you expect from the change? Could you please give us an example?

- *Prompts: positive and negative expectations; effects on decision-making, accountability, day-by-day activities, behaviours, etc.*
10. Can you give us (at least) one example of the effect the change has started producing?
    - *Prompt: what type of information are they starting collecting/what do they see themselves disclosing in the future? Impact on decision making?*
    - *Prompt: has the change legitimated what they were already doing?*
    - *Prompt: if the example is very positive (negative), ask if there is anything negative (positive).*
11. What is your personal opinion on the changes that have taken place? And of those currently taking place?

Charity Annual Report and Annual Review Checklist

Section A: Basic Charity Information

Charity Name:
Document Type:
Accounting Period:

Charity Classification:

What does the charity primarily do?	
1. General charitable purposes	
2. Education/training	
3. Medical/health/sickness	
4. Disability	
5. Relief of poverty	
6. Overseas aid/famine relief	
7. Accommodation/housing	
8. Religious activities	
9. Arts/culture	
10. Sport/recreation	
11. Animals	
12. Environment/conservation/heritage	
13. Economic/community development/ employment	
14. Other	

Who does the charity primarily help?	
1. Children/young people	
2. Elderly/old people	
3. People with disabilities	

4. People of a particular ethnic or racial origin	
5. Other charities/voluntary bodies	
6. Other defined groups	
7. The general public	
8. Acts as an umbrella or resource body	
9. Other	

Section B: Assessing Charity Accountability

Financial Managerial Accountability

Financial:	Nature of information provided
General discussion	
Income by source	
Expenditure by activity	
Income review	
Expenditure review	
Trading activities	
Overall organisational efficiency:	**Nature of information provided**
General discussion	
Management and administration costs	
Spend on charitable activities	
Fundraising efficiency:	**Nature of information provided**
General discussion	
Spend on fundraising	
Voluntary income	

Operational Managerial Accountability

Direct charitable activities:	Nature of information provided
General	
Aims, goals and objectives – ST, MT & LT (Why does the organisation exist? What changes does it seek?)	
What activities does the organisation carry out to achieve its aims?	
What resources does the charity use to make these activities happen?	
Achievements by objective	
Who benefits from the charity's work?	
How does the charity respond to beneficiary needs?	
How do beneficiaries influence the charity's development? (Is the organisation seeking feedback, review and input where appropriate?)	
Performance	
Input	
Output	
Impact/outcome	
Efficiency	
Effectiveness	
Future target information	
Lessons learned	

References

Abbott, W. F. and Monsen, R. J. (1979), "On the measurement of corporate social responsibility: self-reported disclosures as a method of measuring corporate social involvement", *Academy of Management Journal*, Vol. 22, No. 3, pp. 501–515.

Accounting Standards Board (ASB) (1999), *Statement of Principles for Financial Reporting*, London.

ASB (2007), *Statement of Principles for Financial Reporting: Interpretation for Public Benefit Entities*, London.

Accounting Standards Committee (ASC) (1975), *The Corporate Report*, London.

ASC (1988), *Accounting by Charities, Statement of Recommended Practice No. 2*, London.

Aerts, W. (2001), "Inertia in the attributional content of annual accounting narratives", *European Accounting Review*, Vol. 10, No. 1, pp. 3–32.

Alexander, J., Brudney, J. L. and Yang, K. (2010), "Introduction to the symposium: accountability for performance and measurement: the evolving role of nonprofits in the hollow state", *Nonprofit and Voluntary Sector Quarterly*, Vol. 39, No. 4, pp. 565–570.

American Accounting Association (1989), *Measuring the Performance of Nonprofit Organisations: The State of the Art*, Sarasota.

Andon, P. and Free, C. (2012), "Auditing and crisis management: the 2010 Melbourne Storm salary cap scandal", *Accounting, Organizations & Society*, Vol. 37, No. 3, pp. 131–154.

Anthony, R. N. and Young, D. W. (2002), *Management Control in Non-Profit Organisations*, 7th Edition., McGraw Hill, New York, USA.

Ashford, J. K. (1989), "Charity accounts", in *Financial Reporting 1989-90: A Survey of UK Reporting Practice*, Skerratt, L. C. L. and Tonkins, D. J. (Eds.), pp. 23–48, Institute of Chartered Accountants in England and Wales, London.

Austin, M. and Posnett, J. (1979), "The charity sector in England and Wales – characteristics and public accountability", *National Westminster Bank Quarterly Review*, No. 3, pp. 40–51.

Bay, C. (2011), "Framing financial responsibility: an analysis of the limitations of accounting", *Critical Perspectives on Accounting*, Vol. 22, No. 6, pp. 593–607.

Beattie, V., McInnes, B. and Fearnley, S. (2002), *Through the Eyes of Management: A Study of Narrative Disclosures*, Interim Report, Institute of Chartered Accountants in England and Wales, London.

Benjamin, L. M. (2012), "The potential of outcome measurement for strengthening nonprofits' accountability to beneficiaries", *Nonprofit and Voluntary Sector Quarterly*, Vol. 42, No. 6, pp. 1224–1244.

Bettman, J. and Weitz, B. (1983), "Attributions in the board room: causal reasoning in corporate annual report", *Administrative Science Quarterly*, Vol. 28, No. 2, pp. 165–183.

Bird, P. and Morgan-Jones, P. (1981), *Financial Reporting by Charities*, Institute of Chartered Accountants in England and Wales, London.

Boardmatch Ireland (2013), *Charity 100 index*, December. http://www.boardmatchireland.ie/wp-content/uploads/2013/12/Final-Version-CI-100.pdf

Bouckaert, L. and Vandenhove, J. (1998), "Business ethics and the management of non-profit institutions", *Journal of Business Ethics*, Vol. 17, Nos. 9/10, pp. 1073–1081.

Brace, P., Elkin, R., Robinson, D. and Steinberg, H. (1980), *Reporting of Service Efforts and Accomplishments (Research Report)*, Financial Accounting Standards Board, Stamford, USA.

Breckell, P., Harrison, K. and Robert. N. (2011), *Impact Reporting in the UK Charity Sector*, Charity Finance Group, London.

Breen, O. B. and Carroll, J. (2015), "Giving in Ireland: a nation of givers in a largely unregulated arena", in *The Palgrave Handbook of Global Philanthropy*, Wiepking, P. and Handy, F. (Eds.), pp. 190–210, Palgrave Macmillan UK, Basingstoke.

Broadbent, J. and Guthrie, J. (1992), "Changes in the public sector: a review of recent 'alternative' accounting research", *Accounting, Auditing & Accountability Journal*, Vol. 5, No. 2, pp. 3–31.

Brody, E. (2001), "Accountability and Public Trust", in *The State of America's Non-Profit Sector*, Saloman, A. (Ed.), Aspen Institute and Brookings Institution.

Brunsson, N. (1989), *The Organization of Hypocrisy: Talk, Decisions, and Actions in Organizations*, John Wiley & Sons, New York.

Burke-Kennedy, E. (2013), "Charity donations 'plummet 40%' in wake of CRC revelations", December. http://www.irishtimes.com/news/social-affairs/charity-donations-plummet-40-in-wake-of-crc-revelations-1.1626936.

Cabinet Office (2002), *Private Action, Public Benefit: A Review of Charities and the Wider Not-For-Profit Sector: Strategy Unit Report*, London.

Cabinet Office of the Third Sector (2009), *Key Facts on the Third Sector*. http://webarchive.nationalarchives.gov.uk/+/http:/www.cabinetoffice.gov.uk/media/231495/factoids.pdf

Cadbury Report (1992), *The Financial Aspects of Corporate Governance*, Gee, London.

Carter, N. (1989), "Performance Indicators: 'backseat driving' or 'hands off' control?", *Policy and Politics*, Vol. 17, No. 2, pp. 131–138.

Carter N, Klein, K. and Day, P. (1992), *How Organisations Measure Success: The Use of Performance Indicators in Government*, Routledge, London.

Chang, L., Cheng, M., and Trotman, K. T. (2008), "The effect of framing and negotiation partner's objective on judgments about negotiated transfer prices", *Accounting, Organizations and Society*, Vol. 33, Nos. 7–8, pp. 704–717.

Charities Aid Foundation (CAF) (2001), *Tell the Main Story: Guidance on Effective Annual Reporting*, CAF, London.

CAF (2016), *World Giving Index 2016: A Global View of Giving Trends*, London.

Charity Commission (1995), *Accounting by Charities: Statement of Recommended Practice*, Charity Commission, London.

Charity Commission (2000a), *Accounting and Reporting by Charities: Statement of Recommended Practice* (SORP 2000), Charity Commission, London.

Charity Commission (2000b), *Users on Boards: Beneficiaries who Become Trustees*, Charity Commission, London.

Charity Commission (2004a), *RS8: Transparency and Accountability*, London.

Charity Commission (2004b), *The Hallmarks of an Effective Charity*, London.

Charity Commission (2005), *Accounting and Reporting by Charities: Statement of Recommended Practice*, SORP 2005, London.

Charity Commission (2009), *Charity Reporting and Accounting: Taking Stock and Future Reform*, London.

Charity Commission (2013), *Charity reporting and accounting: the essentials*, London.

Charity Commission (2016), *Charities in England and Wales – 31 March 2016*. Retrieved from: http://apps.charitycommission.gov.uk/showcharity/register ofcharities/SectorData/SectorOverview.aspx.

Charity Commission and Office of the Scottish Charity Regulator (OSCR) (2014a), *Charities SORP (FRS 102) Accounting and Reporting by Charities: Statement of Recommended Practice applicable to charities preparing their accounts in accordance with the Financial Reporting Standard applicable in the UK and Republic of Ireland (FRS 102) (effective 1 January 2015)*, London.

Charity Commission and OSCR (2014b), *Charities SORP (FRSSE) Accounting and Reporting by Charities: Statement of Recommended Practice applicable to charities preparing their accounts in accordance with the Financial Reporting Standard for Smaller Entities (the FRSSE) (effective 1 January 2015)*, London.

Charity Commission and OSCR (2014c), *What has Changed?*, London.

Charity Commission (2014d), Charities SORP: Application Guidance for Charity Accounting. http://www.charitysorp.org/about-the-sorp/helpsheets/.

Charity Commission for Northern Ireland (2016), *ACC08 The Trustees' Annual Report and Public Benefit Reporting*. www.charitycommissionni.org.uk.

Charity Commission for Northern Ireland (2017), *The 'Deemed' List of Northern Ireland Charities*. http://www.charitycommissionni.org.uk/Our_regulatory_ activity/List_of_deemed_charities.aspx.

Charity Finance Group (CFG) (2012), *Managing Charities in the New Normal – A Perfect Storm?* CFG, London.

CFG (2013), *Managing Charities in the New Normal – Adapting to Uncertainty*, London.

Clapham, S. E. and Schwenk, C. R. (1991), 'Self-serving attributions, managerial cognition, and company performance', *Strategic Management Journal*, Vol. 12, pp. 219–229.

Clatworthy, M. and Jones, M. J. (2003), "Financial reporting of good news and bad news: Evidence from accounting narratives", *Accounting and Business Research*, Vol. 33, No. 3, pp. 171–185.

Clemens, E. and Cook, J. (1999), "Politics and institutionalism: explaining durability and change", *Annual Review of Sociology*, Vol. 25, pp. 441–466.

Comtois, E., Denis, J. L. and Langley, A. (2004), "Rhetorics of efficiency, fashion and politics: Hospital mergers in Quebec", *Management Learning*, Vol. 35, No. 3, pp. 303–320.

Connolly, C. and Dhanani, A. (2006), "Accounting narratives: the reporting practices of British charities", *Journal for Public and Nonprofit Services*, Vol. 35, No. 1, pp. 39–62.

Connolly, C. and Dhanani, A. (2009), *Research Report 109: Narrative Reporting by UK Charities*, Association of Chartered Certified Accountants, London.

Connolly, C. and Hyndman, N. (2000), "Charity accounting: an empirical analysis of the impact of recent changes", *British Accounting Review,* Vol. 32, No. 1, pp. 77–100.

Connolly, C. and Hyndman, N. (2001), "A comparative study of the impact of revised SORP 2 on British and Irish charities", *Financial Accountability & Management,* Vol. 17, No. 1, 2001, pp. 73–97.

Connolly, C. and Hyndman, N. (2003), *Performance Reporting by UK Charities: Approaches, Difficulties and Current Practice,* Institute of Chartered Accountants of Scotland, Edinburgh.

Connolly, C. and Hyndman, N. (2004), "Performance reporting: a comparative study of British and Irish charities", *British Accounting Review,* Vol. 36, No. 2, pp. 127–154.

Connolly, C. and Hyndman, N. (2013), "Towards charity accountability: narrowing the gap between provision and needs?", *Public Management Review,* Vol. 15, No. 1, pp. 1–24.

Connolly, C. and Hyndman, N. (2017), "The donor-beneficiary charity accountability paradox: a tale of two stakeholders", *Public Money & Management,* Vol. 37, No. 3, pp. 157–164.

Connolly, C., Hyndman, N. and McConville, D. (2013), "UK charity accounting: an exercise in widening stakeholder engagement", *British Accounting Review,* Vol. 45, No. 1, pp. 58–69.

Cornforth, C. (2003), "The changing context of governance – emerging issues and paradoxes", in *The Governance of Public and Non-Profit Organizations: What do boards do?,* Cornforth, C. (Ed.), Routledge, Oxford.

Covaleski, M. A., Dirsmith, M. W. and Rittenberg, L. (2003), "Jurisdictional disputes over professional work: the institutionalization of the global knowledge expert", *Accounting, Organizations and Society,* Vol. 28, pp. 323–355.

Creed, D., Scully, M. and Austin, J. (2002), "Clothes make the person? The tailoring of legitimating accounts and the social construction of identity", *Organization Science,* Vol. 13, No. 5, pp. 475–496.

Czarniawska, B. (2011), *Cyberfactories: How News Agencies Produce News,* Edward Elgar Publishing, Cheltenham, United Kingdom.

Dhanani, A. (2009), "Accountability of UK charities", *Public Money & Management,* Vol. 29, No. 3, pp. 183–190.

DiMaggio, P. (1988), "Interest and agency in institutional theory", in *Institutional Patterns and Organizations: Culture and Environment,* Zucker L. G. (Ed.), pp. 3–21, Ballinger, Cambridge, MA.

Dubnick, M. (1998), "Clarifying accountability: an ethical theory framework", in *Public Sector Ethics: Finding and Implementing Values,* Preston, N. and Bois, C. A. (Eds.), pp. 68–81, Routledge, London.

Ebrahim, A. (2003), "Accountability in practice: mechanisms for NGOs", *World Development,* Vol. 31, No. 5, pp. 813–829.

Eden, R. and Hyndman, N. (1999), "Performance measurement in the UK public sector: poisoned chalice or holy grail?", *Optimum: The Journal of the Public Sector,* Vol. 29, No. 1, pp. 9–15.

Edwards, M. and Hulme, D. (1995), *Non-Governmental Organisations – Performance and Accountability: Beyond the Magic Bullet,* Earthscan, London.

Eldenburg, L. and Vines, C. (2004), "Nonprofit classification decisions in response to a change in accounting rules", *Journal of Accounting and Public Policy*, Vol. 23, pp. 1–22.

Ellwood, S. and Greenwood, M. (2016), "Accounting for heritage assets: does measuring economic value 'kill the cat'?", *Critical Perspectives on Accounting*, Vol. 38, pp. 1–13.

Erkama, N. and Vaara, E. (2010), "Struggles over legitimacy in global organizational restructuring: a rhetorical perspective on legitimation strategies and dynamics in a shutdown case", *Organization Studies*, Vol. 31, No. 7, pp. 813–839.

Etzioni, A. (2010), "Is Transparency the best disinfectant?", *Journal of Political Philosophy*, Vol. 18, No. 4, pp. 389–404.

Falk, F. (1981), "Why not a SSAP for Charities?", *Accountancy*, Vol. 92, No. 1050, pp. 72–74.

Financial Accounting Standards Board (1980), *Statement of Financial Accounting Concepts No 2: Qualitative Characteristics of Accounting Information*, Stamford.

Financial Reporting Council (FRC) (2013), *Financial Reporting Standard for Smaller Entities (effective January 2015)*, July, London.

FRC (2015a), *FRS 102 The Financial Reporting Standard applicable in the UK and Republic of Ireland*, September, London.

FRC (2015b), *FRS 105 The Financial Reporting Standard applicable to the Micro-entities Regime*, July, London.

Freeman, R. E. (1984), *Strategic Management: A Stakeholder Approach*, Pitman, Boston.

Friedman, M. T. and Mason, D. S. (2004), "A stakeholder approach to understanding economic development decision making: public subsidies for professional sports facilities", *Economic Development Quarterly*, Vol. 18, No. 3, pp. 236–254.

Fry, R. E. (1995), "Accountability in organisational life: problem or opportunity for nonprofits?", *Nonprofit Management and Leadership*, Vol. 6, No. 2, pp. 181–195.

Gambling, T., Jones, R., Kunz, C. and Pendlebury, M. (1990), *Research Report 21: Accounting by Charities: The Application of SORP2*, Association of Chartered Certified Accountants, London.

Glennon, R., Hannibal, C. and Meehan, J. (2017), "The impact of a changing financial climate on a UK local charitable sector: voices from the front line", *Public Money & Management*, Vol. 37, No. 3, pp. 197–204.

Gray, R. (1983), "Accounting, financial reporting and not-for-profit organisations", *AUTA Review*, Vol. 15, No. 1, pp. 3–23.

Gray, R. (1984), "Uncharitable view of accounting", *Accountancy*, Vol. 94, No. 1096, pp. 84.

Green, S. E. (2004), "A rhetorical theory of diffusion", *Academy of Management Review*, Vol. 29, No. 4, pp. 653–669.

Green, S. E., Babb, M. and Alpaslan, C. M. (2008), "Institutional field dynamics and the competition between institutional logics", *Management Communication Quarterly*, Vol. 22, No. 1, pp. 40–73.

Green, S. E. and Li, Y. (2011), "Rhetorical institutionalism: language, agency, and structure in institutional theory since Alvesson 1993", *Journal of Management Studies*, Vol. 48, No. 7, pp. 1662–1697.

Guéguen, N., Pascual, A., Silone, F. and David, M. (2015), "When legitimizing a request increases compliance: the legitimizing object technique", *The Journal of Social Psychology*, Vol. 155, No. 6, pp. 541–544.

Guthrie, J. and Parker, L. (1989), "Corporate social reporting: a rebuttal of legitimacy theory", *Accounting and Business Research*, Vol. 19, No. 76, pp. 343–353.

Heald, D. (2006a), "Varieties of transparency", in *Transparency: The Key to Better Governance? Proceedings of the British Academy 135*, Hood, C. and Heald, D. (Eds.), Oxford University Press, Oxford.

Heald, D. (2006b), "Transparency as an instrumental value", in *Transparency: The Key to Better Governance? Proceedings of the British Academy 135*, Hood, C. and Heald, D. (Eds.), Oxford University Press, Oxford.

Hedley, S., Keen, S., Lumley, T., Ní Ógáin, E., Thomas, J. and Williams, M. (2010), *Talking About Results*, New Philanthropy Capital, London.

Hind, A. (2017), "Fundraising in UK charities: stepping back from the abyss", *Public Money & Management*, Vol. 37, No. 3, pp. 205–210.

Hines, A. and Jones, M. J. (1992), "The impact of SORP on the UK charitable sector: an empirical study", *Financial Accountability & Management*, Vol. 8, No. 1, pp. 49–67.

Hirsch, P. M. (1986), "From ambushes to golden parachutes: Corporate takeovers as an instance of cultural framing and institutional integration", *American Journal of Sociology*, Vol. 91, No. 4, pp. 800–837.

HM Treasury (2011), *HM Treasury and Department for Work and Pensions: Green Book discussion paper on valuing social impacts*, London.

Home Office (2003), *Charities and Not for Profits: A Modern Legal Framework: The Government's Response to Private Action–Public Benefit*, London.

Hood, C. (1995), "The 'new public management' in the 1980s: Variations on a theme?", *Accounting, Organizations and Society*, Vol. 20, Nos. 2–3, pp. 93–109.

Hyndman, N. (1990), "Charity accounting: an empirical study of the information needs of contributors to UK fundraising charities", *Financial Accountability & Management*, Vol. 6, No. 4, pp. 295–307.

Hyndman, N. (1991), "Contributors to charities – a comparison of their information needs and the perceptions of such by the providers of information", *Financial Accountability & Management*, Vol. 7, No. 2, pp. 69–82.

Hyndman, N. and Anderson, R. (1997), "A longitudinal study of the use of performance measures in the annual reports of UK executive agencies", *Irish Accounting Review*, Vol. 4, No. 1, pp. 43–74.

Hyndman, N. and Lapsley, I. (2016), "New public management: the story continues", *Financial Accountability & Management*, Vol. 32, No. 4, pp. 385–408.

Hyndman, N. and Liguori, M. (2016a), "Public sector reforms: changing contours on an NPM landscape", *Financial Accountability & Management*, Vol. 32, No. 1, pp. 5–32.

Hyndman, N. and Liguori, M. (2016b), "Justifying accounting change through global discourses and legitimation strategies. The case of the UK central government", *Accounting and Business Research*, Vol. 46, No. 4, pp. 390–421.

Hyndman, N. and McConville, D. (2016), "Transparency in reporting on charities' efficiency: a framework for analysis", *Nonprofit and Voluntary Sector Quarterly*, Vol. 45, No. 4, pp. 844–865.

Hyndman, N. and McConville, D. (2017), "Making charity effectiveness transparent: building a stakeholder-focused framework of reporting", *Financial Accountability & Management*, forthcoming.

Hyndman, N. and McDonnell, P. (2009), "Governance and charities: an exploration of key themes and the development of a research agenda", *Financial Accountability & Management*, Vol. 25, No. 1, pp. 5–31.

Hyndman, N. and McMahon, D. (2010), "The evolution of the UK charity statement of recommended practice: the influence of key stakeholders", *European Management Journal*, Vol. 28, No. 6, pp. 255–266.

Hyndman, N. and McMahon, D. (2011), "The hand of government in shaping accounting and reporting in the UK charity sector", *Public Money & Management*, Vol. 31, No. 3, pp. 167–174.

Hyndman, N., Liguori, M., Meyer, R., Polzer, T., Rota, S. and Seiwald, J. (2014), "The translation and sedimentation of accounting reforms. A comparison of the UK, Austrian and Italian experiences", *Critical Perspective on Accounting*, Vol. 25, Nos. 4–5, pp. 388–408.

Inspiring Impact (2013), *The Code of Good Impact Practice*, National Council for Voluntary Organisations, London.

Irish Nonprofit Knowledge Exchange (2012), *Irish Nonprofits: What Do We Know? A Report by Irish Nonprofits Knowledge Exchange*. http://www.wheel.ie/sites/default/files/Irish%20Nonprofits%20-%20What%20do%20we%20know_%20Report%20January%202012.pdf

Jackson, P. M. (1982), *The Political Economy of Bureaucracy*, Philip Allan, London.

Järvinen, J. (2016), "Role of management accounting in applying new institutional logics", *Accounting, Auditing & Accountability Journal*, Vol. 29, No. 5, pp. 861–886.

Jensen, M. C. and Meckling, W. H. (1976), "Theory of the firm: managerial behavior, agency costs, and ownership structure", *Journal of Financial Economics*, Vol. 3, pp. 305–360.

Jetty, J. and Beattie, V. (2009), *Research Report 108: Charity Reporting – A Study of Disclosure Practices and Policies of UK Charities*, Association of Chartered Certified Accountants, London.

Joutsenvirta, M. and Vaara, E. (2015), "Legitimacy struggles and political corporate social responsibility in international settings: a comparative discursive analysis of a contested investment in Latin America", *Organization Studies*, Vol. 36, pp. 741–777.

Katz, R. (2005), "The not-for-profit sector: no longer about just raising funds", *The Journal of Private Equity*, Vol. 8, pp. 1–10.

Koopmans, R. and Statham, P. (1999), *Ethnic and Civic Conceptions of Nationhood and the Differential Success of the Extreme Right in Germany and Italy. How Social Movements Matter*, University of Minnesota Press, Minneapolis.

Kurunmäki, L., Lapsley, I. and Miller P. (2010), "Accounting within and beyond the state", *Management Accounting Research*, Vol. 22, pp. 1–5.

Laughlin, R. (1990), "A model of financial accountability and the Church of England", *Financial Accountability & Management*, Vol. 6, No. 2, pp. 93–114.

Laughlin, R. (1996), "Principals and higher principals: accounting for accountability in the caring profession", in *Accountability: Power, Ethos and the Technologies of Managing*, Munro, R. and Mouritsen, J. (Eds), International Thomson Business Press, London, pp. 225–244.

Lefsrud, L. M. and Meyer, R. E. (2012), "Science or science fiction? Professionals' discursive construction of climate change", *Organization Studies*, Vol. 33, No. 11, pp. 1477–1506.

Liguori, M. and Steccolini, I. (2012), "Accounting change: explaining the outcomes, interpreting the process", *Accounting, Auditing & Accountability Journal*, Vol. 25, No. 1, pp. 27–70.

Liu, Y., Zhang, C. and Jing, R. (2016), "Coping with multiple institutional logics: temporal process of institutional work during the emergence of the one foundation in China", *Management and Organization Review*, Vol. 12, No. 2, pp. 387–416.

Lumley, T., Rickey, B. and Pike, M. (2011), *Inspiring Impact: Working Together for a Bigger Impact in the UK Social Sector*, New Philanthropy Capital, London.

Mack, J., Morgan, G. M., Breen, O. B. and Cordery, C. J. (2017), "Financial reporting by charities: a matched case study analysis from four countries", *Public Money & Management*, Vol. 37, No. 3, pp. 165–172.

Maguire, S., Hardy, C. and Lawrence, T. (2004), "Institutional entrepreneurship in emerging fields: HIV/AIDS treatment advocacy in Canada", *Academy of Management Journal*, Vol. 47, No. 5, pp. 657–679.

Mayston, D. (1985), "Non-profit performance indicators in the public sector", *Financial Accountability & Management*, Vol. 1, No. 1, pp. 51–74.

McConville, D. (2017), "Transparent impact reporting in charity annual reports: benefits, challenges and areas for development", *Public Money & Management*, Vol. 37, No. 3, pp. 211–215.

Meyer, R. E. and Höllerer, M. (2010), "Meaning structures in a contested issue field: a topographic map of shareholder value in Austria", *Academy of Management Journal*, Vol. 53, No. 6, pp. 1241–1262.

Meyer, R. E. and Hammerschmid, G. (2006), "Changing institutional logics and executive identities. A managerial challenge to public administration in Austria", *American Behavioral Scientist*, Vol. 49, No. 7, pp. 1000–1014.

Mitchell, R. K., Agle, B. R. and Wood, D. J. (1997), "Toward a theory of stakeholder identification and salience: defining the principle of who and what really counts", *Academy of Management Review*, Vol. 22, No. 4, pp. 853–886.

Mumford, M. (1990), "Healthy Light of Public Scrutiny", *Certified Accountant*, January, pp. 32–35.

National Council for Voluntary Organisations/Charities Aid Foundation (2012), *UK Giving 2012: An Overview of Charitable Giving in the UK 2011/12*. https://www.cafonline.org/publications/2012-publications/uk-giving-2012.aspx.

National Council of Social Service (1976), *Charity Law and Voluntary Organisation (Report of the Goodman Committee)*, Bedford Square Press, London.

Nevill, C. and Lumley, T. (2011), *Measuring Together: Impact Measurement in the Youth Justice Sector*, New Philanthropy Capital, London.

Ní Ógáin, E., Lumley, T. and Pritchard, D. (2012), *Making an Impact: Impact Measurement among Charities and Social Enterprises in the UK*, New Philanthropy Capital, London.

O'Brien, C. (2013), *Former CRC Chief Executive Received €200,000 Lump Sum from Charitable Funds*. http://www.irishtimes.com/news/health/former-crc-chief-executive-received-200-000-lump-sum-from-charitable-funds-1.1624374

O'Dwyer, B., Owen, D. and Unerman, J. (2011), "Seeking legitimacy for new assurance forms: The case of assurance on sustainability reporting", *Accounting, Organizations and Society*, Vol. 36, No. 1, pp. 31–52.

Office of the Scottish Charity Regulator (2017), *About OSCR*. http://www.oscr.org.uk/about-scottish-charities/.

Oliver, C. (1991), "Strategic Responses to Institutional Processes", *The Academy of Management Review*, Vol. 16, No. 1, pp. 145–179.

O'Neill, O. (2006), "Transparency and the ethics of communication", in *Transparency: The Key to Better Governance? Proceedings of the British Academy 135*, Hood, C. and Heald, D. (Eds.), Oxford University Press, Oxford.

Osborne, D. and Gaebler, T. (1992), *Reinventing Government: How the Entrepreneurial Spirit is Transforming the Public Sector*, Addison-Wesley, Reading, MA.

Palmer, P., Isaacs, M. and D'Silva, K. (2001), "Charity SORP compliance – findings of a research study", *Managerial Auditing Journal*, Vol. 16, No. 5, pp. 255–262.

Patton, M. Q. (2002), *Qualitative Research and Evaluation Methods*, Sage Publications, London.

Pearson, J. and Gray, R. (1978), "Can non-profit organisations' financial reporting benefit from accounting standards? Part 12, *Accountancy*, Vol. 89, No. 1021, pp. 87–88.

Pendlebury, M., Jones, R. and Karbhari, Y. (1994), "Developments in the accountability and financial reporting practices of executive agencies", *Financial Accountability & Management*, Vol. 10, No. 1, pp. 33–46.

Pratten, B. (2004), *Accountability and Transparency*, National Council for Voluntary Organisations, London.

Randall, A. (1989), "Pressure to Put More Heart into Accountability", *Accountancy*, Vol. 104, No. 1156, pp. 70–72.

Roberts, J. and Jones, M. (2009), "Accounting for self interest in the credit crisis", *Accounting, Organizations and Society*, Vol. 34, No. 8, pp. 856–867.

Roberts, R. and Scapens, R. (1985), "Accounting systems and systems of accountability – understanding accounting practices in their organisational contexts", *Accounting, Organizations and Society*, Vol. 10, No. 4, pp. 443–456.

Romanelli, E. and Tushman, M. (1994), "Organizational transformation as punctuated equilibrium: an empirical test", *The Academy of Management Journal*, Vol. 37, No. 5, pp. 1141–1166.

Sahlin, K. and Wedlin, L. (2008), "Circulating ideas: imitation, translation and editing", in *The Sage handbook of organizational institutionalism*, Greenwood, R., Oliver, C., Sahlin, K. and Suddaby, R. (Eds), Sage Publications, p. 242.

Salancik G. R. and Meindl J. R. (1984), "Corporate attributions as strategic illusions of management control", *Administrative Science Quarterly*, Vol. 29, pp. 238–254.

Saxton, G. D., Kuo, J. S. and Ho, Y. C. (2012), "The determinants of voluntary financial disclosure by nonprofit organisations", *Nonprofit and Voluntary Sector Quarterly*, Vol. 41, No. 6, pp. 1051–1071.

Scott, W. R. (1995), *Institutions and organizations*, Sage, Thousand Oaks, CA.

Sharifi, S. and Bovaird, T. (1995), "The financial management initiative in the UK public sector: the symbolic role of performance reporting", *International Journal of Public Administration*, Vol. 18, Nos. 2–3, pp. 467–490.

Shleifer, A. and Vishny, R. (1997), "A survey of corporate governance", *Journal of Finance*, Vol. 52, No. 2, pp. 737–783.

Silver, I. (2001), "Strategically legitimizing philanthropists' identity claims: community organizations as key players in the making of corporate social responsibility", *Sociological Perspectives*, Vol. 44, No. 2, pp. 233–252.

Slim, H. (2002), "By what authority: the legitimacy and accountability of non-governmental organisations". Paper presented by International Council on Human Rights Policy at the International Meeting of Global Trends and Human Rights – before and after September 11, Geneva, 10–12 January. https://www.gdrc.org/ngo/accountability/by-what-authority.html.

Staw, B. M., McKechnie, P. I. and Puffer, S. M. (1983), "The justification of organizational performance", *Administrative Science Quarterly*, Vol. 28, No. 4, pp. 582–600.

Stewart, J. D. (1984), "The role of information in public accountability", in *Issues in Public Sector Accounting*, Hopwood A. G. and Tomkins, C. R. (Eds.), Philip Allan, London.

Stone, M. M. and Ostrower, F. (2007), "Acting in the public interest? Another look at research on nonprofit governance", *Nonprofit and Voluntary Sector Quarterly*, Vol. 36, No. 3, pp. 416–438.

Strang, D. and Meyer, J. W. (1994), "Institutional conditions for diffusion", in *Institutional environments and organizations: Structural complexity and individualism*, Scott, R. W. and Meyer, J. W. (Eds.), Sage, Thousand Oaks, CA.

Suchman, M. C. (1995), "Managing legitimacy: strategic and institutional approaches", *Academy of Management Review*, Vol. 20, No. 3, pp. 729–757.

Suddaby, R. and Greenwood, R. (2005), "Rhetorical strategies of legitimacy", *Administrative Science Quarterly*, Vol. 50, No. 1, pp. 35–67.

Taylor, D. and Rosair, M. (2000), "Effects of participating parties, the public and size on government departments' accountability disclosure in annual reports", *Accounting, Accountability, and Performance*, Vol. 6, No. 1, pp. 77–98.

The Wheel (2014), *A Portrait of Ireland's Non-profit Sector*, The Wheel, Dublin.

The W. K. Kellogg Foundation (2004), *Using Logic Models to Bring Together Planning, Evaluation and Action: Logic Model Development Guide*, The W. K. Kellogg Foundation, Battle Creek, MI.

Thompson, G. D. (1995), "Problems with service performance reporting: the case of public art galleries", *Financial Accountability & Management*, Vol. 11, No. 4, pp. 337–350.

Tsang, E. W. K. (2002), "Self-serving attributions in corporate annual reports: a replicated study", *Journal of Management Studies*, Vol. 39, No. 1, pp. 51–65.

United Nations (2003), *Handbook on Non-Profit Institutions in the System of National Accounts*, New York.

Vaara, E. (2002), "On the discursive construction of success/failure in narratives of postmerger integration", *Organization Studies*, Vol. 23, No. 2, pp. 213–250.

Vaara, E., Tienari, J. and Laurila, J. (2006), "Pulp and paper fiction: on the discursive legitimation of global industrial restructuring", *Organization Studies*, Vol. 27, No. 6, pp. 789–810.

van Leeuwen, T. and Wodak, R. (1999), "Legitimizing immigration control: a discourse-historical analysis", *Discourse Studies*, Vol. 1, No. 1, pp. 83–118.

Wagner, J. A. and Gooding, R. Z. (1997), "Equivocal information and attribution: an investigation of patterns of managerial sensemaking", *Strategic Management Journal*, Vol. 18, No. 4, pp. 275–286.

Williams, A. (1985), *Performance Measurement in the Public Sector: Paving the Road to Hell?*, University of Glasgow Publications, Glasgow.

Williams, S. and Palmer, P. (1998), "The state of charity accounting – developments, improvements and continuing problems", *Financial Accountability and Management*, Vol. 14, No. 4, pp. 265–279.

Williamson, O. E. (1997), *The Mechanisms of Governance*, Oxford English Press, Oxford.

Yang, C., Northcott, D. and Sinclair, R. (2017), "The accountability information needs of key charity funders", *Public Money & Management*, Vol. 37, No. 3, pp. 173–180.

Index